MEMOIRS OF A BABY BOOMER

Memoirs of a Baby Boomer

A Personal Time Capsule ▪ 1949–1962

Philip Haldeman

English Hill Press

Redmond, WA

Copyright © 2024 by Philip Haldeman

Published by English Hill Press
Redmond, WA
ehpress@frontier.com

Much gratitude to the friends who read and commented on the manuscript in its various stages; to my wife Ann Haldeman for her editing skills and constant love and support; to my son David Haldeman for his always valuable input; to David E. Schultz for the text design; and to graphic designer Sandra Moreano for the cover.

ISBN: 978-0-9846543-5-2

3 5 7 9 8 6 4 2

For David, Laurel, Elliott, and Silas

Foreword

No matter how old you are right now, you've heard the phrase "baby boomer," someone who is part of the very large generation born after World War II. Because the war was such a big deal, the boomers also became a big deal, a part of US history. (And a big deal in their own minds, of course.) If nothing else, there was and still is the sheer number of us. I guess parents, reunited and relieved that the war was over, were having a lot of sex. But after axing the Axis, after the war and the welcome home parties, the threat of a new kind of war—a nuclear war—was always on or in back of everyone's mind. Phil (and I) were raised in a world with grownups who were relieved to have one global conflict resolved, but very afraid of the next. The anxieties led to all manner of apocalyptic stories and movies, at once informing and frightening kids of all ages.

Along with the undercurrent of anxiety, our world carried an enormous helping of a new prosperity. Optimism evolved from investment in infrastructure, agriculture, and communication technology that came with the war effort. These advancements greatly influenced our imaginations, in what we thought would soon be possible, creating even more stories and more movies.

Because of the safe, walkable neighborhoods in which Phil was raised, he was able to go to the local movie theaters often. And among the movies he saw, he took in one fantastical science fiction or horror film after another. Such time spent in a movie theater did not induce idleness. Instead, it sent Phil's imagination soaring in multiple directions. He was influenced and inspired almost every week, as most boomers were, by movies of all kinds, not only about possible futures, but about the past seen through Hollywood Westerns that were as much of a craze back then as was science fiction. I've known Phil for well over 30 years. We met at a Northwest Skeptics meeting in Seattle. Phil gave me a great deal to think about, especially when it came to routine claims of the paranormal—y'know, your psychic phenomena, your ghosts in the attic, your astrological forecasts in the newspaper. Phil is adept at what is nowadays called "critical thinking." In his (and my) youth, it might have been called "logical reasoning" or something like that. It's the ability, or the motivation really, to evaluate evidence, or claims. Phil later became expert at debunking psychics, for example. He has even pretended to be one from time to time for psychology classes. An instructor would present him as a "registered psychic." He is an expert with a technique called "cold reading" wherein the presumed psychic can tell you things about yourself he or she couldn't know without being genuinely psychic. Phil helped me understand the human tendency to fill in facts from mere assumptions or suggestions, deal in selective perception, and ascribe knowledge where none exists. Our inadvertent ability, for example, to believe in an interaction with a deceased ancestor, is actually an interaction with one's own emotional needs. Along with debunking claims, sometimes as a guest on radio and television, Phil reminded me to keep an "open-minded skepticism" and that our intuition can also motivate us to do right by ourselves and others, otherwise the human tribe might have killed itself off long ago. Phil also helped me not to take optimism for granted.

In *Memoirs,* Phil's "boomer" experiences, feelings, and the reasons he had them, are described in wonderful detail. This is related to his extraordinary powers of observation, vivid memories of childhood, and his remarkable ability to think deeply about just about anything. He's a master of detailed observation. As well as having been a professional music critic, Phil can tell the difference between different brands of compact disc players, amplifiers, etc., just by closing his eyes and listening carefully. He trained me to do the same thing. I don't have especially good hearing, especially these days, but by paying attention and focusing on the sound itself, a fellow can get a lot more out of audio as a hobby or otherwise. It is this kind of focus, coupled with deep reactions to, and interactions with, the world around him that makes *Memoirs* a joy to read.

If any of us had a nickel for each time a movie is described as "a coming of age story…," well we'd have a few bucks. This book is not about coming of age with sex, or drinking, or speeding in cars. It's a journal of the life experience of a boy discovering the world around him in a period of optimism, fear, and profound change. What makes you want to read each passage and the next is the detail in each scene along with how the protagonist, a young boy, experienced his reality at each moment.

Memoirs of a Baby Boomer is a superb account of what was on a kid's mind during the 1950s and early '60s. With a young person's curiosity, and especially his imaginings, he describes encounters born of toys, books, movies, music, the new era of television, and youthful encounters with the opposite sex, with a richness that few of us have experienced, let alone been able to describe. Phil's visions of what the world was and could be like are, for me, fantastic.

Take it up. Drink it in. Whether you are young or old, *Memoirs* will allow you to understand how our generation experienced the hands we were dealt, and how so much of our world today has been shaped by the thinking of kids like Phil, who grew up and did their best to simply live life and do the right thing. It's an important story that helps us all learn how we got here from the mid-20th century and on into the 21st.

BILL NYE
Studio City, CA

Preface

Eventually, a person wonders if he or she has a significant autobiographical story—whether it has a genuine plot or merely fragments, relationships, and disconnected scenes. Does it contain a thread of cultural, social, or nature/nurture inevitability?

Most of us lead unremarkable lives. Yet we're all subject to the culture in which we grew up. The cultural 1950s were a time that actually ended in 1963 when President Kennedy was assassinated and the country was plunged into war and protest. The '50s and early '60s have often taken on a warm glow in the minds of those of us who experienced them as children or youth. You who are reading this will be living in a very different world, for in the 1950s there were no home computers, smartphones, video games, big screen televisions, DVDs, school mass shootings, or anxiety about global warming. There were, however, fears: the hydrogen bomb, brutal racism, unsafe automobiles, street gangs, and "acceptable" biases such as limits imposed on women and gays. Yet those of us who grew up in the '50s white and middle class, were usually blessed with a sense of personal security as well as crazily catered to by advertisers, toy manufacturers, movie studios, and television, all in an era that eventually acquired an enduring nostalgia and a yearning for supposedly simpler, more innocent times. We of the post–World War II "baby boom" generation recall those times within the context of childhood— and that, of course, makes all the difference.

What follows is a spontaneous *personal* remembrance, an autobiographical narrative with generous slices of cultural awareness, not a formal accounting of the times that will satisfy everyone's expectations. Aside from a little research regarding the timing of certain events (e.g., the release date of a movie or a hit record) this narrative is merely how I remember things. That also applies to the spoken words, the dialogue being as best as I can recall. It's a child's-eye view, so to speak—with, I hope, minimal commentary from my more knowledgeable adult self. Without that limitation, this would have been longer and more intricate than the most patient reader could abide. Yet I've found, in talking to others, that I have a better than average memory of childhood. I felt the urge to write these memories down, those that for whatever reasons have permanently lodged in my mind, creating a "personal time capsule." If those of my generation find some shared experiences here, and others find something entertaining or interesting, all the better.

§ 1

I not only recall my first memory, I happen to know the exact year, month, date, hour, and minute of that memory. You might ask how one may know such a thing, given that the memory occurred at the age of two. Of course, I didn't know the exact time at that age; the time of the memory was confirmed later.

The initial, abrupt sensation was that of being picked up by my grandmother in a panic. She held me in her arms in the doorway to my bedroom while I watched the water in the bureau fishbowl slosh around and a crack go across the ceiling. Those are the clues to my first memory.

The 1949 Seattle earthquake occurred on April 13 at 11:56 AM local time. To be exact, it was named the Olympia earthquake, a 7.1 with an epicenter between Olympia, WA, the state capital, and Tacoma. It remains the largest quake to hit the Puget Sound area since Seattle was founded.

We lived in a massive 1911 three-story brick apartment building, an "Old English" structure called The Gables, on a Capitol Hill residential street behind red-brick Fire Station No. 7. The inside was intersected with oriental-carpeted hallways that might have been those of a luxurious mausoleum, except that these passages were haunted not by dead souls, but by living ones. I lived there until the age of four or five with my two grandparents, Nels and Emma Hanson, my mother Judy (divorced from my father that same year) and Aunt Evelyn ("Peggy," because as a child she'd walked with a slight limp as if she had a peg leg). But it wasn't the building's faded elegance or its tenants that were the focus of my childhood. My imagination caused some disturbing, surrealistic visions. The images were vague at first, then became more distinct. During a few nights of quiet terror, I came to believe, without previous associations, that hairless human-like creatures were under my bed, and that if I let my arm dangle over, they would grab me and take me under—a common type of childhood fear, I learned later.

Grandfather Nels would sit in his wine red, velvet-flocked overstuffed chair, his head often resting against the embroidered antimacassar while listening to *Amos 'n' Andy* or other radio shows on our new upright 1949 Magnavox radio/record player with its green-lighted dial. It was still the era of radio.

I listened to *The Lone Ranger, Jack Benny, The Inner Sanctum* (with its creaking door), and many others. Grandfather had managed a lumber yard in Bozeman, Montana, and it was said he could tell on sight how many board feet of lumber were on a given railroad flat car.

But in the late '40s, he decided to come to Seattle, partly to find other work, and partly because he was in the habit of moving from place to place, job to job, having lived in several small Montana towns. He started a grocery store named Esperance Market north of Seattle on 225th and Aurora Ave. At that time, the area was woodsy, and my grandmother and I once encountered a bear and her cubs. One of Grandfather's desires was to visit Sogndal, Norway, the area where he grew up on a farm. Moreover, he seemed the sort of person you could depend on for advice.

"Don't let your hand dangle over the edge of the bed," he said.

In the winter, Grandmother and I built a snowman in the open courtyard at the front of the big apartment building. An elderly woman peered down disapprovingly from her window because we were destroying the coat of virgin snow with our galoshes, rolling snowballs, and acting as if the courtyard were our private domain. Perhaps because we lived in an old, distinguished section of the city, our building contained no children other than myself, at least none I can recall.

The hallway on our third floor was carpeted with an intricately-patterned runner, and it led down the hall to the corner I could not see beyond. Near the end of the hall was another apartment. One day the tenant, a man, stared at us for a long time as my grandmother and I arrived upstairs from the main staircase's dark forest of polished mahogany posts and railings. We watched the man turn and walk back down the hall to his door like a drunken passenger lost in the depths of an ocean liner.

At night, I recall my mother saying, "Go to sleep now and I'll leave your door open a crack"—her way of making me feel secure. She and Aunt Peggy shared a bedroom, while my grandmother and grandfather shared another. My room was quite small, probably not intended to be a bedroom, and with the narrow column of light coming from the short hall outside, I put my cheek on the cool pillow and began to sleep, and to dream.

I did not know the whereabouts of my father, nor likely knew I even had a father until a few years later after he had contracted multiple-sclerosis, was confined to a wheelchair, and we began to visit him twice a year.

Grandmother, a healthy 5'2" and wearing her brown plaid overcoat, walked with me to Caroline's Cakes, a bakery on 15th Ave., where I stared into the long glass cases that often contained fresh birthday cakes. The baker sometimes decorated the frosting on these cakes with small plastic cowboys and Indians. But we came for the old fashioned cupcake-size cinnamon rolls; and when walking home, we passed Fire Station No. 7, that old brick building with big double doors. The back of our apartment house bordered an alley directly behind the fire station, and the gridded metal fire escape whose uppermost platform was outside our kitchen window, could be seen winding downward to the alley where the garbage cans were grouped like big aluminum mushrooms near a brick wall. One of the firemen sometimes threw a large white rubber ball decorated with stars, back and forth to me in the alley, teaching me to play catch. He once brought me into the station to lift me up onto the fender of the fire truck—quite a thrill!

At the front of our apartment building, I would with difficulty open the tall, wood-framed glass door to the entry hall. Grandmother took a key out of her purse to check the mailbox. Sometimes I would play on the second- or third-floor landing, or even venture down to the entry hall. One morning while the sun was still low and the light glared through the front-door glass into the hall, I sat on the lower step of the staircase with a toy. A woman was cleaning her apartment and made one or two trips out the back door behind the staircase, now carrying a grocery bag of garbage that smelled of used coffee grounds. I heard the garbage can lid rattle onto the can in the alley, and from her open apartment door I could hear the soap-opera voices of *Stella Dallas* coming from the radio. I knew the show because my grandmother was a lifelong soap opera addict, referring to them as "my programs." The back door closed, and I watched the woman start back down the hallway, then turn. She suddenly walked back toward me, a hurricane of thick makeup and bright red lipstick. She stared at me. Her left eye twitched slightly in its cavity of dry flesh, then she quickly turned, as if from the scene of a crime, retreating toward her apartment with the soap-opera voices, leaving me slightly stunned.

On summer days, my grandmother would sometimes walk me to Volunteer Park and sit me up on one of the two ancient Chinese stone camels guarding the front of the Seattle Art Museum, or take me to the kids' wading pool near the big greenhouse. The art museum was a massive horizontal structure in Art Deco style, more suitable to Oz than to Seattle, with fountain pools at each end and a tall, dazzling metalwork entrance. Looking to the west down the wide steps leading from the entrance was a reservoir the size of a small lake, supplying water to the city spreading out below Capitol Hill. Two lily-pad pools with giant goldfish, nearby banks of flowers, and green lawns completed a scene that seemed otherworldly, though of course I knew nothing of the art of architecture or landscape design.

Looking at the museum, never having been inside, I could not conceive of who occupied such a place or what was done there. The world was mysterious. The people I saw while I was in public were pedestrians on the sidewalks or passengers on the bus that took us downtown where Grandmother would sometimes go shopping. The bus created a powerful memory with its narrow twin doors opening and closing with a "chhhuff!" and a metallic thud upon closure. The seats were brown faux leather with metal bars for hand-holds across their tops. At the front and back of the bus, longer seats faced across the aisle from one another, and when the bus was crowded, people stood and held onto tall metal poles. The uniformed bus driver was the most impressive human being I had ever seen, navigating the city with a huge steering wheel made of Bakelite plastic (known to early plastic aficionados as polyoxybenzylmethylenglycolanhydride), with an impressively large center hub. So, the first thing I ever wanted to be was a bus driver. Aside from that, I was in the habit of singing a Norwegian song in the aisle of the bus and doing a little dance. On one of these occasions, two Norwegian women were sitting across from us and burst out laughing until nearly in tears, when at one point, to emphasize a certain lyric, I forcefully stomped my foot on the floor. I can't recall the line of the song (or any of the song at all) that elicited this ferocious gesture, and I finally had to sit down or fall down.

I don't recall any strong emotions during this period of

my early childhood (other than the temporary fear of creatures under my bed)—not of joy or disappointment, loneli-
ness or great affection. I was apparently content, fascinated
by things around me, which was enough, along with the security of my extended family and my environment both inside
the apartment and in the public places we visited. My world
was one of immediate surroundings, and luckily, having been
born right after World War II, I benefited from a certain sta-
bility: a parent and aunt with dependable middle-class jobs,
and the beginnings of a consumer culture catering to childhood desires. (As I was to find out, a too-crowded population
of those post-war children.)

When I was four or five, my grandfather sold his grocery
business and found a job in a lumber mill, somewhere in the
Scandinavian district of Ballard. He moved our family to the
rented first floor of a classic "Four-Square" Edwardian house
with its second-story "projected" corner bedrooms, hip roofs,
and a small round window in the center of the second story.
This house at 1607 NE Ravenna Boulevard in north Seattle
was about a mile north of the University of Washington. It
faced north because the boulevard went east-west at that
point. The house was set high above the street on a grass embankment behind a retaining wall, with concrete stairs leading
up to a broad front porch. The street itself had a wide median
of lawn with tall horse-chestnut trees that lined the entire
length. This boulevard curved westward here and there all
the way to Green Lake, a large urban lake to the mostly residential northwest—a lake surrounded by a park and neighborhoods of houses. In the early days, a trolley line had
brought people through the University District out to Ravenna Park near our house. I could see the tracks still embedded
in the street along the section of University Way intersecting
the boulevard. I had a rudimentary fascination with these

abandoned tracks. I imagined trolley cars rumbling along—perhaps my first faint notion of a world existing before my birth.

A kind of Dickensian trauma would soon change my life, but for now this old Seattle house was shaping my view of what a house and household should be, with its formal grandeur (grand, certainly to me), heavy woodwork, hardwood and oriental-carpeted floors, formal archways, box-beamed ceilings, yellow-tiled kitchen counter-tops below the painted wooden cabinets, big front porch, and steep, concrete-walled stairs cutting through the grass embankment buttressed at the bottom by a long concrete wall.

At some point, the tenants of the upstairs floor (accessed by separate stairs attached to the back of the house) were engaged to baby-sit me, and so I discovered an architectural detail, by exploration, as I found my way into the central upstairs closet. By some mysterious intent this was the location of the small round window that from the exterior of the house was framed with circular wooden molding. These central round or oval windows were typical of that style of house, and as the light filtered in on me, I felt an unaccountable emotion, something haunting about this odd but seemingly important window with its light coming through to illuminate an otherwise dark closet. Was it a dim memory of birth, or merely due to the nature of the house, with the upstairs closet nearer the life-giving sun, the cellar its subterranean opposite? The strange window became a permanent memory from that large old house.

Other spaces provided refuge. I would sometimes hide downstairs in a corner behind a big overstuffed chair, with a toy or two, and not respond to my grandmother's calls until she came into the living room. Or I would crawl under the long, polished walnut dining table with its thick pillars of ornately carved legs, augmented by the legs of chairs, lying on my back looking at the underside with its complicated mechanism for opening the table for an extension. I would spontaneously escape into this shadowy pavilion after playing on the floor with my toy cars.

"My goodness, *there* you are!" Grandmother would say. "What are you doing under there again?" To which, of course, I had no answer. I merely liked being under the table or behind the chair in my private space. How nice to hide.

The holidays gave me the opportunity to lie under the Christmas tree and stare up at the multi-colored lights in the branches, lights that reflected off the shiny balls and bright lead-foil tinsel my aunt always hung with care. Because of the weight of the material used then, the tinsel hung straight and true. The tree was always a natural Douglas fir, never sheared during growth to make it too dense for hanging decorations. Christmas Eve dinners were of traditional Norwegian food— lutefisk, lefsa, krumkake, and a delicious cream pudding called rommegrot. For a main dish, my grandmother took pity on me and also served meatballs, potatoes, and gravy.

Like almost all kids, I believed in the mystical notion of Santa Claus. Disillusionment would come later, but in the meantime, the world contained fantastic entities such as Santa Claus and the Easter Bunny. I believed in visitations by these mythical beings on the appropriate nights during my first year in the house on Ravenna—beliefs more desirable than the ghastly creatures under my bed.

One evening in winter, half a foot of glowing white snow covered the street, the wide grass median with its chestnut trees, the sidewalks, the lawns, and our embankment. Suddenly the world outside was magical, for it didn't often snow in Seattle. That night, my grandmother and I put on heavy coats and galoshes and went out onto the top of the glistening embankment illuminated by a distant street lamp and the glow from our living room windows. We stood there for a few moments, watching the snowflakes fall. Then Grandmother motioned me to make our way down to the bottom of the embankment where it flattened out along the top of the concrete wall. She said to lie down flat in the snow where the slope began, which I did, while she did the same; then she showed me how to make a snow angel by moving my arms up and down in a wide arc. We again stood where the lawn leveled out near the top of the wall and regarded the magical figures we had made. We left them behind and made our way down to the sidewalk. Gloved hands warmly in pockets, we walked down toward 15th Ave. to look at the snow-covered chestnut trees and listen to the silence. I would remember this night, in its simple beauty, all of my life.

Just before dinner time in those days, my grandfather Nels, tall but not imposing, with a slightly thin face and thinning white hair, would arrive home from the lumber mill. (Aunt Peggy, rather thin, plain and studious-looking with her glasses, worked at the Federal Reserve Bank downtown; my mother Judy, a former high-school beauty queen with silky brown hair and a face more fashionably attractive than my aunt's, was, at that time, a secretary at an automobile dealership.) Grandfather wore a black 19th-century-style pea coat with wide, curving lapels and half-leather sleeves, carried a black lunch pail and smelled wonderfully of fresh cut wood as I ran to hug him. On rare days, he would bring home small blocks of wood, perhaps ends of newly-sawn two-by-four lumber, for me to play with. I had quite a collection and would build little cities for my toy cars—little enamel-painted metal cars I would also play with in the dirt near the foundation of the house. Out there, I had once tried using water to make mud cookies, with the mistake of biting into one of them and having to run into the kitchen to have my mouth washed out with soap for an abnormal reason.

I had a big red and white tricycle. The sidewalk in front of the house went east-west, and eastward it curved upward at a steep angle to the right, southward, passing below other houses on rocky embankments and ending at a high corner. I'd push the tricycle up the curving hill, hop on at the top and zoom down the sidewalk, sometimes making the curve on two wheels or falling off onto the grass of the parking-strip, the tricycle crashing and clattering. Not often the latter, but enough to test the limits of my skill. I loved speeding down that steeply curving sidewalk and, as was more usual, ending just past the bottom steps in front of our house.

Another vehicle of note was my Aunt Peggy's 1950 Ford V-8, a light-green four-door she parked in front of the detached garage out back. The dashboard was gray metal, and when I had the chance to ride in the passenger seat—no seatbelts then—I was fascinated by a detail of the interior design: a tiny futuristic car integrated into the gray window sill next to me. Imagination reigned in automotive design. The nose of the '50 Ford was circular chrome, the hood ornament a small fin of translucent plastic. The seats were originally of gray mohair, but my aunt had purchased two-tone red and green seat covers to protect this material. When she pulled into the gas station, she always told the attendant, "Fill 'er up with Ethyl." This was high-octane fuel, and with it the car could accelerate rapidly with its three-speed manual transmission. My aunt sometimes let me sit beside her and shift the steering column wand with its ivory-colored ball on the end: pull back and down for first gear, way up and a bit forward for second, straight down for third. How the car drove made a huge impression on me, along with being trusted to shift it on my aunt's instruction while she operated the clutch, gas pedal, and steering wheel. My grandmother claimed that my very first words were "ka-kee" ("car key") which, not long before, I'd heard my aunt say. (I suspect "mama" or "papa" came first, but who knows.)

I made a friend next door to the east. His last name had been changed from the German "Goot" to Good, his first name Gary. He and I played cowboys. We had cowboy hats, cowboy bandannas, and cowboy guns. My set of twin Cisco Kid cap guns had black holsters with ruby red jewels in the centers. Sometimes I was the Cisco Kid, sometimes the Lone Ranger. These and other cowboys flooded the radio airwaves with high adventure, and Gary and I ran around behind the house, up and down the concrete alley, taking cover behind wooden garages, fighting bad guys or each other as we played various roles. I even had a small, yellow painted desk in the kitchen we called the "sheriff's desk," with a drawer containing my tin badge, some marbles, and some green-plastic bus tokens left over from WW II. I would sometimes make a little chocolate drink and serve it to myself there, using a Donald Duck tea set. Not very sheriff-like.

The cowboy craze of 1950s childhood had begun. Almost no one had a television, so Western movies and radio shows were the hugely popular method of influencing our minds with the supposed romance of guns, shoot-outs, covered wagons, horses, and stagecoaches. Thus a complex set of circumstances—largely myths of how the country was founded and settled, and the romantically embellished ideals associated with it—passed down the generations in a uniquely American way. Why this fascination with the old west took root in post WW II America I had no clue, nor did I understand the world that was trying to shape my identity or affect my perspective in ways I could barely comprehend.

One day when I was playing cowboy alone, I met the first girl to make an impression on me. Molly was a tomboy (so my grandmother said) who lived in a house somewhere behind us, and who would also run around playing cowboy—or rather cowgirl. She did not have guns or holsters, but hid here and there, spying on Gary and me, and of course we ran away from her. One day I wandered over to her house, found her in the back yard, and we played catch. Molly was freckle-faced, wore flowered dresses, and was lively. She might have been a year older than I, but my attraction to her at the age of five, and with so little exposure to girls, began an understanding that girls could be more than "just girls." We played catch now and then until she moved away—so shortly after I'd met her—yet her lively, friendly personality remained with me forever.

Gary moved away as well. This was a sad event, for I was back on my own, truly now the Lone Ranger. Well, not quite alone. There was Lady, the springer spaniel across the street, with whom I also made friends; but eventually the owner wouldn't allow her to make the journey across the street and wide green median of Ravenna Boulevard. So I took to rolling down the steep grass embankment in front of the house, stopping before the top of the wall.

Soon my Aunt Peggy showed me how to put together simple balsa-wood airplanes that came unassembled. The best of these had the number "74" on a wing that could be adjusted to make the plane circle or fly straight. I would stand at the top of our steep grass embankment, or on the wide front porch, and fly the plane off into the airy stratosphere. Once in a while it would curve onto Mrs. Wine's embankment next door to the west. This involved the serious danger of retrieval, for Mrs. Wine, a cantankerous old woman with wild black hair, would sometimes come out of her house wielding a black bull-whip. She'd flick the thick, snake-like weapon with a loud "SNAP!" to scare kids off her lawn—mostly Gary and me previously—but now only me with my wandering "74." She made my grandmother nervous, for no one knew anything about her origins or background. She lived alone in her large, mustard-yellow corner house and became another sub-

ject of my childhood nightmares—the visitation of a wicked
witch complementing the creatures under the bed.

Yet nightmares were rare, and days were filled with soli-
tary play.

Our house was often filled with music. My mother played the
piano, and in our big living room I loved to watch the US
Capitol Dome spin around and around on a platter. The
dome on the purple label was the trademark of Capitol Records, and my record of choice was "Twelfth Street Rag" by
Pee Wee Hunt and His Orchestra. I became mesmerized by
the spinning record, its purple label, and the Dixieland instrumental, which I played over and over again on a special
45 rpm record player designed by RCA Victor. This player
had been added by my Aunt Peggy to the 1949 Magnavox—
the floor-stander that was both a radio (AM plus shortwave)
and a 78 rpm record player. The little 45 player sat on top, on
the side opposite the lid that gave access to the Magnavox's
record player, but could be lifted down and put on the floor
for me to use. The little player was nearly a cube, only about
ten inches wide, made of black Bakelite plastic (same ubiquitous stuff as the bus driver's steering wheel) and switched on
using a wafer-thin dial at the side. From its center rose a thick
cylindrical spindle designed to fit the large hole of a 45 rpm
record. The tone arm was a short, thick, wide, gold-colored
curvature that looked vaguely Egyptian and gave the whole
player an Art Deco look without genuine Deco motifs. A
dozen records could be stacked on the spindle, supported by
two thin tabs, and these records would drop down one at a
time, one after another as they were played, onto a small red-
vinyl-covered platter while the heavy tone arm whipped over,
down, up, back, over, down, with frightening mechanical violence.

After getting used to this, with the help of my aunt, I

slowly accumulated, as various gifts, a number of 45 rpm children's records, such as the story of "Little Toot" the tugboat (with all the appropriate sound effects), and cowboy songs—one by Tex Ritter titled "Blood on the Saddle." ("Oh, there was bluuuud on the saaaddle, and bluuuud on the ground . . .") and no one seemed to think I'd be harmed for life by all this bloodshed, let alone all our gun play outdoors. Such secure, innocent times. And of course I had some of the Disney record sets, as well, like *Snow White* and *Pinocchio*. I hadn't seen these movies yet, but the records had high production values like old radio shows and made good use of a child's imagination. Nevertheless, it was 78 rpm records that had been, and would continue to be for several more years, the mainstay of our house. My Aunt Peggy had a sizable collection of hits, including multiple-record sets of Glenn Miller, Doris Day, and some Tchaikovsky—a set of 12-inch 78s with a cover drawing of a sleigh and horses traveling through the snow. I wasn't old enough to fully appreciate classical music, but I appreciated something of it regardless, partly because of the cover art. Mostly I played 78 rpm singles like "Sweet Georgia Brown" by Brother Bones and His Shadows, "Aba Daba Honeymoon" sung by Debbie Reynolds, and "The Cry of the Wild Goose" by Frankie Lane. A famous 78 rpm children's record on the Capitol label, taken from a Dr. Seuss story, was "Gerald McBoing Boing" about a boy who could only speak in sound effects! It was narrated by Harold Peary, "The Great Gildersleeve" of radio comedy who narrated a number of children's records. His character of Throckmorton P. Gildersleeve originally appeared on *Fibber McGee and Molly*, a hugely popular radio comedy of the time.

What sort of picture of life did I draw from this bizarre conglomeration? Once in a while, adding to the cowboy motif, my mother would buy me a 78 rpm of *The Lone Ranger* from a series of episodes issued in colorful record jackets.

Western heroes continued to inspire, exercise my imagination, and instill notions of good and bad, good guys and bad guys, without ambiguity. The things I was given—Little Golden Books, toys like the amazing Fort Apache play set, games such as *Candy Land,* puzzles from Disney cartoons, those wooden blocks my grandfather brought home, my records—created an exterior world of things, and an interior world of experiences, always changing, expanding, influencing, and finally of unaccountable and unmeasurable effect.

The Magnavox radio console and 78 rpm record player was especially influential and impressive with its red mahogany cabinet about three feet high. Unlike the former decade's more ornate models, its lines were post-war modern. The clean design was achieved by having a single door that closed over the radio's controls and loudspeaker, and a flat lid that covered the record changer. I learned how to open the front and turn on the radio, also how to play 78s.

Older people recall with great fondness the glowing dials of those big radios, and I luckily experienced the tail-end of the era before television. I knew the meaning of having sound alone coming into the living room each night, and the advantage of words, music, sound effects, and pictures created only by one's imagination. As for the Magnavox, in front were knurled brown knobs, one of which lit up the big rectangular green dial. The bandwidth was AM, supplemented by short wave. FM was just being introduced (there was a selection marked for it, but no electronics installed). A small, round piece of glass was set at the base of the big tuning dial. This was the fine-tuning device, a green glowing light in the shape of a "V" that pinched itself together when a station came into perfect tune. A really strong signal could nearly close the "V" entirely. All this green luminosity was magic to my eyes, the sound to my ears, as the shows and records filled the room with music and entertainment.

More wonder lay in back. Because of the baseboard along the floor, the Magnavox was set a couple of inches out from the wall, and a small person could press his cheek against the wall, close one eye, and peer into the inner sanctum of the cabinet. In that cavern was a fabulous city of warm, glowing vacuum tubes in many sizes. This electronic city of glass and metal created a true sensation of magic—for how other than magic could I knowledgeably relate all the glowing dials and glass tubes to the programs and music broadcast from the outside world? This was civilization.

Although Aunt Peggy had purchased RCA's 45 rpm record player ($12.95 plus tax), she did so as one might buy a new hat. She probably realized that RCA's "war of the speeds" with Columbia's 33 ⅓ long-playing record, would last for a while, so she decided to stick with 78s until the results were in, while I was given 45s. The 45 became the de facto format of the young—leading to rock & roll—while the LP required an entirely new kind of record player.

§ 2

In front of the wine red, velvet-flocked overstuffed sofa was an ornate, rectangular coffee table with a glass top upon which were placed Aunt Peggy's and Grandmother's Bible and a copy of *Science and Health, with Key to the Scriptures* by Mary Baker Eddy. Every Sunday morning, Grandmother and Aunt walked up along Ravenna Boulevard to the Third Church of Christ Scientist where they attended services. I was too young to attend at that time, Grandfather was a former Lutheran, and Mother had failed to be indoctrinated into Christian Science or any particular religion. Christian Science had become a fad in the 1920s, asserting the healing power of prayer and the rejection of medical treatment. When I asked Grandfather why he stayed home from church, he merely smiled.

The rented upstairs of the house had been sealed off from downstairs, but I was playing on the previously functional stairs, bounded down, tripped, fell, and smacked headlong into Grandmother's three-foot-long cedar chest in the entry area below. I struck my head on the corner of the chest, striking it just to the outside of my left eye. I cried, bleeding profusely, causing a panic in the household. A quarter of an inch difference, and I'd have been blinded in that eye. My fall, and the luck with which I'd hit the corner of the chest without going half blind, was told in our family many times as an example of the perils of childhood. But the immediate result, aside from injury, was my singular awareness of the cedar chest *itself.*

Later, I tried to lift the lid, but it was locked. The key was hidden, my aunt said. I was curious but was told only that the chest was never to be opened or tampered with. So it remained a mystery.

My days were those of an only child who learned to keep company with his imagination, his toys, records, the family radio, even the furniture and the house itself. My environment was a cornucopia of pleasures—including green summer, traditional Christmas, rare winter snow, ubiquitous Seattle raindrops seen through a multiplicity of windows, and little curiosities.

Unfortunately, all this came to an end when my mother remarried. Her new husband whom I had never seen, Larry Nelson, sold fire extinguishers and was instantly disliked by my grandparents and aunt. His black hair was combed almost straight back, he had a "strong silent type" personality common in those days, but with an edge that seemed suspicious. He looked something like Fred MacMurray in *Double Indemnity*.

I was five and would have to move away with this new man and my mother to start kindergarten.

One night they came to pick me up and parked my new

stepfather's dark blue Plymouth station wagon on the street down in front of the house. I had a suitcase and a few of my things in boxes that were loaded into the car. I had been much closer to my grandmother than my mother—in fact had always referred to my grandmother as "mom"—and so felt as if I were being taken away to some private orphanage ruled by a stranger I did not know or care to know. They came up onto the big front porch because I would not descend. While my grandmother stood behind me, I panicked, turned, and grabbed onto her dress. I was suddenly in tears. She held onto me and said, "Does he *really* have to go?" My mother said yes while my stepfather stood silently. It must have taken a lot of emotional courage for my grandmother, who had cared for me more than anyone else, to take my arms and separate me from her while I still tried to hold onto her dress. My mother helped with the separation, and I knew it was hopeless, finally, to change something that was now inevitable, and I let go.

That night I was driven away from the security of that big Edwardian house of my grandmother's and grandfather's, and of my life as I had known it. No memory or impression of getting in the car, the ride that night, or the destination, stayed with me.

§ 3

As the trauma of separation from my grandparents faded, my memory of arrival at the two-bedroom house my stepfather and mother had rented, remained vague, though I began to settle into the new environment. The house was in a modest post-war neighborhood called Pinehurst in north Seattle, and I was to attend kindergarten at Pinehurst Elementary School, registered as Philip *Nelson*. My mother had had my last name legally changed to that of my stepfather's. It seemed as if the first five years of my life were to be wiped out and forgotten while my mother attempted to start her new married life. Yet the name change had little impact on my psyche, for I didn't learn to write before first grade anyway—and after a while I could barely connect myself to my original last name.

I didn't know what my real father, Vance Haldeman, handicapped with progressive multiple-sclerosis, thought about all this, for I had rarely been taken to visit him.

Pinehurst Elementary was a single-story, newly built school prepared to accommodate the coming population bubble of post-war children (the "baby boomer" generation). My report card from kindergarten, September 3, 1952–June 10, 1953, was broken down into three categories: Mental Development, Social-Emotional Development, and Physical Growth and Development. Nothing was mentioned under the latter. Under Mental Development, my teacher, Lilian M. Pease, wrote:

> "Philip has made satisfactory progress in all phases of kindergarten activities. He is able to follow a series of directions and to complete a task to his satisfaction and for his age. And his interest in the work period has to do with block building and playing with mechanical toys. When he is required to work with the creative art materials he does a better than average job." Social-Emotional Development: "It has been difficult for Philip to speak before the group but when he does, he tells his 'story' in a logical, orderly way. Philip is always cooperative and courteous. He has a keen sense of responsibility for school and personal property."

The building blocks were big, hollow, varnished plywood cubes about two feet high, and the boys built forts out of them. Art was mostly finger painting, and we were encouraged to express ourselves by smearing vivid colors around on thick paper and then washing our hands.

That is all I recall of kindergarten.

*   *   *

Larry Nelson, my stepfather, didn't quite turn out to be Mr. Murdstone from *David Copperfield*, or Mr. Neff from *Double Indemnity*, yet he was mostly silent and remote, not a good match for my mother, who was used to being talkative and engaging. On the surface, all seemed well enough, but as time passed I became aware of tension in the house. Larry attempted to assume the role of my father insofar as he was able, given that he spoke little, maintained his "strong silent type" creepy persona and was gone most of the time selling Kidde fire extinguishers.

I was given a red and white J. C. Higgins bicycle on my sixth birthday, which was in May, and Larry dutifully taught me how to ride while running along beside me, keeping me balanced until he decided to let go, whereupon I usually lost balance and fell crashing onto the gravel of the unfinished street. The bicycle was too large for me, probably the result of my parents not wanting me to outgrow it for a few years, so this learning process required no small amount of courage. Falling off was painful, but learning to ride a bicycle was a rite of passage, so I attempted to find my balance again and again, without training wheels, depending on Band-Aids applied by my mother until I could keep control—a major achievement, and one shared by every kid.

It was common for kids to ride their bikes to school; but near that time, my parents had rented another two-bedroom house (I never found out why we moved) and Pinehurst Elementary was only a half-block down the slope from our back yard, so I walked there when first grade started that fall.

Before that, during the summer, our next door neighbors bought a miraculous device called a television. Some other neighbors may have had them, as well, but the kid next door invited me over to see theirs, and the pressure was on for everyone to own one of these miracles and experience pictures and sound instead of only sound from radios. The first thing I saw on television was burned into my memory from that day forward: the black-and-white scene of a vast, rolling ocean and a huge white "V" that came out of the distance to announce the title of the World War II documentary series *Victory at Sea*. This program featured actual war footage and was accompanied by the stunning symphonic music of Richard Rodgers and Robert Russell Bennett. No one could resist having sound and pictures like this in one's living room. It is difficult to convey how impressive this was—the beginning of the television age—even though a mere 21" screen was considered large. Yet before my stepfather and mother got a television—and possibly for a while afterward—I would lie huddled in my room before falling asleep, listening to the old radio shows like *The Lone Ranger* that were still on the air. The transition to TV remained incomplete for some time.

Also that summer, I was stung by a bee on my bare foot while walking across our front lawn. The sudden surprise of pain was terrifying. "A bee! A bee!" I yelled, running into the house where my mother removed the stinger and applied ointment to my foot. Pain, other than a sunburn and falling off my bike, was mostly unfamiliar, though I knew bees could be dangerous. For sunburn, protection was attempted with a product called "Skol," a brown, watery antiseptic from a glass bottle that insofar as I could tell did nothing. We sometimes went to a lake on day trips, but my mother wouldn't let me learn how to swim. She had a paranoid fear of the water—for when she was a young girl in Montana, she had witnessed a drowned boy. He was pulled from a lake, horribly discolored and unable to be revived. Traumatized with the horror of accidental death, Mother recounted that the young man had been a friend of hers in school. This led to an overprotectiveness of me that lasted my entire childhood, although she eventually got the courage to take me to formal swimming lessons. I failed because of the fear of getting water up my nose and the feeling of suffocation. My stepfather then tried unsuccessfully to teach me, believing in strict methods—once threatening to throw me into a deep part of the lake, as some fathers had been known to do, to "make" the kid swim. Of course my mother was appalled, and arguments ensued as to how to raise a child.

Why some parents wouldn't allow their children to develop according to their own schedule and comfort level I didn't know, but I later learned to swim on my own, at the age of ten, in a motel swimming pool after my mother bought me a nose plug and a face mask. With one or the other of these I was swimming and diving around in the pool like a champ, and yelled at my stepfather, "Hey, I can swim!" But he merely stared at me, waved weakly, and afterwards lightly ridiculed the items that had alleviated my fear—items I eventually learned to do without, at least most of the time. Later, though, he seemed to understand, and we swam together in motel pools while on vacations. Still, Larry expressed almost no sympathy toward me or my mother for whatever inconvenient emotions we experienced, though he wasn't a tyrant. He had grown up in a small mid-western town named Manhattan, Kansas, and had been imbued with certain conventions of husband or fatherhood. He had married the wrong woman, probably attracted by her looks, and she had obviously married the wrong man. In time, it became clear that both of them were trying to raise the wrong child.

What I knew was that I'd become wary of my stepfather's moods, and his arguments with my mother—not usually about my upbringing, but about finances and god knows what, and these arguments got worse and worse, until, after arguments, it became Larry's habit to go for several *days* without speaking. Mother would try to talk to him, but he refused to say a word, staring into a newspaper or a book, not responding. Eventually, things would get back to relative normalcy. But partly as a result of his behavior toward her and me, in summer of '53, at the age of six, I was allowed to return to my grandparents' house on Ravenna Boulevard. Again, I stayed comfortably with my extended family, but only until first grade began in the fall; thereafter on weekends if I desired. This became the pattern throughout my childhood, staying with my grandparents and aunt in summers and on weekends.

The downside was having to go to church on Sundays to be indoctrinated into Christian Science. My grandmother, aunt, and I would walk to church south along 17th NE, which still had the wide median grass and tall horse chestnut trees of Ravenna Boulevard. Sundays in the fall, on the way home I would load my pockets with fallen chestnuts, marveling at the shiny wood-patterned capsules of the seeds, though not having any uses in mind. The church was a brick, two-story block-shaped building that looked more like an ornate bank than a church. Sunday School was held in the daylight basement, and over the following years I learned to memorize "The Scientific Statement of Being" as propounded by the church's founder, Mary Baker Eddy: "There is no life, truth, intelligence, nor substance in matter. All is infinite Mind and its infinite manifestation, for God is All-in-all. Spirit is immortal Truth; matter is mortal error. Spirit is the real and eternal; matter is the unreal and temporal. Spirit is God, and man is His image and likeness. Therefore man is not material; he is spiritual."

Philosophers who later addressed the difficult subject of consciousness (David Chalmers for example) might have agreed but for the inclusion of "God" and "Spirit"; indeed, modern physics found little or no "substance in matter"—at least at the sub-atomic level—but unfortunately, Mrs. Eddy's non-scientific idea was used to reject medicine and medical care in favor of "mind healing." According to Mrs. Eddy, illness and disease were merely the result of faulty materialist thinking—referred to as "error." Healing could even be done remotely via Christian Science "practitioners" who would be called upon to "know the truth."

More than a few children of strict Christian Scientists died as a result of medical neglect while their parents or practitioners tried to "know the truth." Luckily, I was not one of them, for my mother would have nothing to do with medical neglect—one advantage of her over-protectiveness. (Aside from her fear of water, she had a fear of intestinal constipation, a fear shared by my grandmother for reasons I did not know at the time, and had no problem giving me a mild laxative or other necessary medication. She rejected Christian Science "mind healing" even for a common bowel problem.)

My grandfather usually stayed home from church, for as I mentioned, he had been raised as a Lutheran and seemed to remain neutral insofar as my grandmother's and aunt's beliefs. Or perhaps he was more or less not allowed to discredit their beliefs. I had no idea. Even so, his attitude toward religion and the Bible would later become more apparent—as would Mrs. Eddy's unintended effect on my philosophical interests.

Although we were taught the basic principles of Christian Science, the Sunday School teachers mostly sat with us around little wooden tables in the church basement and read Bible stories to us. These stories were much like other fairy tales I had heard as a child, so I didn't much mind while I glanced at the big clock on the wall, waiting to be released. I didn't take all this very seriously, though I did not have the intellectual wherewithal to judge or disbelieve in what I was being told. Neither did I necessarily *believe* what I was being told.

When first grade began in the fall, I was back at Pinehurst Elementary. The school-age population was growing rapidly, and having been born in 1947, I was near the leading edge of the baby boom. Since Pinehurst had been newly built, we sat at comfortably wide desks two by two, but there were already "portables"—portable classrooms outside the main building, boxy wooden structures with a row of windows on one side. After school, while the weather was still comfortable, the boys played marbles by drawing a circle on the ground, placing marbles in the center and shooting others at them by balancing a "shooter" on the inside of the forefinger and launching it with the thumb, winning those marbles that could be knocked out of the circle. The nastiest shooters were the "steelies"—not marbles at all, but actual ball-bearings, heavy instruments of destruction brought by unscrupulous kids who tried to foist them off as legitimate. Some of us refused to play and drew our own circles for competing with ordinary colorful marbles, including prized "puries" (transparent) and "cat's eyes" that came in two sizes, using the larger as shooters. Because Aunt Peggy worked at the Federal Reserve, she somehow procured for me a small, brown, Seattle First National Bank money pouch with a drawstring to carry my treasure of marbles.

The most important thing about first grade was falling in love. Did other boys or girls have these feelings? I had no idea. The girl who unconsciously captivated my affection was named Andrea—the most beautiful name because she was the most beautiful, sweetest girl I had ever seen. I would have told you, had you asked, not to think for a moment that a six-year-old was incapable of falling in love. Andrea was an artist's angel, shorter than I, with light-brown hair, blue eyes, a soft, lovely face; and she seemed, perhaps, to like me. I would try to catch her attention subtly, unobtrusively, ridiculously, and if she smiled at me I experienced a meltdown. How I survived the year without dying of these tender feelings, I didn't know, for what could I do about a girl in the first grade? I did not even quite know what this was about, only that these secret feelings welled up inside me. I would have married her any day, in a playground ceremony, had there been such a thing.

On a weekend during the fall, my mother and stepfather took me to my first "live action" movie, apparently deciding that I was old enough at six to see something other than a Disney movie such as *Bambi* or *Pinocchio*. And our theater of choice was the Northgate Theater, a cornerstone of the nation's first large regional shopping center, called Northgate Center (later Northgate Mall) with a big department store and a couple of dozen shops lining the wide walkways. The theater, along with the mall, had been built in 1950 and was completely modern, but in a couple of odd ways. The large, wide marquee across the front looked like a giant set of Venetian blinds where the movie title and actors' names were displayed in huge red or black letters. The inside was given over to an American Western motif in homage to the most popular movie genre of the time, with tepees, horses, and figures of Indians painted on the walls, and restrooms with lighted signs over the entrances marked "Braves" and "Squaws." Even at my age, I found this rather amusing.

We saw many a Western (and many a science fiction) movie at the Northgate Theater as I grew up, but that first experience could never be repeated in the mind for sheer spectacle, for *The Robe* was the first movie filmed in Cinema-Scope, with a screen so wide it could have embraced the parting of the Red Sea. Appropriately so, for it also began the 1950s fascination with so-called biblical epics, many of which had little to do with the Bible—including *The Robe*. At the very beginning, Jesus is already being crucified, and the rest of the film centers around characters played by Richard Burton, Jean Simmons, and those hunting for his garment that had fallen to the ground during that first scene. Today, this movie plays almost like science fiction on another planet, but it's quite good if not taken seriously. At the age of six, I took it quite seriously of course and was terrified by one of the nastiest villains ever to chew scenery in a motion picture. Just who the actor was who played Caligula, the Emperor of Rome, I didn't know (his name was Jay Robinson) but his sneering, sarcastic degeneracy taught me something about . . . well, sneering, sarcastic degeneracy. And in the end, he who rules over his fellow man condemns poor Richard Burton and Jean Simmons to death.

As with my first exposure to television, "the big screen" impressed itself not only on my visual senses, not only on my apprehension of adult human nature, but on my life generally—and with a power I had yet to understand.

Now, for some reason my mother was especially fond of science fiction movies. This was incongruous, for she never read science fiction, science fact, or anything other than *Readers Digest* condensed books, of which she and my stepfather had quite a collection. Yet movies were entertaining, and she liked to go out. My stepfather always wore a suit and tie to the movies, which was still the custom in the early '50s. He usually took us to dinner ahead of time and didn't mind walking into the theater late, if need be, believing that we could "catch up" to the plot. My mother objected, so we were usually on time.

One evening I saw my first science fiction movie. It was a rather mediocre movie called *Riders to the Stars*, yet the final minutes gave me nightmares for months. The plot concerned three astronauts sent into space in separate spaceships (those 1950s ones with fins) to capture meteoroids by way of scoops that opened up in the noses of the ships; the idea being to catch up to a meteoroid at matching speed, scoop it up, and bring it back to Earth. One of the ships explodes when it tries to grab a meteoroid that's too big, the astronaut is blasted free—and his space-suited body ends up floating in front of the viewport of one of the other ships. Inside the helmet, the flesh had been dissolved off his face, apparently because his suit had been punctured, leaving only a skull. I was terrified. And not only me! The other astronaut panicked at the sight of his dead companion, mentally snapped, and suddenly thought he was back in World War II needing to bail out of his plane. He loses control, and his ship hurtles off into the black void forever. Only one astronaut is left, he succeeds in snatching a meteoroid, crash lands on Earth, and the final scene is of the sparkling, multi-colored meteorite glowing in the receiving chamber of the ship, rescuers standing in awe.

I was six! Outer space was mysterious and frightening, and I did not have the critical sense or ability to distance myself from such scenes in the movies. There would be many more to come, and although we had not seen the best science fiction films in that early cycle of the 1950s (*The Thing from Another World, The Day the Earth Stood Still, War of the Worlds*) I was sufficiently impressed by what I did see—not only science fiction, but movies such as *The Robe, The Egyptian,* and *Shane,* a classic Western (not to mention John Huston's version of *Moby Dick* a few years later) that they had the power to imprint scenes upon my memory equal in seriousness to reality. So it seemed. Yet I also laughed wildly at Danny Kaye in *The Court Jester.* Movies had become a cornerstone of my life.

§ 4

After we got our own television, we began having dinner in the living room on folding TV trays. This was a normal American ritual. At the time, there were two networks broadcasting in Seattle. Soon, a third came along (ABC or NBC), and late in the evening all the stations simply went off the air, replaced by test patterns—one of which was the profile of an American Indian in a headdress, with lines and numbers along the margins, and when called upon at other times helped the TV repairman adjust the picture.

Television hoped to bring culture into American homes, and I watched "live" teleplays with my mother and stepfather: *Studio One,* and later, *Playhouse 90* were two of these as I was growing up. The other kinds of shows we watched were *I Love Lucy, I've Got a Secret, You Bet Your Life, The Jack Benny Show, Ozzie and Harriet, The Life of Riley, This is Your Life,* and *Disneyland.* But the most consistently popular program of the early '50s, besides *I Love Lucy,* was the detective show *Dragnet.* And this show may have led to an incredible incident in the neighborhood where I stayed with my grandparents.

Nels (I called him Papa), Emma (I called her Mom), and Aunt Evelyn (she was always Peggy), had moved into their own 1908 craftsman-style house after Papa had been working for a while in the lumber mill in Ballard. The house at 6323 14th NE, just south of NE 65th St. was technically in the craftsman style, but a plain example without much fancy interior woodwork, although it did have beamed ceilings on the first floor and a mantled fireplace. I was so happy to stay with my extended family again, partly to get away from my stepfather, that my mother reluctantly decided I would live there in the summer and while attending second grade starting in the fall. I was home again.

Here, on both sides of the street (unlike the previous location on Ravenna Boulevard on only one side), the houses were built high up on retaining-wall embankments with concrete steps leading up to front porches. Across the street lived the Brandt family—husband, wife, and three kids, and like most of the television mass audience, they were used to watching *Dragnet* on Thursday nights at 9:00. I had turned seven in May, so along with my extended family, I watched shows on the new Zenith television my aunt had purchased. *Dragnet* was a favorite. It had a compelling documentary realism taken from actual L.A.P.D. files, and a police detective, Sergeant Joe Friday (Jack Webb), who solved cases without ever cracking a smile. Its gritty procedural approach was completely different than other detective shows: "The story you are about to see is true. Only the names have been changed to protect the innocent," ran the intro, followed by: "It was two forty-five. We were working the day watch out of homicide . . ." Certain lines of Joe Friday's dialogue entered common usage: "Just the facts, ma'am."

In these days of television, residential sidewalks were nearly abandoned at night, and the glow of television sets could be seen in the houses while people sat entranced in their living rooms in front of the black-and-white hearth. Such was true of the Brandts across the street, who had no idea what was about to happen.

The story, as told by the Brandt kids, went as follows: A Seattle criminal known as The Dragnet Burglar had become aware of the optimum, statistically ideal period of time when a huge number of people were likely to be frozen in place in their living rooms, unaware if someone was sneaking into the back of a house whose rear window or door might be left unlocked. The Dragnet Burglar had become an efficient, calculating, and maddeningly systematic thief, who, during the thirty minutes of Joe Friday's investigations, was a real-life criminal entering through back doors or windows into bedrooms where he'd find cash or jewelry. It might have taken awhile for the police to recognize that the burglaries were happening during a particular television show; but eventually they did, and on the night in question, Mr. Brandt had taken a moment during a commercial break to go into the kitchen for a snack. He heard a noise coming from the bedroom, and having read the newspapers, figured it could be the notorious

Dragnet Burglar. He went back into the living room, made sure his family was all there, and called the police. Minutes later, a squad car pulled into the concrete alley up the short, steep grade at the side of his house, while the Burglar exited through a rear window, running east in the dark alley toward 15th Ave. a half-block away. The police had already gotten out of their squad car and gave chase. They drew their guns, yelling for the man to stop. He did not. And he was shot dead trying to cross 15th Ave.

Was the story true? How much of it was true? My search of the *Seattle Times* archives many decades later turned up nothing!

§ 5

I began second grade that fall. My grandmother walked me several blocks along NE 65th until I made the rest of the journey to Ravenna School myself, about a mile from our house. Although, along with most kids, I had learned to read from the *Dick and Jane* books in first grade, or perhaps kindergarten, and at home I had *My First Dictionary* with pictures next to the words, it was in second grade that I learned more completely how to read and write, and also do simple addition and subtraction. We were given sheets of paper, blank in the upper half, with wide lines in the lower; we were expected to make drawings in the blank space, and write in the lower. I carefully formed printed letters, imitating what the teacher had done on the blackboard, while she, a rotund elderly lady with her hair in a bun, went up and down the aisles guiding us. During the first couple of weeks of the school year, we temporarily shared desks that had been designed to seat only one. They were very old wooden desks with built-in metal ink wells in the upper right corners, though the ink wells were not used now. Rather, we had dark blue pencils that seemed to have been made for the hands of giants. When the "porta-

bles" arrived outside, our class was divided up, and I was assigned the original classroom. The student crowding, usually
thirty to a classroom after arrangements were completed, was
of course due to the post-war baby boom. But this flowering
of little humans, resulting in the sharing of desks and textbooks, didn't strike me as odd, for I had no idea I was in the
forefront of a unique population bubble that would affect
me, more often as a hindrance, as I tried to make my way
through life.

Not much about second grade lodged in my memory
other than writing, spelling, simple math, playing at recess,
and an occasional classroom game of "musical chairs." Indoors at home, I built log cabins from a set of Lincoln
Logs—actual notched wooden logs of varying lengths up to
about nine inches. These sets were hugely popular. So were
Plastic Bricks, a precursor to Legos but far more realistic-
looking once a building was completed.

Movies and TV shows created a shared environment outside of school, and much of children's television became legendary. Walt Disney's *Disneyland* was watched every week by
millions of kids, not to mention adults, and one could be sure
that almost every kid in class the next day had seen it. Shared
watching was a feature of childhood throughout the early
years of television because we had limited choices with only
three major networks: ABC, NBC, and CBS. I watched *Howdy
Doody* featuring Buffalo Bob with various marionettes, along
with its iconic live audience of kids called The Peanut Gallery.
Another was *Andy's Gang*, also known as *The Buster Brown
Show*, from radio days. Heavy-set, gravelly-voiced cowboy actor Andy Devine hosted this strange show featuring Froggy
the Gremlin, Midnight the Cat, and episodes of a jungle adventure series called *Gunga, the East Indian Boy*. For some crazy reason, the show's opening was unforgettable, as Devine's
voice intoned "Plunk yer magic twanger, Froggy!" And a

puppet frog would appear from a puff of smoke, saying, "Hiya, kids! Hiya, hiya, hiya!"

No less memorable were all the Saturday morning cowboy shows, most of which had evolved from western movies and radio shows: *Hopalong Cassidy, The Cisco Kid, The Lone Ranger, Roy Rogers, Gene Autry,* and *Annie Oakley,* the latter becoming a role model for millions of girls.

This phenomenon of TV culture also resulted in one of the most incredible fads of the 1950s—the astonishing popularity of a historical backwoodsman named Davy Crockett.

Toward the end of 1954, I watched "Davy Crockett: Indian Fighter," the first of a three-part *Disneyland* mini-series, seen by 40 million Americans. The second installment in January, "Davy Crockett Goes to Congress," captured fully half of the entire TV audience that night. Millions of kids went nuts buying Crockett's iconic coonskin cap—a soft, fuzzy, fur cap complete with a striped tail—and something like 3000 other Crockett items such as lunch pails, T-shirts, blankets, wallets, guitars, all manner of toys, even toothbrushes. "The Ballad of Davy Crockett" sung by Bill Hayes was the number one selling record for an entire month—and by that time I had my own record player. The player was like a little suitcase, red and cream faux leather, with its own loudspeaker at the front, and I played the Bill Hayes hit over and over again, as I had done years ago with "Twelfth Street Rag." Concerning the fad itself, Stephen Spielberg, who was my age at the time, recalled the series—which ended with "Davy Crockett at the Alamo"—in an interview in *Rolling Stone*: "I was in third grade at the time. Suddenly the next day, everybody in my class but me was Davy Crockett. And because I didn't have my coonskin cap and my powder horn, or Old Betsy, my rifle, I was deemed the Mexican leader, Santa Anna. And they chased me home from school until I got my parents to buy me a coonskin cap."

Unfortunately, Crockett dies at the Alamo, and everyone I knew was heartbroken. Disney was pretty good at traumatizing children with movies like *Bambi*, and now Crockett was left for dead at the Alamo—although his actual killing at the hands of Santa Anna's army wasn't actually shown. Instead, he was left swinging his rifle on the battlements. His sidekick George was shown dying, however, and it was a shock, for we had grown fond of that character played by Buddy Ebsen.

The Disney people were caught completely off guard by the fad and could legally only copyright and control items with "Walt Disney's Davy Crockett" or with images of Fess Parker, the actor who played him, because the person of Davy Crockett was a historical figure in the public domain. Yet the studio made huge profits. And every kid dreamed of going to Disneyland.

After the fad had all but ended, Disney came back with two "prequels": "Davy Crockett's Keelboat Race" and "Davy Crockett and the River Pirates." But that wasn't until nearly the end of the year.

In the meantime, as summer began, my stepfather Larry and my mother had moved into a rented two-bedroom house at 6234 37th NE, just south of NE 65th in the Bryant district of northeast Seattle, not far from my grandparents in Ravenna. In late August I was shuttled back to my parents, and I would start third grade at Bryant Elementary School in the fall. My mother had taken on the customary role of housewife and mother. We had a dog, a male Great Dane named Willie, who was very gentle but too big for my mother to care for, and expensive to feed. Although we loved Willie, he was eventually traded for a Welsh Terrier, a rambunctious little dog we named Barney, who was always digging under the white picket fence and escaping, causing my mother further trouble.

My childhood was again divided between my grandparents' house in Ravenna (weekends and summers) and my parents' house in Bryant. The street of my parents' new neighborhood was typical of north Seattle, with curbs, grass parking strips, sidewalks patterned with a subtle double row of squares, and in this case, modest single-story houses that on our side of the street had been built in the '30s or '40s. In other words, partly an early suburbia within the city limits. Our house was painted white, had a small entry porch, and a corner window typical of the style.

I became best friends with a kid named Dean who lived three houses from me to the north. He wore glasses and had a full, pleasant, slightly squarish face, his black hair cut in a "flattop" at the time. His father, a WW II veteran—described by Dean as a "grease monkey"—a Navy mechanic of some sort—owned a Henry J., a small white automobile at odds with the big Detroit rocketships purchased by most Americans. Dean's last name was Nordstrom, so everyone always asked him if he was related to the Nordstroms of Seattle clothing store fame (he was not). We played guns, trading our cowboy weaponry for World War II firearms, and then went through a period of dinosaur hunting—battling the *Tyrannosaurus rex*, escaping through the imagined jungles of our back yards, camping out, and getting called in for dinner by our mothers before it got late.

Sometimes a couple of kids would come over from the next block to play army. We pretended to fight Germans or "Japs" with our quite realistic-looking guns and ran around the neighborhood ducking behind trees or bushes. Perfectly normal behavior. One kid actually had his father's M-1 rifle from World War II (with a plugged barrel) and no one would have thought to call the police in fear of a maniac, even though we freely ran through front and back yards, and on the sidewalks, carrying these weapons.

World War II had ended only a decade before, and since

most kids' fathers had served, the war invaded our consciousness in many ways, including playing war and building
model airplanes and ships.

§ 6

It wasn't long before I (now age eight) was taken by Aunt
Peggy and "Mom" (grandmother Emma) to visit my real father, Vance Haldeman, whom I had seen only two or three
times since his divorce from my mother when I was two. He
lived in a small, modern house that had been built next door
to his parents' two-bedroom farmhouse in what was then rural Alderwood just north of Seattle. His parents, my grandparents, Charles and Bessie Haldeman, raised chickens in a
large walk-in hen house out in back of their farmhouse. I was
nervous around the chickens, but especially the roosters, for
it seemed that they all wanted to peck sharply at my legs; and
the strong, acrid smell from inside the long wooden hen
house was something I wasn't accustomed to. Nevertheless, I
enjoyed the small farm and didn't mind visiting my father
who, because of severe multiple sclerosis, was cared for by
Charles and Bessie and a part-time nurse.

Vance had been a Navy flyer in World War II and co-
piloted a PBY Catalina flying boat in the South Pacific. The
PBYs would go out with fighters and bombers on strikes and
linger at the edge of the target area until the combat planes
started to return from their mission. If any planes went down,
the PBY could swoop down and land on the surface of the
ocean for a rescue operation, which they were often called
upon to do.

Vance's rescue plane was carrying a crew of eleven when
a terrible accident occurred. He was quoted in the newspaper
later, saying: "Our plane cracked up in a storm two miles off
Tikopia, an island fortunately inhabited by friendly natives.

Lots of times we'd dropped cigarettes and bed sheets and ra-
zor blades as we flew over that island on another mission and
the natives—who had learned a bit of English from a mis-
sionary—had drawn notes in the sand, 'NAVY PILOTS WE
THANK YOU'. We didn't think we'd soon be thanking *them*.
But if it hadn't been for them that day, the three of us who
survived the crash would never have come home to tell about
it. The plane went down instantly, carrying eight men with it.
The rest of us hung onto fragments of the tail section. It went
down just before the natives came out to get us in canoes. On
the beach I stood up and waved my skivvy shirt at one of our
planes overhead. Luckily the pilot saw me. We were taken out
that day."

But my mother told a different story. I didn't have the
nerve to ask my father about it, though he wasn't at fault in
any case, though perhaps engaging in a minor cover-up. Her
story, obviously gotten from him, was that the pilot of the
plane had decided to show off for some native girls on the
beach by steering the plane in a tight, circling turn, too close
to the surface of the ocean. An unexpected wave caught the
wingtip, causing the plane to spin violently, crash, and break
apart. Was this the truth? I didn't know for sure, and I wasn't
about to get involved with this conflicting story while seeing
my father in his wheel chair. Neither could I quite imagine his
past life, other than through my mother's descriptions and an
album of black and white photographs taken during their
brief marriage.

Father was about forty now, with thinning dark hair
combed straight back, his head a bit cocked to one side. He
was dressed in a white shirt and tie, with brown slacks and
braces on his legs, but he wasn't able to rise out of the wheel
chair on his own. I stood kind of dumbly, close in front of
him. He smiled at me. I took his hand, which he offered in an
awkward motion due to his disability. He had always affec-

tionately referred to me as "Fup" when I was little, and did so again, perhaps as a kind of jest. It was OK. I was sorry that his speech was badly slurred, though. I told him a few things about school, my friends, our dog Barney, and what I was doing. I pushed his wheel chair over to a kitchen table where Grandma Bessie had placed some cookies.

Bessie soon brought out a set of checkers, placing the board on a tray she attached to the arms of father's wheel chair. He was not able to well grasp or move the checkers himself, for his hand and arm movements were undependable; but he was able to motion me to make the moves for him. My grandparents and aunt sat in the living room making small talk until it was time to leave. I had accepted the situation of this visit, and others to come, gratified that I had some connection to my father; but the estrangement wasn't reparable, and his condition continued to deteriorate.

Neighborhoods, parents and grandparents, friends, and kid activities were the center of my life, and my awareness of life was expanding. Until about third grade, I'd known almost nothing of the world beyond my immediate surroundings: Eisenhower was President, the Korean War had been fought, the communist revolution in China was complete, Einstein had died, the double-helix was discovered, the Supreme Court ruled on *Brown v. the Board of Education*; the list was endless. I didn't know much about science or nature, the extent or complexity of the world generally, or where children came from specifically. I was almost exclusively engaged in being eight-years-old: playing board games, building plastic model kits (World War II ships and planes), "playing guns," and learning further how to read and write in school. The 1950s were geared toward raising a massive number of children, including the selling of toys and entertainment to them. Much of what one knew about the world was filtered through this

post-war culture (including educational TV, such as the Bell
Systems science series hosted by Dr. Frank Baxter—"Our
Mr. Sun" a favorite episode of mine—and the science demon-
strations of *Watch Mr. Wizard*). Overall, if one were white and
middle class, it was something like heaven, because it pan-
dered to us and was secure and free from harm. Except for
"the bomb." More specifically, the hydrogen bomb. Because
by the beginning of third grade, I clearly understood that everything I knew might be instantly obliterated. I became especially aware of this during one of the live television dramas
that depicted a family like those I knew in my own neighborhoods awaiting a nuclear holocaust via incoming ballistic missiles—one of the first things on TV that truly frightened
me—while in our classroom we practiced "duck and cover"
under those wooden desks with the obsolete ink wells.

And the summer before school started, while I lay on my
back resting on the lawn, hands clasped behind my head, enjoying the warmth of the sun with my eyes closed in some
sort of reverie, a neighbor kid of about six years old sneaked
up and smashed me on the face with a water balloon. In that
startling instant I thought the hydrogen bomb had exploded!
Was I dead?! Oh, wow. Not quite. "Thanks a lot, Billy, you
little creep!" I jumped up angrily and chased him all the way
to his house.

§ 7

Bizarre experiences tended to crowd out more ordinary ones
and leave the most lasting impressions. That September,
around Labor Day, I was taken by my aunt and grandmother
to the Western Washington State Fair. The Puyallup Fair, as it
was more commonly known due to its location in a town
southeast of Tacoma, was a gargantuan affair of prized do-
mestic animals, rodeo riding, local agriculture, greasy food,

shameless hucksters, Ferris wheels, crowds of crazed humanity, and sawdust. Amazing to me were several acres of a traditional American amusement park. This included a massive white-painted wooden roller coaster built in 1935 called The Cyclone, indoor bumper cars smelling of ozone, a "tunnel of love" called The Old Mill with boats floating through a dark, winding water canal inside, and an elaborate two-story Funhouse right out of early Ray Bradbury. These structures had a mysterious aspect, especially at night when the fair was blazing with the multi-colored lights of carnival rides. The Old Mill was the size of a large, sprawling house with brown shingled siding and a huge center windmill. These traditional examples of amusement park Americana were built to last like real structures (which they were, of course) but with cockeyed details and crooked windows in odd places.

Entering the Funhouse for the first time, I walked into a black, narrow tunnel with a solid wood floor that contoured up and down in several waves in the darkness. My face brushed against strings hanging from the ceiling that felt like spider webs. A twisting staircase led up to the second floor where I emerged onto a balcony overlooking the carnival scene below. People were staring up at this high balcony, watching people walk across it, and laughing as women's dresses were puffed out, some quite far, by a blast of compressed air actuated by a man with a devious smile standing at ground level with a pull-cord in his hand.

I quickly crossed over the balcony and turned left into a hall of mirrors, where everyone was creating distorted images of themselves via warped full-length reflections. Eventually I found my way out through a brief maze of Plexiglas and mirrors into the stuffy attic of the main interior. One could go down steep wooden stairs to the main floor or take the longest slide I had ever seen—from high in the attic all the way to the bottom floor. The long, undulating slide was made of narrow strips of varnished wood, like those of a bowling alley, and one could slide down seated upon a square of thickly woven cloth. I hesitated, for it was a scary drop. But other kids were going down, so down I went, as well. And of course I wanted to go down again (!) which was OK, since one could go back up the stairs alongside the slide and wait in line. The second time was less frightful and more fun. Looking around on the main floor at the bottom, I followed another path that led to a rolling barrel of a tunnel one had to pass through, then through some crazy gates and a floor with spinning discs that caused one's feet to twist and turn. All this lay under the gaze of several strange clown faces painted on the wall—strange because the smiles expressed a touch of the insane. I went out into the cool air again amid the smell of sawdust and the colored blaze of the rides.

Late that night on the long walk back to my aunt's car parked among many others in a dark grassy field, the fair seemed to blend into the town itself. Rows of old houses with their dimly lit windows seemed as strange, and equally mysterious, as the Funhouse or The Old Mill. In my imaginative mind, there was no strict boundary in the mysterious night.

§ 8

I soon settled into the routine of walking several blocks to Bryant Elementary school. We had no dress codes I was aware of. Boys usually wore blue jeans with plaid flannel cuffs turned up like buckets. Patterned flannel shirts were preferred. Shoes were often U.S. Keds "tennis shoes"—white or black. Leather shoes also permissible. Socks of any color. Coats of any type, but they had to be fairly warm during winter.

My third grade teacher at Bryant was Miss Partington, an older lady who had the unfortunate distinction of reminding me of Mrs. Wine, the mad woman with the bullwhip. Miss

Partington, her black hair in a bun (did all grade school teachers have their hair in a bun?) wandered up and down the aisles (we no longer had to share desks) encouraging and cajoling, or if dissatisfied, rapping a student's hand with a ruler. My friend Dean had been rapped and was none too happy about it.

Weekday evenings were spent watching television and doing homework, in that order. My favorite show later that year was *Science Fiction Theater*. The show began with an orchestral fanfare while the camera panned over a room full of scientific equipment, then cut to an authoritative-looking man: "How do you do, ladies and gentlemen. I'm your host, Truman Bradley." In suit and tie, Bradley did a fascinating scientific experiment that related to that particular episode. The series was low budget, did not rely on special effects but had a true speculative quality, with intelligent plots and familiar actors. Much of what we kids were exposed to in those days traded on our imaginations, not superficial action, explosions, and such.

One spring weekend, at the suggestion of one of our parents, Dean and I walked up the hill on NE 65th to an appliance store and dragged home a huge cardboard shipping box designed for a refrigerator. This was something kids could do, girls and boys, because these giant boxes for refrigerators or stoves, when set on the lawn, in our case horizontally, could be made into little houses, stores—or, by us, a spaceship! Dean and I used crayons to draw gauges and controls. We cut portholes. We made a view screen out of white butcher paper and pasted it inside at the front of the ship. With our toy ray guns, we imagined adventures loosely based on TV's *Tom Corbett, Space Cadet*, or Buck Rogers and Flash Gordon serials, zooming into space and landing on other planets.

Interest in rockets and outer space also penetrated my dentist's waiting room. To amuse children (and probably himself) Dr. Boler had built a realistic-looking slanted control panel with working gauges, dials, buttons, levers, and lights—

and had a black ribbed chair to go with it. He also had a glass case with his own model airplanes in it. What a cool guy!

Unfortunately, dentistry in those days wasn't quite space age. Drills were operated by motor-driven pulleys, and filling a cavity could take an hour of sheer torture—the drilling, the horrible high-pitched sound, the smell of burning tooth enamel. And I had a lot of fillings while growing up, supposedly the result of too many cookies or ice cream (though I was always slim, so it couldn't have been that much). The only satisfying part was to rinse out one's mouth at the end and spit in a round porcelain bowl next to the dentist chair. Later they got rid of those, because eventually they were considered unsanitary and inconvenient to clean.

Speaking of '50s fads, my friend Dean and I might have become millionaires that year. We were in the habit of flying the lid of a large cookie tin back and forth across the street. One day, Dean hurled it especially hard over my head, over the white picket fence in front of our house, and right through the corner dining room window with a crash of breaking glass that sent my mother outside to find out who had done it. That evening, my stepfather talked Dean's father into taking responsibility for his son's mistake, which was controversial, for as Dean said, "We were both playing with it!" Nevertheless, his father graciously repaired the broken window. And Dean and I failed to invent the *Frisbee*. Or did we? In any case, I was the first on the block to purchase a Pluto Platter (the early name of the Frisbee) and Dean and I continued as usual, but with the official item and no more broken windows. Not without further mischief, however, for we painted the Pluto Platter with luminous paint, came out after dark, and flew it over cars coming down 65th, hoping to fool people into thinking they saw a UFO.

During the third grade, I began to learn multiplication, and to write of my own simple experiences using those same sheets of paper that were blank on the top half, with ruled lines on the bottom half. Miss Partington demonstrated math on the blackboard as we tried to understand the principles. We made drawings, and I was quite good at drawing dinosaurs, my special interest at a time when these awesome, gigantic, extinct creatures were not quite as popular with kids as they later became. Miss Partington didn't know what to make of me, for I also learned on my own to spell the names of the better known dinosaurs, and these proudly peppered my ordinary spelling papers. My favorite book was one of the "All About" series for young readers: *All About Dinosaurs* by famous naturalist and explorer Roy Chapman Andrews. Another was the children's book *The Shy Stegosaurus of Cricket Creek* by Evelyn Sibley Lampman.

My interest in dinosaurs led to the first item I had to save my weekly 50-cent allowance to buy—and I did save for weeks until my mother finally kicked in the remainder of the purchase price that spring. It was a large, heavy book published by *Life* magazine called *The World We Live In*. The pages were directly reprinted from that large-format magazine's beautifully illustrated science articles—mainly on geology, natural history, meteorology, zoology, and astronomy. The text of the book was on too high a reading level for me, generally, but I was captivated by the wonderful paintings and photographs used for the illustrations, several of which were fold-outs of magnificent proportion. The fold-outs of the dinosaurs were stunning, with a *Tyrannosaurus rex* prominently featured along with a *Triceratops, Brontosaurus Stegosaurus*, and others from that time; and another fold-out extravaganza with an *Allosaurus* eating a recent kill; and many other dinos, large and small. A third fold-out showed the monstrous reptiles that inhabited the sea. And the astronomical illustrations in the opening sections of the book were by the famous illustrator Chesley Bonestell, whose photo-realistic stellar and planetary crea-

tions—imaginary landscapes of other worlds—became legendary among science, as well as science fiction fans. But
more than this, the book had a lasting impact on my growing
awareness of my place in the universe, perhaps an effect I did
not count on. This was exemplified near the beginning of the
book by an imaginary illustration showing the earth in multiple images, first spiraling out of a solar dust cloud as it is
born, then in the foreground at the present time, then moving
away as it ages and finally dies. The caption for the illustration
impressed itself on my eight-year-old mind. It read:

> "The life of the earth is shown from its probable origin in a pri-
> meval cloud of cosmic dust to its final entombment in the void.
> At the center the planet is pictured condensing out of the original
> cloud. For more than 4 billion years it rolls through the starry
> cosmos, through the ages of mountain building, ages of ice. In
> the foreground is the young earth today. As it journeys through
> time and space, its continents change their shape. At some distant
> time the sun will redden and swell, boiling away the earth's seas
> and atmosphere. Then, as the solar fires wane, the scorched
> planet will circle, cold and lifeless, around the dying sun."

Not only my own death, or the death of all those I knew,
but of the planet itself, was impressed upon my tender psyche. So the third grade was a time of expanding awareness
and learning, but not all at school. Books, television, and
movies seemed equally important. Parents not so much, but
even though I wasn't completely conscious of it, positive values were instilled by *all* these sources (including the fictional
cowboys of my earliest years!). Since I was an only child—
unusual at the time—I was alone a lot, which meant I had to
develop my own interests. "The only child" was a topic of
(often negative) discussion in those days, when most families
had about three children. "The only child" was considered
automatically spoiled. Having a step parent also seemed a bit
odd, but being adopted was rarely commented upon. Perhaps

I was a bit spoiled, or overprotected, by my mother, but that didn't prevent intellectual growth, making friends, riding my J. C. Higgins bicycle wherever I pleased, or having a somewhat adventuresome nature.

I was at my grandparents' one Sunday in April of 1956 when, after reading the comics in the newspaper, I turned to the movie page and saw a nearly full-page ad for a science fiction movie called *Forbidden Planet*. A year before, my parents had taken me to see the interstellar spectacular *This Island Earth*; but this new one, whose plot was based on Shakespeare's *The Tempest*, was to make a more lasting impression. Dean and I were dropped off by my mother at the Orpheum Theater in downtown Seattle, where he and I waited in a line that went nearly around the entire block. We sat in the dark theater, kids all around us, everyone mesmerized by the mind-expanding scenario of *Forbidden Planet* involving the ancient Krell civilization of Altair 4. The Krell planetary technology and the subconsciously driven "Monsters from the Id" were terrifying as well as fascinating, and for both Dean and me, the movie contributed to much play with our ray guns and space age paraphernalia. The only other movie to make such a powerful impression was Disney's *20,000 Leagues Under the Sea* during the Christmas holidays of 1954. Perhaps it was no coincidence that like *The Robe*, these were big budget productions in CinemaScope. Television simply could not compete with the spectacle—that's the way Hollywood met the challenge of TV—and the stories were superb. *Forbidden Planet* played in its first run for months, and I went back to see it two more times. (The only movie I saw more often during its initial release was *The Seventh Voyage of Sinbad* in 1958, my returning to the Neptune Theater in the University District three times after first viewing.)

§ 9

After we graduated from third grade, a bright idea of mine nearly got Dean killed.

At the end of our block to the south, the relatively quiet cross street of NE 62nd turned into a steep hill down a half-block eastward to another cross street. Brad, our other play-mate, a kid with short-cropped blond hair who always seemed a bit aloof, joined us while Dean and I had been riding on our old childhood scooters, one foot on the narrow wooden plat-form, the other pushing along on the sidewalk. The scooters had handlebars and a fairly useless mechanical lever for a brake that rubbed against the rear wheel. Brad did not have a scooter, but we decided we could share two, and in any case, we needed an extra person to implement my idea to go shoot-ing down the steep 62nd St. hill, just as we'd done on our sleds when the streets were layered with snow during the winter. My idea was to sit down on the scooters, reach up to hold the handlebars, and balance on the way down the hill. Brad would stand at the bottom of the hill and warn us if any cars were coming along on the cross street. We had a great time, trading the scooters so Brad could ride, and taking turns.

The third or fourth time, Dean and I readied ourselves at the top of the hill. Brad waved all clear at the bottom, and off we went. I didn't know exactly how fast we were going at the halfway point, but suddenly Brad started yelling, "Car! Car!" My momentum seemed unstoppable, but I managed to get my hand back on the brake lever until I realized in panic that it wasn't going to stop me, so I rolled off and let the scooter go, bloodily scraping my arm on the concrete as I slid into the curb.

I was vaguely aware that Dean continued to speed straight down the hill, weaving only slightly this way and that. How exactly he parted from his scooter I couldn't tell, but on the last part of the hill, at the fastest point, he slid on his stomach right into the intersection in front of the oncoming car. Brad had jumped aside while waving his arms. The sound of screeching brakes was deafening as the driver, in the last possible instant, hit the brakes as he saw Dean slide in front of him. Dean came to a stop on the concrete—right under the front bumper of the car, directly in front of the left tire.

We ran to him. His eyes were wide, like a frightened animal's. The man got out of his car, slammed the door and quickly determined that no part of Dean had been crushed under his tire. "What the hell are you kids doing?!" he yelled, pulling Dean out from under the car. Brad seemed in a state of shock, for he'd failed to stay in the street and flag down the driver, it all happened so fast. Apparently the car had quickly backed out of a driveway, turned, and headed for the intersection. Brad had been looking in the other direction and was aware only in the last few seconds.

Dean's parents were, to say the least, unhappy with this escapade. Dean was mad at Brad—and for a while not too happy with me for inventing the foolhardy idea in the first place. But we were bandaged up and suffered only minor injuries. We also learned that one's life could depend, one way or another, on a second of time.

Days later, Brad, who always seemed a little shifty, became the target of an intense force within me I didn't know existed, at least to the extent it did.

One day he and I were playing a game of "hide the jeep" in our living room, where one of us would hide a tiny toy jeep and the other would try to find it, getting clues of "warm," "cool," "cold," "hot," "hotter," etc. Brad happened to bump into an end table and knock over a lamp that crashed to the floor. My mother heard it from in the kitchen. She came in, picked it up, and asked what happened. I answered matter-of-factually that Brad had accidentally knocked it down.

"No I didn't," Brad said, nervously looking at my mother.

That was a surprise. Was he about to blame me instead? Was he afraid of getting scolded?

"Yes you did," I said.

"No I didn't."

This lie triggered a spontaneous, acute anger in me all out of proportion. I felt heat rise into my head. The unnecessary, blatant lie triggered my judgment of immorality in a surprisingly profound, spontaneous way.

Brad just stood there.

My mother looked at me. Within those seconds, I began to stiffen with rage, my face turned red, and my fists clenched. Mother raised her voice: "Get control of yourself, Philip." Then she said, "You'd better go home, Brad." Brad had turned pale, I stared at him with such intense anger. He slipped by me and out the front door. Mother took me into the kitchen and rubbed a cold wet rag on my forehead. "You must never lose your temper like that again!" she said. "You might have burst a blood vessel."

Though I had never attacked anyone, I had felt a powerful urge: perhaps it was lucky Mother had stopped me. She admitted later that my behavior had frightened her. I discovered that I could not tolerate a liar.

A couple of weeks later, Brad and I were playing together once again.

§ 10

The summer of 1956 was a watershed season in many ways as my existence shifted back to my grandparents' neighborhood on 14th NE and I began to play with children in my "new" neighborhood: Craig "Buzzy" Brandt and his brother Jimmy, across the street, both slightly younger than I; Ted and Nora Graham, across and north on the corner of 65th, both older than I; Ronny and Stacey Hatch, brother and sister one house south of the Brandts; the Hambly sisters—Pam, Mary, and Nancy—whose back yard was at the end of the paved alley that sloped up between the Brandt's house and the side of the Hatch's garage across the street. The Hambly house fronted busy 15th Ave. to the east (where the Dragnet Burglar had been shot); and to complete the population of kids in that neighborhood, a young psycho who bullied me and who was, in '50s vernacular, a juvenile delinquent. Not a romantic type like James Dean, either.

My first memory of this psycho kid was that he and a pal of his had grabbed a couple of two-by-fours and chased Nora up onto the Hatch's flat garage roof next to the slope of the concrete alley, viciously striking at her. Upon hearing Nora screaming again and again, one of the neighbors called the police, and within minutes a squad car pulled up next to the garage, causing the boys to run up the alley toward 15th— exactly as the Dragnet Burglar had supposedly done. Only they were not shot. Neither were they caught.

Sometime later, I witnessed a parallel event in the industrial south end of Seattle. My stepfather had taken me on one of his business calls in the Georgetown District along a street that was lined with old brick factory buildings. While he was inside, presumably trying to sell fire extinguishers, I wandered out onto the sidewalk. The neighborhood must have had some residential housing nearby, for in a minute I saw a young, about thirteen-year-old Black kid (we called them Negroes)—the first I had ever seen in person—running down the sidewalk toward me, then into a vacant lot. Two white kids, maybe a year or two older and wielding metal pipes, chased him. They cornered him while I peeked around the corner of the sooty building. The white kids started shoving their victim, threatening to beat him. I was frightened and didn't know what to do other than go and get my stepfather

Larry, but I was transfixed, frozen.

The Black kid, terrified, was shoved against the wall. Then he said something I never forgot. He cried out, *'What have I ever done to you?!'*

They started beating him on his arms. But at that moment my stepfather emerged from the building. I yelled to him. He walked over, saw what was going on, and his face took on a dark, angry aspect I had never seen before.

"Knock that off!" he yelled, taking a couple of steps into the vacant lot.

The white kids had been unaware of him, so they turned, then stopped beating the Black kid.

"Get!" said Larry.

They stared for a moment, then ran.

The Black kid also ran—across the street where he disappeared between buildings.

The sober expression did not leave my stepfather's face. He looked at me, and what he said made a lasting impression: "Those stupid kids think they can beat up on a Negro because of the color of his skin. It's nothing but ignorance."

He barely said another word as we drove home.

§ 11

My awareness of the inhumanity and wickedness of certain children climaxed with the release of a disturbing 1956 movie. Theaters insisted that "Children will not be admitted to the theater unless accompanied by an adult," and it was easy to understand why. *The Bad Seed* starred Patti McCormack as a cute little girl who had murdered an elderly woman, drowns her grade-school classmate in order to steal his penmanship medal, then proceeds to murder another adult by setting a fire. Her mother, who'd been adopted, discovers that her cute daughter is actually the grandchild of a female serial killer who died in the electric chair. It was the most frightening movie I'd seen yet. Because of the idea.

A born psychopathic child was believable to audiences at the time, while in later years the notion of such genetic propensity fell out of fashion—then returned as the pendulum swung back toward genetic inheritance. That some were born without normal emotions was disturbing, yet I'd not only witnessed the cruelty of certain children, I'd been bullied by a girl in my grandparents' neighborhood. She would kick or punch for no reason, and we boys were taught never, ever to hit a girl. Avoidance was the only option. Luckily, this "bad seed" moved away, and the neighborhood improved as most of the kids got to know each another.

No one, boy or girl, was left out of games such as hide-and-seek or kick-the-can; and as summer began to wane, the two bullies who'd chased Nora onto the garage roof stayed to themselves, nowhere to be seen. It was just the beginning of a special neighborhood at my grandparents' that would largely define the childhoods of everyone who grew up there.

During that summer, my grandmother and aunt took me on an automobile trip east, with the goal of visiting cousins in Boise, Idaho. Aunt Peggy drove her '50 Ford at a frightening pace, giving me the "willies" around a couple of curves; so a better part of the trip was when I was introduced to a cousin who was my age. He and I got along well, playing board games and going to the park, while our adult relatives visited with each other. Later, it was decided that I should stay overnight at his house across town from the motel where my grandmother and aunt were staying. That night, I was taken by my cousin's mother to a small upstairs room with a newly made bed and a dim shaded lamp. Maybe it was the unfamiliarity of a strange room combined with the distance from home in a strange city—but I suddenly felt an unexpected, fearful separation. I looked out of the window into the darkness at the edge of town and was overwhelmed with what seemed like an immense gulf between myself and that of my grandmother and aunt. My thoughts edged into the irrational. Where exactly were they? Would they be able to find me again? Would they have to leave without me? A phobia-like panic caused me to go back into the upstairs hallway and stand there, not knowing what to do, whether to find my cousin and explain this excessive anxiety. Finally, I went downstairs and found his mother in the kitchen. She must have seen a certain look on my face, for she seemed to know something was wrong.

"I think I'd rather go back to my grandmother and aunt tonight," I said, trying not to show my level of discomfort.

"Oh, is something wrong?"

"Well, no. I don't know. I . . ." But I couldn't explain without sounding crazy or cowardly, yet I knew I wasn't making sense.

"Shall I call them?"

"I guess so."

I was now on the brink of nausea for fear of embarrassment; and then my cousin came in. He looked at me, cocked his head and kind of smiled. Again, that something was wrong must have shown on my face. Was I pale? The situation was unbearable; it made no sense either, for I was worried about being abandoned, being lost, a fear resulting from something deep within me, an unexpected apprehension I couldn't stifle.

My cousin's mother found a piece of paper with the name of the motel where my grandmother and aunt were staying. She looked in her phone book and dialed the number from the kitchen telephone while I waited, unable to explain myself to my cousin.

"Hello, Emma? I think your grandson is having a bit of homesickness."

Oh? Was *this* the right definition of my mental state? I knew of the malady, but did it fit the intensity of what I was feeling? I could do nothing but stand there and accept this spontaneous diagnosis.

My Aunt Peggy came to get me, and we all had a little laugh over it when she arrived. My cousin was perplexed but said nothing to make me feel bad. I was grateful, but I just wanted to get out of there and avoid further embarrassment. Nothing much of this trip would I later recall but the memory of this night. Why had it happened?

Having nothing to do with me, my grandmother decided to cut short the vacation. The small towns of Montana where she, Grandfather, Aunt Peggy, and Judy had lived for so many years weren't too far from Boise; but Grandmother no longer enjoyed long trips, and since she and my aunt had visited those towns only a few years before, they now headed back to Seattle, for which I was (also) grateful.

§ 12

I moved back to my parents' neighborhood when fourth grade began at Bryant Elementary School. Fall weather was refreshing as cool air began to sweep aside a summer of Popsicles, hopscotch, hide-and-seek, and squirt-gun fights; while as days passed, wind in the trees and a scent of first rains initiated a subtle intoxication with the change of the season. I would still ride my bike to school until the rain became routine. On those rainy days I would walk wearing a hooded jacket. Dean, Brad, and I remained friends while school lapsed into the ennui of sitting at a desk most of the day, learning what we were given, and hoping for recess, the occasional fire drill, or learning square dancing in the gym. Yet it wasn't long, near the end of the day, before I would impatiently watch the big black-framed clock on the wall in its endless approach to 3:10 when the bell rang and school was let out. By mid-October, I didn't like sitting at that old wooden desk all day, or in the lunch room surrounded by other children (and this year, no girls cute enough to fall in love with), yet school wasn't intolerable or *especially* unpleasant, and the teacher, Mrs. Egenes, was typical of the middle-aged women who taught elementary school and did well with the children.

The approach of Halloween provided a reprieve from routine as we decorated the classroom with orange and black streamers, paper pumpkins, skeletons, and scary crayon faces. My primitive drawings on those large sheets of thin paper were always variations of the same scene: a broad landscape with a tall haunted house beneath a high quarter moon, a twisted brown tree, bats in the paper background sky, and a wooden fence across the lower part of the picture, with a black cat and pumpkins sitting on the posts. One drawing added ghosts floating out of the windows of the house, for the idea of ghosts inhabited a dark closet in my mind and remained a question to be pondered over. ("No, I don't believe in ghosts," my mother answered to my question.) At least my simple crayon drawings captured the picturesque quality of Halloween I most appreciated, and my standard scene symbolized the imaginative thoughts and anticipation of the night to come.

What was it about Halloween that so deeply resonated? Nothing about being nine years old was quite as captivating or delightfully strange as a holiday about haunted houses, ghosts, witches, demons, cemeteries, and midnight clocks. This landscape of fearful things was also a catharsis for my imagination, memories of old Mrs. Wine and the closet with the mysterious oval window. But it really all began with the unmistakable smell of a fresh pumpkin when the cut lid was yanked off and that pumpkin aroma filled my nostrils. I removed the interior guts gushily, carved a scary face with a kitchen knife, dripped candle wax into the deep interior, blew out and reached the candle inside onto the melted wax. I relit the candle, replaced the lid, turned off the room lights and set the glowing jack-o'-lantern on the fireplace hearth. On our walls we had put store-bought decorations of witches, pumpkins, and black cats made by a company called Luhrs.

October 31, the night of trick-or-treat, Dean and Brad came over to join up while my mother fussed about whether I could see properly out of the eye holes she'd cut in my ghost costume—traditional white sheet with arm holes, one hole of which allowed me to hold an orange pressed-cardboard pumpkin with a wire handle. These hollow, store-bought pumpkins were for collecting treats, and the holes for the eyes and mouth were backed with a colored paper insert. Rumor had it that certain idiot kids tried to put lighted candles into them and caught their houses on fire. Undoubtedly an urban legend, for the coated hollow-shaped cardboard must have been fireproofed. But who knew?

Into the All Hallow's night we ran in our disguises, going from house to house, ringing doorbells or knocking on doors we would never have approached at any other time. The air was chilly, the moon high and clear, and this was *the* night when ghosts and goblins were supposed to rise at midnight. But the sensation of trick-or-treat was one of extraordinary *freedom*. Partly it was because of being in disguise, and also because we could run and open private gates, hurry up dark unfamiliar walkways and visit every neighbor's house on both sides of the street and on neighboring blocks. Once or twice, trick-or-treaters were invited into a house for something homemade, such as cupcakes with orange frosting, or hot apple cider. Of all nights, it was our night, and coming back home, pleasantly exhausted, there was more hot apple cider and the treats we'd collected in our round orange pressed-cardboard pumpkins. I dumped my stash like pirate treasure onto the dining room table: treat-size Hershey and Three Musketeers bars, packs of Double Bubble bubble gum, Junior Mints, Dots, Tootsie Pops, multi-colored M&Ms, and all the rest. Dean and Brad went home to assess their own take of treats.

Not long afterward, long before the witching hour, I was in an untroubled, pleasant, nightmare-less sleep.

In the morning, the desolate streets and the passing of this mysterious holiday gave an unusually empty feeling. Too bad that Halloween couldn't come back for one more night.

Yes, this of all holidays was strangely fragile and unique. The scary masks, wispy ghosts, haunted houses, and cemetery ghouls of legend faded back into the underground dark of the subconscious where they mostly resided. They were symbols of death, after all, not often to be entertained. Why was I so attracted to this time of the season? Did my experiences in that big old house on Ravenna Boulevard have something to do with it? I had no clue, but it seemed that I was spellbound by old houses, possibilities of ghosts, the feeling of windy days, the change of the season, and Halloween.

Not long afterward, I began to be abnormally absent from school. Like most children, I'd had the mumps (both sides) and the measles (my mother had kept my bedroom dark) but whenever I had a cold, a sore throat, or the flu, I convinced myself, for days after I was reasonably well, to remain "sick" and home from school. "I still don't feel good," was my mantra at these times, and I was able to claim this ill feeling until my mother finally realized that not only was I no longer suffering any symptoms and hadn't had a fever for quite some time, but that I was actively playing with toys or games, not to mention reading books or lying on the living room sofa watching *Midday Matinee*—an hour-and-a-half dedicated to old movies. But by the time of her conclusive awareness, a week had gone by.

This pattern had been established earlier than fourth grade, for in the third grade, Miss Partington had written on my final report card: "The level of Philip's work has dropped off considerably lately due to his frequent illnesses. He loses interest when he is absent so much. When he returns, he is dreamy and wastes his time."

This was, had I known what to call it, a moderate rebellion based on a vague dislike of school. Or was it merely a new way of hiding behind the chair in the corner of the house on Ravenna when I was five? Or hiding under the dining room table? My desire was to be left alone with my models and books. I did what I needed to do to at school to learn the material and get along; but similar to my extra-curricular study of dinosaurs in third grade, I began to read what I wished, choosing my own books by checking them out of the library. Most important to me were the Landmark Books, a non-fiction series put out by Random House starting in 1953. Bennett Cerf, co-founder of Random House, corralled some of the best non-fiction authors of the day to write these books for young readers. The first one I read, perhaps predictably, was *Davy Crockett*. Another was the earliest of the series, *The First Men in the World*, an anthropological narrative of early humans. Others I read, starting in fourth grade and into the fifth, were *Custer's Last Stand*, *The Battle of Britain*, and my favorite, *The Monitor and the Merrimack* by Fletcher Pratt, about the first Civil War ironclads, which I read twice more during the next couple of years.

I was not introverted. I played normally with other children and mostly enjoyed all the activities at school. How many children, had they had the opportunity, would have remained absent from school as long as they could? I had no real idea. Quite a few, I suspected. What I didn't know was that my pretext for staying home longer than other children was enabled because of my mother's uncommon compulsion to closely monitor my illnesses, especially if a stomach upset or vomiting was involved, and that this concern had to do with the locked cedar chest at my grandmother's house.

In the meantime, it was undeniable how little I knew at the age of nine, yet how much I was learning; how limited my understanding of the world, yet how exposed to events past and present. I began to realize how little of life was under our control. The nature of my experiences was manifested in the times and culture. Through various means, including my father Vance's history, I was aware of being born soon after the end of WW II; therefore, during my upbringing, the war got more and more into focus as a precursor to the world in which I existed currently. Much of my free time at my mother's and stepfather's house was spent building plastic models of World War II ships and planes. This hobby was true of other boys, as well. Echoes of the war were not only on television and in books, but there on the dining room table where my models were assembled; and the kit instructions in the boxes always had a brief history of the model being built. The first plane I built was a P-40 Warhawk with the Flying Tigers shark-mouth decal on the nose, so I learned about The Flying Tigers stationed in China, as well as facts about other planes and ships I built. The first ship I built was the USS *Buckley*, a destroyer escort famous for a battle with a surfaced German submarine. After a gun battle, the *Buckley* rammed and sunk the sub, then picked up the German survivors. Many ship models followed. The preferred brands were Revell and Monogram kits with their outstanding illustrations on the box lids and highly detailed parts. It wasn't long before I learned how to allow gun turrets to rotate. After putting the turrets' anchoring pins through the holes in the deck, I would light a match and carefully melt the ends of the tips sticking through the underside. In other words, I did not glue the gun turrets into the holes but created a small blob of melted plastic on the underside so that they couldn't be pulled out, yet rotated freely. The deck was then glued onto the hull. The turrets were fixed into the holes but could turn in any direction, and so I amazed my friends with rotating guns that would normally have been solidly glued on. *Voila!*

Winter was approaching, and that Christmas of 1956 I was to receive what was universally considered the greatest toy any boy could ever receive, and often did. But before the day of opening presents was the trip into busy downtown Seattle and the two grand department stores, Frederick & Nelson and The Bon Marche, each with eight floors of merchandise and an ornate profusion of Christmas decorations difficult to mentally encompass. These two competing giants went all out to attract customers. The Bon Marche interior was designed with Art Deco motifs and had a top-floor restaurant with white table cloths and a fashion show every hour. Frederick's had thick red carpets on the main floor; a book store and toy department on the fourth. The Bon had a sporting goods department (you could even buy a canoe) and a record department with listening booths. Frederick's had the best Santa Claus—a red-velvet costumed, white-bearded, gentle-faced, large ruddy fellow sitting on his throne surrounded by elf helpers and piles of presents and colorful decorations in his street corner window. The Bon's large corner window on the northeast Fourth Avenue side had a huge display of Lionel electric trains flying through tunnels and around mountainsides—absolutely my favorite display, for I had to be literally dragged away. Both stores had a shoe department, a beauty salon, a barber shop, escalators, and elevators with women operators sitting on fold-down stools. "Step to the back of the car, please. . . . What floor please?"—and I would say, "Four, please"—the floor with both the book store and toy department at Frederick's. The Bon had a first-floor games department where one could buy decks of cards, chess sets, cribbage boards, and other paraphernalia from a clerk behind the counter. Frederick's was slightly more upscale with its red first-floor carpets and a brass-buttoned, uniformed doorman on the sidewalk in front of the main entrance. They had also created a character called Uncle Mistletoe, an elf mannequin figure placed in display areas encountered while riding the escalators. Both the Bon and Frederick's had cafes. Frederick's had the Paul Bunyan Room downstairs, a budget lunch-counter cafe with murals of Paul Bunyan and Babe the Blue Ox. The Bon had The Corner House with large windows on the northwest Third Avenue side, a 1930s deco-style cafe with polished metal trim around the tables and counters. Waitresses wore gray uniforms with little white-fronted caps, since the Bon's signature color (for shopping bags and gift boxes) was gray, while Frederick's was green and white. Frederick's had their famous Frango Mints that became a traditional Seattle treat. The Bon had an extensive sixth-floor kitchenware department and a third-floor hobby shop selling model planes and trains. Everywhere, gifts could be put on "layaway" for later payment or shipped anywhere in the world. This was still the era of the big city, grand department store, with an opulent, romantic, civilized resplendence I had no idea would fade and vanish with the rise of suburban populations and the bland convenience of shopping malls.

The day arrived when we opened presents on Christmas Eve after our traditional Norwegian dinner at my grandparents' house in Ravenna. The previous week seemed like the longest week of the year, for I spent Christmas vacation at my grandparents' and had to be patient as presents began to accumulate under the tree. A large, heavy present had appeared for me.

Years later, the moment of this particular gift opening

would disappear from memory, but this was the night I received, from my mother and stepfather, a genuine Lionel train set of the kind I had seen in the big display window of the Bon Marche. Leading up to Christmas, these amazing trains with heavy, black metal locomotives mimicking reality in miniature, were advertised on television with multiple trains and extensive track layouts no kid but the richest could imagine owning; yet here was the fulfillment of an unaccountable desire, shared by almost every boy and not a few male adults.

Soon after the new year, when school had been in session for a week or two, my stepfather Larry built a long table for the Lionel train in the basement of our Bryant house. His unusual involvement with an interest of mine was, I believed, to fulfill his role as my father. He built the table in one day, and it was sprung on me as a surprise, with my mother watching with approval. Larry's effort was genuinely appreciated by my mother and me.

My friend Dean had also gotten an electric train—an American Flyer, a budget brand similar to the Lionel. We spent many hours, together and separately, arranging and rearranging track, making cardboard tunnels, and buying additions such as plastic train stations and crossing gates. I learned to connect wires between the transformer—the speed and direction control unit with its red and black handles—and the track, which was 0-27 gauge (meaning that the curves were of a 27" radius).

A year or two later, our friend Brad received an HO-scale train set—a remarkably small train, it seemed to us, running on remarkably small track, the whole thing beautifully delicate and realistic looking. This scale of train eventually became the default standard in terms of elaborate layouts with mountains, bridges, towns, railroad yards, and a zillion accessories. Later, even smaller scale trains would be introduced from Europe, making HO scale seem of normal size and 0-27 seem huge. In the meantime, Lionel was king, and it gave endless hours of pleasure, sometimes integrated by me with other play sets such as Fort Apache or buildings of Plastic Bricks.

In January, it tended to snow in Seattle; so Dean, Brad, and I would head for that same hill where Dean had nearly been crushed under a car. Could anything go wrong again? Of course not! Brad was on watch again at the bottom intersection! Anyhow, I loved my trusty Flexible Flyer sled, which, as in the classic film *Citizen Kane*, was my "Rosebud" symbol of childhood winters; because from the age of four or five I would sled down the short embankment in front of the old Ravenna house and stop before going over the retaining wall. Or my grandmother would pull me along the front sidewalk. Wooden sleds with metal runners were far superior to the uncontrollable plastic tubs that arrived years later. Flexible Flyers and Yankee Clippers were real sleds—fast, exciting, and steerable—and never more so than on a really steep street or downhill park trail. The most exciting sledding would come during junior high; but for now, our challenging neighborhood hill was sufficient, and enough kids were sledding down it to signal the few cars venturing out that a play zone had taken over the steep street. No one got killed.

During fourth grade, aside from the occasional playground bully and the prospect of being incinerated by the hydrogen bomb, my most frightening event of early 1957 was *The Incredible Shrinking Man,* a movie I saw one night at the Lake City movie theater. A typical suburban man gets dusted with radioactive mist while on his boat and begins to shrink in size, eventually reduced to about an inch, then gets trapped in the basement of his house. Unfortunately, he soon becomes aware he *isn't alone.* Sharing his dark, isolated environment is a big spider whose web protects the only food source—a piece of cake left on a work bench. The final confrontation with the horrific spider was a nightmarish climax in which the man, trapped beneath the spider, shoves a straight-pin into the spider's belly just as he was about to be eaten. So many movies then were made to terrify nine-year-olds and teenagers—if not adults—and they did the job well, partly because audiences had never seen anything quite like them (although many adults were frightened by *King Kong* in 1933, let alone *Dracula* and *Frankenstein*). The most frightening movie of the middle '50s was *The Invasion of the Body Snatchers* starring Kevin McCarthy and Dana Wynter trying to escape from a town of people who had been replaced with look-alike duplicates. Although it may have had political undertones (fear of communists taking over), on a deeper level it dealt with the more diabolical threat of forced conformity: Are you one of *us*? This issue was much discussed in those days; and in school, for example, one had to dress and appear like everyone else or be laughed at or ostracized. I'd only heard about *The Invasion of the Body Snatchers*, and thankfully hadn't seen it at the time. *The Incredible Shrinking Man* and *The Bad Seed* were quite sufficient for my delicate sensibilities.

Unfortunately, the movies—along with certain aspects of reality itself—weren't my only source of fear. In my bedroom, before going to sleep, I developed an irrational feeling of terror that seemed to cause my mother more than ordinary concern: For a couple of weeks, I felt certain that I wasn't alone in my room. No creatures under the bed or something hiding in the closet. Rather, I had an intense feeling, verging on certainty, of an invisible *presence*. It was an invisible person or thing I could not see, watching me from next to the wall or in the corner. When my mother came in to turn off the light, I was afraid to say anything, and somehow, after a period of time, I managed to fall asleep with this terrible notion. But when the feeling didn't go away, I finally told my mother, and of course she tried to comfort me by explaining that it was in my imagination, that imagination was a powerful thing, and that I seemed to possess more than my share. But after several nights of this, I could tell by the worried look on her face that she was wondering if I might be going a little nuts. Eventually I accepted her confidence that a mere idea had taken over my mind, and after a couple of weeks the feeling of *presence* went away.

About this time, because of my frequent absences from school, some discussion developed between my teacher, Mrs. Egenes, and the school principal, about having me repeat fourth grade. My mother was informed, and she informed me. All other concerns vanished under the threat of having to repeat a grade—the most terrifying event that could befall anyone at that age, other than polio, and with the knowledge it would stigmatize one for the remainder of his or her life. How could I keep my friends? How could I get along with students a year younger than I? How could I tolerate repeating all the lessons I'd already learned? What would it feel like sitting in the same classroom for another full year? Nothing could be more devastating. My mother must have felt some guilt about indulging my lengthy absences, and she told me I must not miss another day of school if at all possible. She didn't seem as concerned as she might have, however, and as the weeks went by I heard nothing more about it. Had she and the teacher consulted? Conspired? Were they trying to put pressure on me to return to school as quickly as possible after an illness? I never knew, and neither did I know of certain family circumstances that influenced my mother's own culpability in my absences.

But one day while staying for the weekend at my grandmother's and grandfather's, I asked Aunt Peggy about the low, locked cedar chest occupying a location in a short hallway near the foot of the stairs to the right as one entered the front door. I would pass the chest every time I went upstairs to my room in the house on 14th Ave., and I'd sometimes recall the time I struck my head on its corner and almost lost my eye.

"What's in the cedar chest?" I asked Aunt Peggy, who, only thirty-six at the time, silently looked at me through her round glasses. Before answering, she gave no sign I'd broached a taboo subject.

"Inez's things," she said.

I recalled hearing the name, as one might hear the name of a relative in passing.

"Inez would have been a second aunt of yours," said Peggy. "That's her baby photograph on the wall in the dining room."

The old photo, a very large one under convex glass in an oval frame, was that of a small child sitting on a chair. I'd seen it many times but always assumed it was of my aunt or mother.

"I guess no one told you the story," said Peggy.

"I don't think so."

"Inez died when she was twelve years old, a month before her thirteenth birthday. She was Mom's and Dad's first child, and of course they loved her more than anything in the world. Inez got sick and had some pain in her abdomen, and after Mom and Dad understood what was happening, they tried to get her to the hospital in Lewistown. They were living in Roy where Papa and Uncle Pete had a general store, and the Montana roads turned very muddy after a hard rain, so the car got stuck. Dad got it free and they finally made it to the hospital, and the doctors tried to save her but it was too late and she died the next morning because she'd had a burst appendix. Mom keeps Inez's clothes, her doll, and a few other things in the cedar chest, and it's never opened. Judy and I have our early memories of Inez. I don't know how Mom and Dad lived through such a sad thing, but here they are, and here you are, and they love you very much, too."

I didn't reflect at the time how Inez's death of appendicitis had likely created my mother's concern for my own health involving any hint of gastric distress, upset stomach, flu symptoms, or even a simple fever. Eventually I understood how Inez's death affected my mother's worries. So here were two things involving death—the drowning of a high school friend and a sister's burst appendix—that caused my mother's over-protectiveness.

"There was another Hanson child, too," said Peggy. "Arthur Francis, who was born a year before Judy. But he only lived for a month, and that was also in Roy, Montana." She sighed and kind of shook her head. "So many risks for children in those days. So sad."

In these ways, mysteries were revealed and explained, providing me with clues to the thoughts and behavior of my family.

§ 13

It was common in those days to have "a family encyclopedia" (as they were referred to), mainly for the young, and so my mother purchased a 1957 *World Book Encyclopedia* in hard, dark red bindings, while Dean's parents bought him *The Book of Knowledge*. I loved the encyclopedia, the pages of which were luxuriantly glossy, and I used it for school assignments and to satisfy my curiosity.

On the other end of my reading spectrum were Uncle Scrooge and Donald Duck comic books (the former with its beloved mix of adventure and satire) and in between comics and Landmark history books, Hardy Boys mysteries and Tom Swift science fiction novels (the prose of each, I found out later, having been somewhat simplified from the earlier, original series).

I was only vaguely aware of the public uproar over gory horror and crime comics that became part of a 1954 Senate subcommittee hearing on juvenile delinquency and the supposed harmful effects of such comic books on children. The fear about horror comics in particular was considered a joke by kids in school; yet some of the stories and covers were truly horrifying—even depicting bloody dismemberment—and so the comic book industry had created a Comics Code that tempered the worst of the gore and violence by the time I was a comic book fan aware of the controversy.

Another public concern thought by many adults to corrupt children was introduced to me by my "suitcase" record player: rock & roll.

Back in September and October, 1956, we'd all watched Elvis Presley on *The Ed Sullivan Show*. Sullivan showed Presley only from the waist up to avoid his hip-thrusting gyrations. Whatever else it may have been, rock & roll was about rhythm and movement. My mother, bless her, bought me Elvis's hit 45 single "Hound Dog," a rhythm and blues number I played over and over again, the beginning of my—and my generation's—life-long love of music that broke all the rules of decorum. Yet rock & roll also delivered rapturous melody, harmony, and joy, particularly in the "doo wop" subgenre. But regardless of genre, in the coming year my mother and Aunt Peggy would randomly add 45 rpm singles to my collection, such as 'Oh, Boy!" by The Crickets (with Buddy Holly), "Reet Petite" by Jackie Wilson, "Good Golly Miss Molly" by Little Richard, "Hard Headed Woman" by Elvis, and softer numbers like "Donna" by Richie Valens, and "Venus" by Frankie Avalon. Most songs we simply heard on the radio (station KJR in Seattle), because most kids didn't have sufficient allowance, i.e., budget, to buy more than a few records a year. We'd sometimes get together, pool our collections, and play them in bedrooms and basements—another aspect of kids' and teenagers' culture. Nevertheless, when at my grandparents' I still played the old 78s of Glenn Miller and others Aunt Peggy collected and played on her '49 Magnavox. Her tastes were mostly "pop," however, and so I wasn't always treated to the best jazz or classical. Those I'd have to discover on my own. I don't recall my mother or stepfather playing music at all.

In the spring of 1957, I was growing up in the middle of an era that would, a mere decade later, become mythic. We sometimes drove to an archetypal drive-in restaurant called Burgermaster where we'd eat dinner in our car. Waitresses didn't zip around on roller skates, but they did come out to the cars to take orders and serve food on trays attached to the window sills. Drive-ins were usually family restaurants, not quite the cool car venues depicted later. Yet the mythic '50s culture was half true, at least. Drive-in movies were popular, legendary among teenagers, but seasonal in Seattle because of the rain. Once spring arrived, Dean's parents were more inclined to go to drive-in movies than were my own, and a neighbor once took several of us kids in the back of his pickup truck. We had a great time on the way, joking around in the open truck bed, feeling the wind, no seat belts (seat belts were for jet pilots and race car drivers), being backed in toward the movie screen and putting blankets on ourselves to stay warm.

The school year was ending, and thank God I wasn't forced to repeat fourth grade. Maybe it was just a bluff, anyhow. My attendance improved, and the only medical oddity in my life was mental. It had to do with sidewalks. Walking to school, I noticed that the sidewalk was made of a pattern of squares in a double row. The squares were defined by shallow indented lines, and I got the idea that if I stepped on a line with one foot, I had to step on a line with the other foot to keep the total even. Or nearly even in the sense of having to sort of balance each of them. This feeling was quite strong, and I'd step oddly to keep "in balance" until I reached school. If I walked with Dean and Brad, I was distracted enough to forget about it, and when I mentioned it to my mother, she brushed it off. What I didn't know was that it hinted at a serious malady known as obsessive-compulsive disorder, or OCD. At that time, the habit faded away, but far worse symptoms, a different manifestation of the disease, would emerge much later in life, in middle age, and only then did I realize what the need to step equally on lines meant, and how lucky I was to escape the malady in my youth.

§ 14

Summer of 1957 was the real beginning of "the neighborhood" at my grandmother's. I returned to stay with grandmother, grandfather, and aunt in their craftsman-style house on 14th Ave. NE in Ravenna, a north-south street just below the NE 65th arterial. The neighborhood was defined not only by the street, but by two branching alleys going behind the rows of modest, early 1900s houses set above grassy or rocky walls and embankments. A quirk of our block was that it ended in a "T" just to the south. Anyone turning off of 65th St. to go south would have to zig-zag to one direction or the other at the end of our long block, the result being that traffic down our street was insignificant. Also, as I looked down to the street from my grandparents' front porch, I saw what could be described as a long, natural amphitheater with only a handful of parked cars along the curbsides next to grass parking strips. I was unaware how this geography contributed to the character of the neighborhood—that contrary to the norm, all of the kids, boys and girls alike, and of differing ages, began to play games together in the street. These kids, as usual, included myself (age 10), brothers "Buzzy" and Jimmy, their sister Sue whom we rarely saw (ages 9, 8, and 10 respectively), Ted and Nora (ages about 14 and 12), Ronny and Stacey (ages 10 and 9), the three sisters whose house fronted 15th Ave. to the east—Pam, Mary, and Nancy (ages 12, 10, and 8), Dale and Odessa (ages 8 and 7) and little Stevie (age 6, too young to play with the rest of us but was notable for crashing his tricycle trying to make the corner down the short concrete alley hill across the street).

The game of choice in the street that summer was kickball, played like baseball but with a soccer ball pitched—that is, rolled fast—toward the kicker, who kicked it into the air and ran around the bases. The ball could be caught, putting the kicker out, or picked up and thrown at the kicker for the same result. The game needed a lot of kids. Maybe that was the reason everyone, boys and girls alike, was welcomed into the games. There was no supervision at any time for anything we played, so we made up our own rules. Disputes had to be settled without adults. We did. And no one took their ball and went home.

On those warm summer nights, we'd come outside and play kick-the-can. An empty coffee can was placed in the middle of the street. Someone was chosen "it" and covered his or her eyes while counting slowly to ten while everyone else ran away and hid. "It" then began to search for others while keeping an eye out to guard the can. If "it" found someone, he or she ran back, jumped over the can, and yelled "Over the can on Jimmy!" and Jimmy would have to come out and sit under the street lamp (a shaded light attached high on a wooden telephone pole). The game ended in favor of the hiders if someone could sneak out without getting caught and kick the can before whoever was "it" could jump over it first. Then someone else would be "it" and the game would start again and continue until about 10:00 PM. As with "playing guns" or squirt gun fights, neighbors' yards were, with a few exceptions, fair game for running through or hiding out, either for kick-the-can or hide-and-seek. Aside from a couple of crabby old neighbors, everyone knew the kids were just playing, so not a thought was given to noticing some shadow running through a back yard, creeping through a gate, or jumping over a fence. For us, especially at night, the sense of freedom, combined with the act of concealment, was intoxicating. Especially if a place could be found to keep an eye on "it" and wait for the perfect moment to run out and kick the can. Sometimes "it" would see you emerge and a race developed to get to the can first. One way or another, there was no more satisfying a moment than victoriously kicking that can noisily a half-mile down the street.

Another game we played was called redlight/greenlight. Several kids would stand behind an imaginary line on the grass parking strip while the one who was "it" would walk about twenty feet or so and turn his or her back on the others. Whenever she said "Green light!" the others would start to walk and sneak up on her. She could say "Red light!" at any time and turn around, causing everyone to freeze. If she saw anyone move, that person would have to go back to the starting line. Now and then, some fool would try to walk really fast and nearly fall on his face trying to stop when "it" turned saying "Red light!" Whoever could make it far enough to tag "it" without being caught moving would win. The game was similar to "statues" where people were hurled around in a circle and let go, having to freeze into statues wherever they happened to end up.

I still rode my J. C. Higgins bicycle, and we all rode or walked down to Craigen's Drug Store (not a soda fountain drug store, unfortunately) to buy squirt guns at the height of summer. Having squirt gun fights, running through sprinklers in swimming trunks, and jumping into inflated plastic pools were ways to keep cool when the temperature climbed. Grandmother would make a pitcher of Kool Aid and pour it into an ice cube tray, putting toothpicks halfway into each of the tray's cells. After freezing, we popped out the cubes and had Kool Aid popsicles.

Before the high point of summer in July or August, the movies injected themselves back into my life. In early July I experienced the most terrifying movie I would ever see as a child—or partly see—thanks to my mother, who reluctantly brought me at my own insistence, because I didn't know what all the fuss about Frankenstein movies involved. But *this* Frankenstein was on a level of horror altogether unexpected, and not only by me, but by audiences generally. The poster outside the Neptune theater said, "IT WILL HAUNT YOU FOREVER!" Little did I know they weren't kidding.

The Neptune theater, built in the 1920s, was a very special theater in the University District. Beyond the candy counter down a wide hallway, the green-padded doors to the auditorium had brass-framed portholes. Another entrance to the auditorium started at the left of the candy counter and curved down a steep, carpeted slope past a rather mysterious door in the wall, then through heavy curtains into the lower part of the theater. Inside, above the proscenium, was a frieze of King Neptune. What could be more impressive? I was to spend many compelling hours in this theater during my youth.

This day, however, the movie I had insisted my mother take me to was the first in a series of horror films that set a new standard for the genre. *The Curse of Frankenstein* was a newly conceived British version made by the soon-to-be-notorious Hammer studio; and what set it apart was that it was the first gory horror movie in color—not an insignificant development, as audiences were to find out because of the red blood and other realistic putrid details. The early 1931 *Frankenstein* with Boris Karloff was legendary among adults who'd seen it as kids, so I'd been curious to see this new one. My mother could not have known of the severe criticism in the British press the movie had acquired for being far too gruesome, or that the blood and gore of a color horror movie might come as a shock. The movie was ghastly enough as the creature was created and then left dormant, completely bandaged up, floating in a large tank of water. Soon enough, Victor Frankenstein, played by Peter Cushing, hears a crashing sound coming from his laboratory. Although he assumed he'd failed to bring his creature back to life, he nevertheless rushes down to find out what had happened. He opens the door, and there is the creature standing in the middle of the laboratory, wrapped up like a mummy in bandages, including the face. And just as the creature reaches up to rip the bandages off its face, the camera zooms in, and what is suddenly revealed is so horrible, the face so sickening, that my heart leapt into my throat, as the saying goes, and I covered my eyes and ducked down as the audience screamed. This moment of horror was likely the equivalent, for my generation, to when Mary Philbin removes the mask from Lon Chaney in the 1925 *Phantom of the Opera*. I peered over the seat in front out of one eye as the hideous creature, played by Christopher Lee, tries to strangle Peter Cushing.

Witnessing my shock, mother asked if I wanted to leave, I said "oh, uh, OK," so we made our way back out into the carpeted hallway and sat down on a sofa while I steadied my nerves. It was the only time I'd been so frightened in a movie that I had to leave the theater. Yet after a few minutes, I peeked back in as the creature made its way through a forest. But I was in no mood to continue watching, so we made our way past the candy counter and out into the Saturday matinee daylight.

The fallout from this experience was four-fold. Partly expected was the nightmare of Hammer's newly conceived Frankenstein monster, which made it almost impossible for me to go to sleep on time—this lasted for about a month. Unexpected, subconsciously perhaps, was that I'd instantly become a fan of Peter Cushing—in this film the very definition of an unscrupulous anti-hero, but also the epitome of British style in speech, mannerisms, and velvet-trim Victorian attire. Third, regardless of my terror, or perhaps because of it, I'd become enthralled, against my more sensitive nature, by the horror genre. And fourth, the movie got me in serious trouble back in my grandparents' neighborhood.

My sin was telling (in lurid detail) *all* about *The Curse of Frankenstein* up to the time I had fled the theater, to Buzzy and Jimmy. I was ten, Buzzy was nine, Jimmy was eight, and it seemed as if I'd been far too enthusiastic in relating the horror, particularly when Christopher Lee rips the bandages off his face. Buzzy and Jimmy's mother, Mrs. Brandt, complained to my grandmother that I had frightened her children, and furthermore, that I should try in the future to emphasize the finer things of life.

I had no idea how my grandmother reacted to this chastisement, because it was only through Buzzy and Jimmy that I heard about the complaint. In any case, though not for this reason, I was temporarily bounced back to my parents' neighborhood in Bryant where Dean and I played guns and board games. Dean complained about my leaving too often to stay with my grandparents, for there was only his younger brother and Brad to play with while I was gone. It was also true, however, that Dean was sometimes taken out of the neighborhood, and when he returned, he couldn't stop babbling about his wonderful friend Terry McCardle who was SO much cooler than anyone else he knew, implying me. No matter, we had a pretty good time while we were able to join up.

It may also have been that I was shuttled back and forth between houses because my mother and stepfather weren't getting along. Now and then I would hear my mother yelling or complaining, once or twice about the rent not being paid, and then Larry would retreat into silence, sitting in the living room chair hiding behind a magazine or newspaper. I was never informed how well or badly Larry's fire extinguisher sales were going, whether he was salaried or on commission, or anything else about his life, and he wasn't interested in sharing. Or in conversation generally. Whereas my mother talked a great deal, mostly to her friends on the telephone during weekdays. We had what was known as a "party line," where to save money, two customers used the same phone line although the numbers were different. Now and then I would pick up the phone to call Dean or someone, but the other person would be using the line. If I didn't hang up right away, I'd get a "Get off the line!" because they could hear the phone being picked up. Of course, this also worked in reverse, although I didn't much care if anyone wanted to listen to me asking Dean if he wanted to play.

One day, my stepfather's brother, Myron, pulled up in front of our house in the most beautiful automobile I'd ever seen. He'd bought a brand new '57 Pontiac Star Chief convertible in two-tone aqua and cream. The car was dazzling. It looked like a rocketship with those red taillights, streamlined design, and chrome trim. Myron was younger than Larry, had a flat-top hair cut, and gave me a ride in his new car. Everything about that car—the beautiful exterior, the amazing instrument panel, the fancy vinyl upholstery, the power of the V-8 engine—was nothing less than a fantasy on wheels. American cars in those days were about style and imagination. With each change of the model year, everyone wondered what would come next. Nevertheless, after Myron had dinner and left, Larry was critical of him for spending such money on a new car. Envy? Larry still had his old faded blue Plymouth station wagon. Yet it sounded like Myron had blown his savings. Who could blame him? I asked myself. Who could resist?

I'd had nearly a month of vacation by the time the Fourth of July rolled around. On the morning of the Fourth, back at my grandparents' Ravenna house for the rest of the summer, I awakened to the start of celebrations—kids setting off firecrackers in the neighborhoods. When a big BOOM was heard in the distance, as if a chemical factory had blown up, Grandfather would delightedly say, "That was a big one!"

No one went to the Indian reservations to buy firecrackers—even for the red "two-inchers" that were like little sticks of dynamite—because Seattle had yet to ban these things. Commonly, people set off "one-and-a-half-inchers" in backyards or on picnics, but it was always an adult or teenager who would light off an entire strand of 500 and throw them into the street where they flashed and exploded like automatic gunfire for a full minute or more. We might as well have been in China on Chinese New Year.

The fireworks stand on 65th, set up on a vacant lot, was a fantastic cornucopia of skyrockets, Roman candles, missiles, pinwheels, fountains, firecrackers, aerial bombs, sparklers, and those delightful black snakes of ash that would come squirming out onto the sidewalk when the pellet was lit. The Fourth was like the Devil's Xmas. We loved every minute of it!

That night, we drove in Aunt Peggy's '50 Ford down to Green Lake to watch from a high vantage point the big display over the lake. And back home, Peggy revealed the colorful fountain she'd purchased at the fireworks stand. The family gathered in the backyard, lit sparklers (me making big circles in the dark) and then set off our tribute to a day that seemed to last forever, with the glow of the large fountain lingering on our faces.

I got ready for bed around midnight, knowing I was comfortable in this house, in this neighborhood, and that the majority of summer still lay ahead.

§ 15

By August, I had learned how to swim in a motel pool on vacation with Mother and Larry, so Mother sometimes drove over from Bryant to take me and Buzzy and Jimmy, or Dean and I, to Green Lake to go swimming. Rather than swim in the lake, we preferred to use Evans Pool, an Olympic-size indoor pool next to the lake. I reeked of chlorine for hours afterward.

The first week in August, Aunt Peggy was getting ready to watch the Unlimited hydroplane races on television. Every year, she got a race program with a score sheet and kept score as each "Heat" of racing completed. This was a Seattle tradition like no other. In 1950, Seattle had no major league sports team. But an unexpected event took place that brought the city—already a boating mecca—into the big league of powerboat racing. As told by sports writer Fred Farley:

> In the early hours of June 26, 1950, an event transpired that caught the racing world by surprise. An Unlimited Class hydroplane with the unlikely name of *Slo-mo-shun IV* set a mile straightaway record of 160.323 miles per hour on Lake Washington near Sand Point, which raised the former standard by nearly 19 miles per hour. A trio of Seattleites, owner/driver Stanley S. Sayres, designer/riding mechanic Ted Jones, and builder Anchor Jensen, had toppled Sir Malcolm Campbell's world mark of 141.740, established in England in 1939 with *Bluebird K4*. The era of the three-point suspension design of hydroplane had assuredly arrived.

My grandmother recalled that shortly thereafter, someone came to our door in the older house on Ravenna Boulevard asking for a donation to send the *Slo-mo-shun IV* to Detroit to compete for the prestigious Gold Cup powerboat trophy. Grandmother had no idea what a "Slo-mo" was, so she declined. But the money was raised, and Stanley Sayres took his boat and crew to Detroit, where it was decided by "experts" that although the *Slo-mo-shun IV* could go fast in a straight line, it couldn't possibly run quickly enough through the corners. This seemed logical because this new kind of race boat literally flew across the water on the tips of two forward sponsons integrated into the mahogany hull, and the propeller in the rear, causing a high, spectacular "roostertail" of water behind the boat. The roostertail was generated by the half-submerged propeller turning at many thousands of rpm, driven by a WW II Allison aircraft engine originally used in the P-38 Lightning and P-40 Warhawk fighter planes.

Seattle, without a major league sport, was immediately captivated by the *Slo-mo*'s world speed record, and the city would compete in the Super Bowl of powerboat racing—a sport additionally romanticized by the participation of eastern celebrities such as Horace Dodge, owner of the Dodge automobile company, the popular big-band leader Guy Lombardo, and other wealthy sportsmen of the day. Not to mention the dare-devil drivers themselves. Farley reported from Detroit:

> *Slo-mo-shun IV* won all three 30-mile heats of the 1950 contest with Ted Jones driving. In the first heat of the day, *Slo-mo* lapped the entire field, which included the 1949 Gold Cup winner *My Sweetie*. Not once in the 46-year history of the event had the Gold Cup winner hailed from any other locale farther west than Minneapolis (in 1916). Immediately, Sayres announced plans to defend the cup on his home waters of Lake Washington.

Seattle went wild. It would play host to the Gold Cup the following year and for several years thereafter, won by *Slo-mo-*

shun IV and the newer *Slo-mo-shun V*, while other Seattle boats were being built to compete. The rivalry between Seattle and Detroit became legendary, with the largest crowds *ever to witness a single one-day sporting event* lining the lengthy shores of Lake Washington, with estimates at the time of 500,000. In 1955, the Cup was taken back to Detroit with a win by *Gale V*, but the city inaugurated the Seattle Seafair Race to take its place in 1956. *Miss Thriftway* won the Gold Cup back for 1957, and our family was ready to watch it "live" on television that Sunday.

Not only the crowds on the shoreline, nor the thousand pleasure craft along the backstretch of the 3.75 mile-around race course (in later years 3 miles), but a huge television audience, as well, enhanced my passionate dedication to this sport by the summer of 1957. The race was so important in Seattle, that KING TV, anchored by sportscaster Bill O'Mara, interrupted regularly scheduled programming—most often a soap opera—in the middle of the day whenever a boat came out on the water to qualify for the Sunday race. People could hear the distant roar of those aircraft engines all over the city. Kids made wooden hydroplanes, painted them in the colors of their favorite boats, attached them with string to the backs of their bicycles and raced each other in streets and parking lots. Often we simply ran with them, trailing them behind us down along the concrete alley from up near 15th.

I also built a realistic wooden model kit of the *Miss Thriftway*. The design of that 16" kit mimicked the construction of the real thing, with several inner bulkheads, rear transom, engine compartment, decking, sponsons, and all the rest. Older kids sometimes added a .049 gas engine and used the kit's brass hardware, including propeller, to create a real working model. I was satisfied with a boat, sans propeller and propeller shaft, that we ran with on a string, up and down on the grass parking strip around a couple of "buoys," attempting to beat each other's time.

That Sunday in August of 1957, Aunt Peggy kept score of the points for each heat of the race that was again broadcast on KING TV, and the *Miss Thriftway* driven by Bill Muncey won the Gold Cup for the second time. The Cup would be back again in 1958 with an incident no one in Seattle would ever forget—but that was in the future.

For now, summer of '57 was nearing an end, and before returning to my parents' house on NE 37th to start fifth grade, I continued to play in the street with the other kids, walk up the concrete alley across the street to see what was going on near the Hambly sisters' house (they often had a badminton net in their back yard), ride my bike here and there, and at home learn how to play *Monopoly* with Aunt Peggy. In fact, all the kids started playing *Monopoly,* the most ubiquitous of board games. I played variously with Ted, Ted's sister Nora, Ronny, "Buzzy," and maybe one or two others, on my grandparents' big front porch. We would play for hours at a time.

Light-fingers Ronny, my own age but with a blond crew-cut, would now and then try to steal a $500 bill from the bank and hide it under his Hawaiian shirt (his customary attire), then try to sneak it into his pile of cash. Ted or I would usually catch him. "Where did you get that $500, Ronnnny?" We'd make him put it back in the bank, roll our eyeballs, and groan. That was Ronny. You had to watch him like a hawk. We also noticed that he had a quirk. If he tried to lie about the money, he could not look you in the eye. He simply could not. I thought maybe it was because his family were Mormons who could not look you in the eye while lying. It was just a theory.

One day, Ronny said he had something to show me in his garage. Right. Foolishly, I stepped into the garage ahead of him. After hearing the click of the latch behind me, I found myself locked in, more embarrassed than angry at being tricked—and too self-respecting to yell for the mischievous creep to let me out. I strained to see into the shadows. The garage was almost empty but for a few garden tools, as I could see by a crack of light between the twin garage doors, but then I discovered that Ronny's parents were storing a *lot* of gasoline in there. Nervously, I could make out at least a dozen gallon containers. "I have somethin' to *show* you," Ronny had said before I stepped ahead of him into the trap. Was it the gasoline he wanted to show me? I wondered. Naw. But it was creepy.

After a minute or two I banged on the door. Then I took a deep breath and sat down on a relatively clean area of the concrete floor. In about a half hour, I heard someone. A dark shadow covered the thin crack of light between the big wooden doors facing the street. I heard Ronny's father's low voice.

"Philip, are you in there?"

"Yesss," I said as resentfully as I could.

The latch clicked open, light flooded in, and the slightly overweight, balding man peered into the garage.

"Ronny locked me in," I said.

"He told me a couple of minutes ago. He's sure as hell in trouble. How long have you been in here?"

"I don't know. A half hour, I guess."

Saying nothing for a moment, Mr. Hatch motioned me outside. I squinted into the afternoon brightness and stepped out onto the sidewalk while he closed the doors. I had only a vague impression of him as a person. He wore a Hawaiian shirt like Ronny's. But maybe he was an understanding father with a miscreant son. Then, as I thought of the gasoline again, it was a potential arsonist who put a thick white hand out and rested it on my shoulder.

"There's no excuse for what Ron did. We've put him in his room. He's going to stay there for two days. We're going to serve him meals in his room. Scant meals. He's allowed to come out to use the bathroom, but that's all. When he comes out for good, he is going to come over to your grandparents' house and apologize to you for locking you in the garage."

Not enough, I thought.

"Ron may be a little wild sometimes, but he's a good kid. We want him to be aggressive and self-sufficient. I hope you don't take this shenanigan too seriously." His expression was confident, contemplative, and he had the tone of someone giving thoughtful advice. "The Russians have a lot of missiles pointed at us, you know. And we have a lot of missiles pointed at them." The lines on his forehead deepened as he focused on me. "We have a lot of missiles pointed at each other. You know?"

I nodded understandingly at this incomprehensible leap in subject matter. We walked a few paces toward a heavy wooden gate that led into his back yard.

"When the next war comes, it's going to be pretty tough, and only those who are prepared will survive."

I thought of how we kids played "army" and tried to connect this with what Ronny's father was saying. I also remembered the rumor from early summer that Ronny's parents had built a bomb shelter under their back yard. No one believed it. It turned out that they *had* built one—in their basement—stocked with food and supplies. Maybe the gasoline had something to do with it, too.

"We have to be prepared for any eventuality," he continued. "Ron will be prepared to survive the next war."

"Sure," I said, trying to imagine how cheating at *Monopoly* would help.

Ronny's father looked down at me with his round, tanned face (maybe, I thought, that tan explained the Hawaiian shirts) and smiled knowingly. "You kids are all good kids, but you have to be tough. Maybe it wasn't so bad you got locked in that garage after all. Maybe you'll learn something from it. OK?"

"Sure." And thought: What I've learned is to avoid your bratty cheater of a son.

"But we'll see it doesn't happen again."

"Yeah. I gotta go now."

"All right, Philip." (No one but my own family called me Philip; for friends and neighbors it was always Phil.) Tell your grandparents we're disciplining Ronny."

"Sure," I said. "Bye."

And off I ran.

Ronny never showed up at my grandparents' to apologize (though he probably told his father he had), and as September arrived I prepared to move back to my parents' house to start fifth grade at Bryant Elementary School.

An interlude came when my aunt, grandmother, grandfather, and I went to Long Beach on the Washington coast, where I saw the ocean for the first time.

I got an exciting, anticipatory glance of it from the rear passenger window of Aunt Peggy's '50 Ford, but it wasn't until we'd parked—it was in front of an old gray-shingled hotel—and I made my way over the sand dunes, that the full impact occurred. Here was a vista of waves, sky, and horizon I'd only seen in films and photographs, and it was one of the most memorable moments of my life. No less the immense *sound*.

We were given an attic room in the weathered two-story hotel, and that first night it rained while we slept—or tried to sleep amid the sound of the wind, the rain, and the distant breakers.

The sun came out the following afternoon, and I spent my time wading in the surf and building a primitive sand castle using a small metal bucket and shovel my aunt had purchased for me. I was in awe of the bigger waves breaking in the distance, for it was a gently sloping beach and a long way to the foaming tops of the more distant breakers.

Two days went by, and on the morning of the third, just before we left, I noticed a pretty girl with sandy-blond hair looking down at me from a wood-framed second-story window. I hadn't seen her before now, noticed that she seemed to be about my age, and that she made an attractive impression I romantically associated with the ocean, wind, and sky. With a turn of her head away, then back to gaze beyond me toward the dunes, she was not at all self-conscious, no longer even aware of my presence, and alluring in a way I didn't quite understand. I wanted to meet her, make friends, build a sand castle with her, but it was impossible because my folks were about to leave; and then she turned from the window and, like a vanishing spirit, was gone.

§ 16

At my parents' house in Bryant, I got ready to walk to school. I was again aware that life's transitions are marked by the seasons: the beginning of fall when school begins, the darkness of winter and the coming of the holidays, the start of spring, the freedom of summer.

The summer of '57 and its concluding trip to the ocean was now replaced by those old wooden desks with the dry inkwells. The desks were still in rows in the new classroom, but they could not camouflage a significant transition from fourth to fifth grade or hide the impending fall weather seen out of the tall second-floor windows of Bryant Elementary.

I got lucky, so I was told by Dean, because I'd been assigned to Miss Loschen's class, the door of which was located near a corner of the second-floor hallway. Seats were not assigned alphabetically, and I was given a seat in the middle of the left-hand row near the windows. I would soon become aware of my fellow students, some of whom I'd known from fourth grade. But it was Miss Loschen who attracted my attention. She was not the elderly "schoolmarm" type I'd always had before, but a great-looking twenty-something brunette. She had somewhat shorter hair than typical of the time, swept pertly back, and often wore white blouses with fashionable Chantilly lace collars, modest length skirts; but mostly, she was the best looking teacher I'd ever seen. Or just as important, a warm, nice person. The latter is where the "luck" came in, for Miss Loschen was not likely to rap one on the knuckles with a ruler. Rumor also had it that she played classical piano, which added a level of cultivation to her attractiveness.

I was not in love with Miss Loschen that I knew of (or could admit to?), and in any case, falling in love with one's teacher was rare, ridiculed, or just dumb. But no doubt I wasn't used to being around a pretty woman every day (my attractive thirty-eight-year-old mother not counting). It also turned out that she was actually Mrs. Loschen, not Miss Loschen. So that was that.

Aside from reading, writing, and arithmetic, two things had my attention during the first month of school: cars and girls. Or rather, cars and girl.

Insofar as the cars, we boys were again scrutinizing magazine photos of the new models, if only to see what Detroit had come up with. The '58 models showed significant changes: most impressive were the newly conceived '58 Ford Thunderbird and the '58 Chevy Impala, the latter with its triple-taillight lenses set in a remarkable curving surround.

The girl was named Sue. When I became aware of her sitting in the middle row of the classroom, a feeling of déjà vu came over me. It was impossible, so it seemed, but the more I looked at her the more I was convinced that *she* was the very girl I'd seen at the ocean looking out of the window. I tried to gaze surreptitiously out of the corner of my eye. Could it really *be* her? Coincidences do happen, I thought, or maybe I was engaged in wishful thinking. I'd seen the girl in the window only for a moment. But the resemblance was remarkable. Sue was a sandy blond with the same look to her. But it was too much to think she was the same person. An unremarkable co-incidence was that her name, common enough, coincided with my new 45 rpm record, "Wake Up Little Susie" by The Everly Brothers, which I played over and over and was a huge hit on the radio—this having little or nothing to do with the Sue in my classroom. Yet I now associated her with that song *and* the girl at the ocean. The only thing left was to ask her at an opportune moment if she'd been to Long Beach during the summer.

Whatever the case, she was appealing; if she was appeal-ing to other boys in the class, I didn't know. Boys did not di-vulge attractions to girls or they'd be razzed to death. As in first grade with Andrea, I could do nothing to attract Sue's attention as the year progressed, but I did manage to ask her the question that was haunting me. After a week or two, I came up to her in the hallway.

"Hi," I said.

"Hi," she said, somewhat startled.

"I was, ah, wondering if you were at Long Beach this summer."

She gave me a funny look.

"I saw someone who looked like you there," I said,

"Not me," she said.

"Oh, OK," I said.

And off she went, while in my mind, now mildly suspi-cious, I thought it still might have been her. And yet, alt-hough my wishful brain conflated the two girls, I knew deep down that the girl at the ocean was now a lost reality, yet an unforgettable image forever looking out of that window in my memory.

§ 17

At home, my mother and stepfather watched the nightly news with Huntley and Brinkley. ("Goodnight Chet. Goodnight David.") At school, we still read *My Weekly Reader*. Of politics, the memorable image was of Eisenhower playing golf. Like almost every kid my age, I didn't care or think much about current events but was focused on school, homework, hobbies, reading, and watching TV shows like *Jack Benny, Burns & Allen, Wyatt Earp, Gunsmoke, The Millionaire, Alfred Hitchcock Presents, The Adventures of Ozzie and Harriet*, a new show called *Leave it to Beaver*, plus quiz shows *I've Got a Secret, You Bet Your Life* (with Groucho Marx), and *What's My Line?* My parents usually selected the shows, and we were in front of the TV almost every night.

It all seemed normal and natural, for there was a TV antenna on every roof. Once in a while, especially if the TV had been newly adjusted, or when we upgraded our antenna, my stepfather would get out the ladder, go up onto our roof and try to make a fine adjustment, rotating the antenna slightly left or right. It was supposed to be pointed at the tall broadcast towers on Queen Anne Hill, but in the Bryant district we had no direct line of sight, and my mother would complain of "ghosts" in the picture—vague double images. So my stepfather would ascend into the stratosphere and yell down: *"How about that?"* And mother would stand in front of the television and yell as loud as she could toward the open window: *"No. no! Wait! Hold it! Wait a minute! That's better!"* And so it went, although the picture could never be made perfect.

Television newscasts didn't completely dominate as the source of news. Newspapers and magazines were still primary sources, since national TV news was limited to a half-hour of the proverbial "6 o'clock news," and in morning shows like *Today* with the intellectual-looking Dave Garroway.

The bombshell news that hit during the first week of October overshadowed everything else—an event that changed history, including the educational trajectory of every kid in America, mine too. Fantastically, the event concerned an object somewhat larger than a basketball.

The launching by the Soviet Union of the first artificial satellite, Sputnik 1, into orbit around the earth, was an unprecedented achievement, catching our own rocket scientists off guard. This little metal ball with its long wire-thin antennae, sent out a self-important beeping signal as it orbited the globe—taken as a demonstration to the world how scientifically advanced the Soviet Union—our Cold War enemy—had become.

The technological and educational implications had immediate impact. Since early childhood, the boomer generation had been exposed to movies and TV dealing with the mystery, adventure, and possible terrors awaiting human beings journeying into outer space. An orbiting satellite had been the purview only of science fiction until Sputnik.

In the collective imagination of the 1950s, our main orientation to space, aside from the moon, was dominated by the nearby planets. I had read in the *World Book* that in 1877, Italian astronomer Giovanni Schiaparelli discovered what he described as *canali* on the planet Mars. The Italian word could mean either canals or channels, but the word canal meant something intelligently constructed rather than a natural feature, and this became the accepted description. Soon, other astronomers confirmed Schiaparelli's observations. Most impressive were Percival Lowell's drawings showing a weblike pattern of straight, interconnecting lines. For some, the lines seemed to indicate irrigation canals possibly bringing water from the polar caps into the drier regions of the planet. Dark green areas seemed to enlarge and recede with the seasons, and these were thought to be patches of planetary vegetation.

By the time I began to read about Mars, the canals had become controversial—perhaps, some said, an illusion having to do with naked-eye observations through telescopes of high power but unable to sufficiently resolve Mars's surface. Even in 1957, however, Martian canals—and therefore the real possibility of a Martian civilization—was an acceptable hypothesis that stirred one's imagination. So too the influence of the notorious *War of the Worlds* radio broadcast of 1938 that sent thousands of people into a panic in the belief that Martians had landed in New Jersey and were invading the earth. I hadn't yet read H. G. Wells's 1898 novel that was the basis of Orson Welles's infamous radio broadcast, but sightings of flying saucers were routinely in the news, as well as the popular notion of an alien saucer landing on the White House lawn. The possibility of an imminent landing or invasion had been common since the start of the modern UFO phenomenon in 1947, the year of my birth, and abetted by movies such as *The Thing from Another World* (1951), *The Day the Earth Stood Still* (1951), and *Earth vs. the Flying Saucers* (1956). In June of '47 (nearly coinciding with my May birthday) pilot Kenneth Arnold had sighted a group of nine UFOs flying near Mount Rainier; and in July of 1952, as I learned later by reading *The Report on Unidentified Flying Objects* by Capt. Edward J. Ruppelt, mysterious objects were seen at night over the Washington D.C. capitol, both visually and on radar, resulting in the scrambling of F-94 Starfire jet fighters. On the second weekend of the incident, one of the pilots reported over the radio that he was surrounded by the targets; and as a result of this incident, a national news conference at the Pentagon attempted to explain—or, as many would say, explain away—the incident as unusual weather phenomena. That temperature inversions disappeared when jets approached and returned when they retreated, wasn't explained. Or that such temperature inversions were common in the area and never reported as targets on the radar screens. Nor did the radar operators at three different locations appreciate being told they couldn't tell weather from solid objects. Yet the incident, happening on two consecutive weekends, remained of national concern. What seemed likely to many Americans, including people in the military (let alone the radar operators at Washington National Airport and Andrews Air Force Base) was that the Pentagon was trying to suppress flying saucer reports, mainly for two reasons: First, the Air Force feared public loss of confidence in national security; and second, they simply didn't know what to do, yet were responsible for US airspace—especially over the capital! Shockingly, it was a matter of incompetence that on the first weekend of the event, it took two F-94 fighters over three hours to respond to targets nearly overhead of the White House and Capitol Building, having to fly from Delaware because the runways at Andrews were under repair. My own amateur opinion of various events, including this Washington D.C. incident, was that the UFO phenomenon remained unsolved.

In the 1950s no one knew what might exist in outer space, even on the planets of our own solar system, let alone if UFOs proved to be extraterrestrial spacecraft.

Even the planet Venus was a source of mystery. In the fifth novel in the Tom Corbett, Space Cadet series, *The Revolt on Venus* (1954), I read of Tom, his friend Roger, and a big Venusian fellow named Astro, hunting in the Venusian jungles for *Tyrannosaurus rex* (no less). And on my grandfather's bookshelf was a book published in the very same year called *Man and the Planets* by Robert S. Richardson, an astronomer connected with the Mount Wilson and Mount Palomar observatories. Although he noted that the atmosphere of Venus had been found to contain too much carbon dioxide to support life, and that the surface temperature was speculated to be 170 degrees Fahrenheit due to the greenhouse effect (turning out to be a low estimate), he left open the possibility that the thick layer of Venus's atmosphere might render the data inconclusive.

"If you don't like this picture of the planet," Richardson wrote, "you are welcome to dream up a lush tropical world filled with as many flowers and dinosaurs as you like. For when it comes to actual conditions on the surface of Venus *there is nobody who really knows.*" [his italics]

Amid these abiding uncertainties and imaginative possibilities, the space race began with the launch of Sputnik 1.

My first clue as to how quickly national security panic in the United States over Sputnik had taken hold (including demands for more science education) came when Mrs. Loschen was absent from class one day. Our substitute teacher was a wool-suited, balding man with glasses and (perhaps appropriately) a subtle German accent. Mrs. Loschen had instructed him to let us read our library books and then give us a spelling test.

"Instead of following normal procedure," said the sub, going to the blackboard, "I'm going to discuss something more important and then give you an overnight assignment." With a thick piece of chalk he drew an outline in the shape of an electric lightbulb. He filled in the outline with a filament, then drew a pair of wires from the side and bottom of the quickly drawn screw thread at the base to each end of a separate, cylindrical object. "This cylinder here," he said in a clipped, confident tone, "is a battery." He looked back at the slightly bewildered class. "Now, I'm sure you all know that electricity is what causes this lightbulb to light." (I smiled.) "You may not know that the electricity must be carried on what is called an electrical circuit." His demeanor was a little brassy at this point, and I wondered what Mrs. Loschen might think of his usurpation. "Now, I want you all to go home tonight, and by tomorrow write a definition of an electrical circuit, including a drawing. I don't know if I'll be here tomorrow, but if so, we'll talk about other important subjects."

At first, I was skeptical of this sub, but his sudden injection of a lightbulb into our reading and spelling was a novelty of the first order, and fifth graders liked nothing more than novelty. I was excited to go home and find out about electrical circuits in the *World Book*. Which I did. And the next day, the sub was back, and we all turned in the assignment he gave us. He lectured us on electricity and then allowed us to read our library books, but he neglected the spelling test. When Mrs. Loschen returned the following day, she asked what we'd been doing in class. Quite a few hands were raised; she was informed and seemed fine with what we'd been given to do. She then told us to number the usual two columns on our paper for the twenty-word spelling test.

That was pretty much it insofar as science education was concerned, at least for the moment, but the wheels had been set in motion by Sputnik 1, and it orbited the earth for nearly three months before re-entering the atmosphere. American plans were being made for more science education.

In December, we watched television news film of the attempted launch of a Vanguard rocket that was to put our own satellite into orbit. As the rocket started to lift off, it failed, fell, and crashed in a gigantic explosion. Newspaper headlines were merciless: "Flopnik" "Stayputnik" "Kaputnik".

Nevertheless, in my parents' house during this humiliation, daily matters continued as usual; my mother and stepfather argued about things that passed without a trace through my memory, other than Larry's long spells of silence. One argument was certainly down to earth. It was about my eating habits. Larry wanted to force me to eat a greater variety of food, putting things on my plate such as half a cantaloupe, that he knew I couldn't stand. I wouldn't touch it, so what could he do as mother took my side and told me I didn't really have to eat it? He also scowled at my ridiculous habit of eating out the soft part of the toast and leaving the crust. My mother just didn't care, nor did she believe in forcing a child to eat something unwanted. Eventually I began to eat the crust, but never cantaloupe. Throughout my childhood, all of my family members (other than Larry, who had little sway) tended to leave me to my own devices. One day, however, Larry had me alone at a cafe counter and tried to force me to eat a banana split, which he ordered against my wishes, knowing I also hated bananas. I did my best by taking three or four spoonfuls, while he insisted I include a banana slice in each. I suddenly felt as though I might have to throw it all up, so rather than do that, I spit out the next bite into the bowl. Larry was furious, took me by the collar, pulled me off the stool, and hustled me out of the restaurant, refusing to speak all the way home. We never really got along after that—not that we'd gotten along too well before, and although I felt a bit inadequate as a son, I didn't regret my behavior, or that I didn't like bananas or cantaloupe.

Although I had a stepfather and a grandfather, neither were role models. Certainly I loved my grandfather, who was still working in the Ballard lumber mill, and he taught me a few things like how to hammer a nail or saw a board. Larry bought me a baseball mitt and played catch. But these things were fleeting and insubstantial in terms of identifying with or wanting to be like someone. I didn't know what sort of person I really was and failed to acquire an identity from the male members of the family.

Not realizing I had a particular psychological need, I began to look elsewhere for a role model, and like most everyone my age, I liked Westerns and Western heroes. After all, I had "played guns" from age four, so naturally I gravitated to

Old West motifs—and in the fall of '57 there was a plethora
of Westerns on television. From the Old West to the beginning of the space race; movies, television, and children's
books spanned the heroic male gamut. But it was a new kind
of TV Western, and a different kind of romanticized hero
that provided me with the first character I actually had a
yearning to *be*. The new show was called *Maverick,* and it was
different. James Garner played a slick, nattily-dressed poker
player named Bret Maverick who preferred to avoid trouble
but could be cleverly heroic when necessary. My kind of hero,
for this guy was the opposite of John Wayne and other he-
men, whom nobody could live up to. So I liked the balance
struck by Bret Maverick; and as the series became a big hit, its
episodes began to contain more touches of comedy and satire. One bit of dialogue made use of a Western cliché:

Cowboy: "We can head 'em off at the pass."

Maverick: "What did you say?"

Cowboy: "I said we can head 'em off at the pass."

Maverick (slightly astounded): "That's what I thought you
said."

I read that Garner had ad-libbed his response to that line,
and they decided to leave it in. Whatever the case, my identification with James Garner as Maverick peaked when Grandfather Nels taught me how to play poker. I practiced card
shuffling and dealing five- and seven-card stud and five-card
draw with him, playing for those archetypal red, white, and
blue chips. I understood that Grandfather had played a little
poker in Montana when he and Uncle Pete owned the general
store in Roy. Furthermore, such towns were pretty wild back
in Montana in the 1920s. Horses and wagons were still routine, traditional modes of transportation even as the automobile became more and more common.

Maverick always kept a $1000 bill pinned under the front
of his jacket, and I decided to do the same with play money

when I wore my tweed sport jacket to Sunday School—the last year I attended. Or church of any kind.

I wasn't swayed away from church by *Maverick*, it was just that Christian Science didn't take with me. I had learned to pray before bedtime, but the more I did, the more it seemed I was delivering my entreaties into the dark void of outer space. Or that the Christian Science notion of neglecting medicine in favor of "knowing the truth" might not be such a grand idea. It's hard to maintain an idea like that when everyone you know outside of your grandmother and aunt thinks it's nuts.

Neither did my grandfather help my grandmother's or aunt's wishes for me to become a Christian Scientist. Once, when my grandmother encouraged me to read "the lessons" from Mrs. Eddy's blue-leather-bound *Science and Health with Key to the Scriptures*, my grandfather, sitting in his big overstuffed chair, gave me a subtle wink. Or did he? I thought he had. I was sure he had. Yet I'd seen him reading the Bible, and although I was told he was a Lutheran, I understood it was long ago. How little it took to reinforce my mixed feelings—a maybe wink, a subtle look of amusement when we were off to church with or without him. And then, one day he quoted one or two self-contradictory passages from the Bible, placed the book on his lap, slightly raised his left eyebrow and gave that same amused look. Not once did he *say* a word against the Bible or religion. Yet we seemed to have established a silent bond of skepticism that sanctioned intellectual independence from the church and its doctrines.

Eventually we gave up poker in favor of checkers; and Grandfather soon quit the lumber mill when he accidentally sawed one of his forefingers off. Quick surgery attached it back, but it was always pale whitish and dysfunctional.

§ 18

The truly unexpected happened again on the evening of November 11, 1957—an astonishing event that made the pages of *Life* magazine. And to my own amazement, it occurred directly in front of my grandparents' former house (the one with the little round window) on Ravenna Boulevard. Newspapers and television accounts told the story, and I read the news carefully. It was a Monday evening when the phone rang at Charles Meyer's house across the boulevard from where we had lived. An agitated voice sounded on the other end of the line. "Charlie, this is Marty next door. You'd better move your car."

"Move my car?"

"Yes, you'd better get outside and move your car before it falls into the hole."

Meyer had hung up the phone, gone outside, and discovered the beginning of the strangest event ever to befall Seattle. By the dim light of the streetlamp on the corner, he could see his '48 Plymouth sedan parked at the curb. Beyond was the wide median strip where a huge, familiar chestnut tree grew. Meyer stared into the night and couldn't quite believe what he was seeing. The wide, grassy median strip had sunk several feet along with the tree, and a section of pavement had buckled. He nervously got into his car and backed it all the way down the block from the depression. The police showed up to examine the sinking ground. Meyer, somewhat amazed, not knowing why the street had sunk but thinking everything was under control, went to bed.

When he and his wife looked out the window the next morning, there was no chestnut tree, no corner streetlamp, no concrete curb where their car had been parked. There was, in fact, no *street*. In place of these supposedly permanent objects was a gigantic *pit,* 100 feet long, 66 feet wide, and 40 feet deep. At the bottom was a brown, oozing, slimy pool of quicksand. Nothing else could be seen down there. Just the quicksand.

I knew none of this at the moment, of course, or that ten blocks west along the boulevard, the custodian of John Marshall Junior High arrived at work to turn on the building's furnace and discovered that the basement was flooded with four feet of water. The school was quickly closed.

City workers were mobilized. Something strange, they'd heard, was happening in Ravenna. It was like the beginning of a Grade B science fiction movie. A crew arrived with a large power shovel, and the decision was made to pour sand into the huge, incredibly deep hole. Barricades were erected around the pit. City engineers said that the hole must have been caused by a ruptured sewer line 145 feet below the level of the street—the Ravenna Tunnel section of the North Trunk System. The sewer had cracked, perhaps at the time of the great 1949 Seattle earthquake—perhaps earlier—creating unstable soil in the tunnel from the sandy underground. A cavity formed, then grew, and kept growing until everything just got sucked down because of the cavity's immense size and the subterranean quicksand.

The next night, Tuesday, a water main broke. But it was on Wednesday night at 11:00 that all hell broke loose.

"I was upstairs," said Dale Gross of 1621 NE Ravenna Boulevard, "when I heard a rumble. The whole house shook as if we were having an earthquake. I ran outside, and the sidewalks had disappeared!"

Residents of the boulevard rushed to their windows to see what was happening at the pit. People who had assumed they were far enough from the hole watched in horror as huge sections of the street began to disappear downward.

The hole was increasing in size every few minutes.* With the help of surrounding neighbors and University of Washington fraternity students along "frat row" on the upper boulevard, families along the affected street started to evacuate their homes. The Meyers began carrying furniture out their back door and then began handing things out the back windows. "You could hear the rumbling sound as new sections of ground fell into the pit," said Meyer. "Every few minutes we looked out the front window to see if the hole had gotten any closer to the house."

So busy was everyone at the big sinkhole that no one could have imagined what was about to happen several blocks southeast between NE 51st and NE 53rd streets. Under the immense pressure of the continuing cave-in, about 8,000 cubic yards of previously trapped sand, bricks, and timbers were suddenly being forced southward through the Ravenna sewer's six-foot-wide tunnel.

"I was awakened by a jingling noise," said W. D. Burdick of 5212 Ravenna Ave. NE, "apparently the lid of the manhole bouncing around before it was blown off. When I looked out, sand and water were gushing 15 feet into the air from the open manhole."

The Burdicks' rockery and most of their lawn were suddenly washed away. Other homes were also caught in the flood, eight of them having to be evacuated. At the Carnation Company, downhill a mile or so to the southeast, the night shift found their parking lot turning into a lake of water, sand, and sewage. Then the line plugged up again with compressed sand.

Back at the huge pit, two gas mains broke and were shut down. A power shovel that had been left near the hole almost dropped below into the quicksand. Charles Meyer's front

---

*The reader is encouraged to google "Great Ravenna Sinkhole" for photos.

door was about 15 feet from the edge of the precipice. The pit had doubled in size to engulf the entire city block. It was now an ominous 200 feet long, 175 feet wide, and 60 feet deep. The city was losing a war against one of its own sewers. "We can't do anything now except watch," said City Engineer Roy Morse, whose staff had been working around the clock. "There's a real danger of triggering more caving with any jarring. We could lose two or three houses right away." Since Monday, Morse had been working to bypass the break with an emergency sewer line through Cowen Park, giving them time to repair the damage. Assistant City Engineer James Robertson said, "The job won't be done in a matter of hours, but we've got to put a line around that Ravenna hole or we may lose a whole neighborhood."

The media had a field day. At my parents' house in Bryant, I wondered if the kids in my grandparents' neighborhood had gone to see the pit several blocks away. A small sinking of the ground on Ravenna Boulevard had grown into an monstrous calamity. Thursday's headlines were apocalyptic: 75 FLEE THEIR HOMES; NEW CAVE-INS THREATEN WHOLE NEIGHBORHOOD; NINE HOMES EVACU-ATED AS HUGE CAVE-IN SPREADS. In a frail effort to quell nervous residents, the *Seattle Times* quoted City Engineer Morse as saying he was "reasonably certain" there were no other underground caverns in the Ravenna area.

Almost immediately, a new depression appeared at Ravenna and Roosevelt Way, caused by the backup. The Green Lake Field House, a couple of miles to the north, flooded. Green Lake had risen six inches in two days. The lake was still rising, and park department officials did not rule out the possibility that it might overflow its banks, since the North Trunk System was the only drainage.

I was stuck at my parents' house in Bryant, in school during the day and unable to witness anything firsthand, looking forward to the weekend when I could go to my grandparents' and bicycle to the pit about a half-mile south down 15th Ave. In the meantime, I was dependent on the news as the incredible drama continued. Morse, Robertson, Assistant Superintendent of Sewers Gil Byrne, Nat Mayhew of the water department, contractor E. H. Lindstrom and others—individuals few people had ever heard of—were thrown into the limelight. They assumed roles that might normally have been reserved for Kenneth Toby of *It Came from Beneath the Sea*, about the giant octopus that ate San Francisco. *What would they do?* Strategy meetings were held. For days the drama unfolded. Emergency water and gas lines were installed to replace broken mains, families were relocated, Cowen and Ravenna parks were closed, pumps were brought in to unplug the sewer south of the bypass connection, and Mrs. John Siewick, who refused to leave her home at 5603 17th Ave. NE, served coffee to policemen standing 24-hour watch at the pit. And the pit was still growing.

Then, Robert H. Burns, Project Engineer, suggested using the Joosten Process, a method of chemically solidifying the quicksand by injection.

If they couldn't fill it in, maybe they could kill it.

In my grandparents' neighborhood at last, on the weekend, I grabbed Buzzy and Jimmy, we jumped on our bikes and rode down 15th, across the 15th Ave. bridge and to the site of the pit. We stood in awe behind the makeshift barriers to watch what was going on. I could see our old house down the block to the right. The edge of the pit hadn't collapsed the grass embankment, but as reported, it had come only a few feet from the houses on the other side of the street. No wonder they were afraid of losing those houses! Seeing pictures was one thing. Being there to witness the immensity of the sinkhole was another. The huge chestnut trees were really gone, along with cars, all swallowed up 60 feet down in the quicksand. It was truly like a science fiction movie.

Two 30-foot steel towers were erected 100 feet from each side of the hole. A cable was strung between them upon which rode a wooden platform carrying a man armed with a high-pressure grease pump and a long nozzle. A mixture of sodium silicate and calcium chloride was forced into the quicksand. The quicksand would solidify into a hard cocoon. The long job of filling it in and repairing the line could begin.

The monster hole had been destroyed. But in the tradition of any good '50s science fiction movie, there was a warning for the future: "More than 1,200 miles of sewer pipe—some of it 70 years old—crisscross under Seattle streets," reported the *Times* in an interview with retired city sewer maintenance engineer William P. McNamara. "There are several tunnels even deeper than the line under Ravenna Boulevard."

Tick . . . tick . . . tick.

§ 19

Back to school at Bryant Elementary!

The filling of The Great Ravenna Sinkhole proceeded through the holidays. In late January, America successfully launched its own satellite, Explorer I, and the space race was on. I was back to my routine, sitting in class and sometimes getting further lessons in square dancing in the gym. I also completed two memorable projects for fifth grade: I'd built my best plastic model ship, the USS *Missouri* battleship upon which the Japanese had signed the World War II surrender. My model had all rotating turrets, a teak-colored deck, and a perfectly done waterline-masking job along the hull. It was a show-and-tell that Mrs. Loschen left on display in the classroom for a week, causing me great pride.

The second accomplishment was my first short story, a

detective tale of three or four handwritten pages created under the influence of one of the first TV detectives, *Richard Diamond*—the show being unique because of Mary Tyler Moore's shapely legs under the desk, the only part of her shown on screen as she answered the phone in a breathy voice. I had no idea what sex was, at least not in any detail, but somehow the concept, via this or that movie or TV show, started to get through. My short story, on the other hand, had nothing to do with a sexy secretary, but climaxed, inevitably, in a gun fight.

The drama of movies and television was always in the background as fifth grade wound down, and my eleventh birthday prompted Mother to occasionally drop Dean and me off at the Saturday movie matinees. This was usually at the Neptune or Egyptian theaters in the University District. One of the matinees was *Invaders from Mars* from 1953, and it had creepy aliens putting a metal implant into the necks of a kid's temporarily kidnapped parents. This made the parents villainous and totally under the control of a small, super-brained octopus creature in a glass bubble! This early science fiction color movie dominated the nightmares of thousands of kids, even when it was eventually shown on television.

Outside of kids' matinees, I developed a love for submarine movies, triggered by *Run Silent, Run Deep* starring Clark Gable and Burt Lancaster. But aside from that World War II sub-genre (pun!), the film that attracted every kid or teenager in town was *Thunder Road* starring Robert Mitchum as a moonshine whiskey runner driving a hot-rod '50 Ford—later in the film, a '57—being chased by revenue agents led by Gene Barry who'd previously starred in George Pal's *War of the Worlds*. The movie became a low-budget phenomenon and generated a hit record, "The Ballad of Thunder Road," sung by Mitchum himself. After I saw the movie, I rode my bike down to Standard Records and Hi-Fi in the Roosevelt district near my grandparents' house to buy the 45 rpm hit for 69 cents.

Standard Records became a very important place, for although the store was known for its huge stock of classical LPs (which I would come to appreciate years later) it was also where 45s were sold. My 50 cents a week allowance wouldn't allow for buying all I wanted, but I managed, as the year went on into summer, to increase my collection with "Poor Little Fool" by Ricky Nelson, "Splish Splash" by Bobby Darin, "Little Star" by The Elegants, "When" by the Kalin Twins, "26 Miles" and "Big Man" by The Four Preps, "Peggy Sue" by Buddy Holly, "It's Only Make Believe" by Conway Twitty, and a crazily popular "The Purple People Eater" by Sheb Wooley, along with others. I played these on both my Zenith "suitcase" record player and Aunt Peggy's trusty 45 rpm "cube" atop her Magnavox console. Not to mention hearing all the hits I and almost everyone younger than thirty listened to on the radio.

My mother and stepfather did not have a record player then, and their taste in furniture reflected the "colonial" fad of the '50s. Most everything in our house was purchased at Cooper's Maple Shop in the Northgate Mall. The beige fabric sofa and chair had high backs and frilly trim around the bottoms. End tables were rock maple in a light-brown, natural finish, along with the "cobbler's bench" coffee table—a bizarre affair with thick splayed legs, a set of raised drawers on one end, and a circular, unsupported leather inset at the other end that one dared not set a drink on (it would stain the leather or just fall over). The television had a "colonial" maple cabinet with twin doors and fancy little ring knobs for opening and closing. The "ginger jar" lamps on the end tables had big fabric shades with a similarly frilly trim as the sofa and chair. Next to Larry's chair was a reading lamp, somewhat smaller than the two adjacent to the sofa, with a "planter" base in which miniature cactus plants tried to survive. I assumed that the light from the lamp was supposed to substitute for the desert sun, and my mother dutifully watered the little cacti every so often. Without success.

Our dining room table was more modest—gray Formica with brushed aluminum trim and a set of four matching chairs with gray vinyl seats. My mother would spread a tablecloth out when guests came over to play canasta—a card game that was a 1950s fad, the most elaborate of gin rummy games; and I sometimes sat and watched, fascinated.

Larry had quit working for Kidde and gone into business for himself, selling sprinkler systems. One day, a potential client of his came over for dinner and parked his sports car in front. I'd never seen a car exactly like it, though I was aware of the type. It was a small Austin Healey (British) sports car, and when our guest noticed me looking out the window at it, he asked if I wanted a ride. "Sure!" So in a few minutes, we were zooming up and down the 65th St. hill, and it was exhilarating—nothing like the big American cars that were by comparison so isolating and cumbersome. That ride in the Austin Healey changed forever my automotive predilections and began my love of sports cars. Or perhaps it actually began with a CinemaScope movie I'd seen: *The Racers* with Kirk Douglas and Gilbert Roland, about Grand Prix racing that had impressed me a few years earlier.

My stepfather Larry had other things on his mind, and whatever the outcome of our guest's business, the fact was that Larry's choice to leave Kidde and strike out on his own was a difficult transition. And secret, as well. For he and my mother were behind on the rent, him sometimes lying to her about having paid it. The situation had also been kept secret from me, of course. In those days people rarely spoke of family troubles, especially to their children. I did know that Mother saved all her spare change. She'd been a child of the

Great Depression, and this was the cause of her emphasis on saving every nickel she could. What I didn't know was that she eventually had to "front" for Larry to the landlords—an older couple—and was forced to absorb the pecuniary embarrassment. Otherwise, Larry would have remained silent. His general behavior I was well aware of, and until it was announced that we had to move, I'd been left completely in the dark by both of them. It would be the third time I'd have to unexpectedly change elementary schools.

Naively perhaps, I didn't think there might be other things kept hidden. I expected no divorce announcement, or any expectation of moving far away—and indeed, no such announcements came.

Yet the unexpected always seemed to happen. Our little Welsh terrier's habit of digging under the white picket fence and escaping finally caught up to him. One day, Barney made his usual escape but didn't make it across the street. He was hit and killed by a car during my last week at school. Mother called Larry, and he rushed home to take care of things. Barney's little body had been taken away by the time I got home, and although the unruly dog hadn't been my greatest buddy, I was profoundly saddened. The loss of him, especially in that way, upset me. And it was not only that, but having to move came as a shock as I recovered from the loss of our dog. On the other hand, having to move overruled in some small measure my upset over the loss of Barney. And now school was out, so for me it was mostly about leaving my friends Dean and Brad. Loss upon loss.

Luckily, I supposed, Mother and Larry did not move far away, and it was promised that I could visit my old friends, or they could visit me. The new residence was a two-story, two-bedroom apartment in Laurelon Terrace, a large urban enclave of about two dozen dark-brown, four-unit shingled buildings with pitched roofs, mullioned windows, and shared

front lawns. The whole assemblage covered an area of about
four landscaped acres below a steep hill that began its upward
slope right on the eastern boundary. Atop the hill was Children's Orthopedic Hospital, newly built of glass and steel in
1954. Beyond and to the southwest toward Lake Washington
was a hilly area of old English-style houses called Laurelhurst.
We were now a modest, barely middle class family living in an
apartment on the outskirts of one of the wealthiest neighborhoods in Seattle. And next fall, I would be attending Laurelhurst Elementary School.

§ 20

As if in compensation for turmoil at my parents', I began to
spend the warm, enjoyable summer of 1958 with my grandparents and Aunt Peggy back in Ravenna. The Ravenna district was as close as one could get in Seattle to a congenial
small-town atmosphere. This part of north Seattle retained its
early twentieth century appearance, with streets of modest
but classic older homes. A couple of blocks from us was
Cowen Park lined with maple trees on three sides and the
15th Street bridge on the east traversing the Ravenna Park
canyon. A "ma-and-pa" grocery store toward the south, positioned on Ravenna Boulevard, supplied our summer thirst
with bottles of Coca-Cola, Dad's Root Beer, and Orange
Crush shimmering in the icy water under the lid of a bright
red, floor-standing Coca Cola chest with an attached bottle
opener. Nothing was as refreshing as pulling a bottle of Orange Crush out of that ice-cold water, popping off the cap,
and drinking it down in gulps.

Our house was about three blocks distant from this store,
the route to the store jogging to the right at the "T" southern
end of our street facing a row of houses, then left after a half-
block west, then passing along the tree-lined street of the

park. The houses on our own block, as I mentioned, were built above street level, red rhododendron bushes in bloom, the street's pavement paralleled by curbs, grass parking strips, sidewalks, and an occasional parked car. Again, the scene of our street games.

Several blocks west along 65th (that street traversing at the north end of our block) was the intersection with Roosevelt Ave. Shops were spread along both streets and included Craigen's Drug Store, Standard Records and Hi Fi, a modest two-story Sears outlet, a hobby shop, a dentist's office, and other places of interest. Virtually a small town square kind of place.

It was at the beginning of this refreshing summer that I lay, as was my habit, with hands behind my head on the backyard grass, looking up at the blue sky and the white drifting clouds, when I became intensely conscious of the brilliant sun. I knew not to stare at the sun directly, but in a peripheral way, and at that moment I became fully aware of its existence as a *star*. Knowing this from a science book was one thing, but in this moment of meditation, while my mind was at ease, this knowledge was something else entirely, an awareness of reality I'd not fully comprehended until then. "A star," I whispered to myself. "That is a *star*." And I was suddenly overwhelmed by the sense of awe and deep cognizance, by the idea of being near an immense star that was, in fact, a single dot of light among billions of others in the vastness of space. A daylight epiphany.

And at the age of eleven, summer was an endless allotment of free time. Each morning I would rise, dress, and join my grandparents and aunt in the dining room, usually for a breakfast of bacon and eggs, or sometimes oatmeal—food that my grandmother would prepare each morning. Then I'd dash back upstairs to my room or down into the basement to find something to play with or to continue with some project, such as another model ship or plane. But it wasn't long before I was looking out the front window to see if anyone was hanging out across the street, maybe sitting on the Brandt's steps next to the alley, waiting with a ball. The kids would gather one or two at a time, most every day, until it was decided to start our usual game of street kickball. If I was in my room, and the doorbell rang, my grandmother would yell up the stairs, "Philip, the kids are here!" And I'd run downstairs, nearly tripping, and out to play.

Our neighborhood continued its uncommon tradition of including, in nearly everything we did, boys and girls alike, any age who could play the games. The kids our street games included, at various times, were brothers "Buzzy" and Jimmy; sisters Pam, Mary, and Nancy; brother and sister Ronny and Stacey; brother and sister Ted and Nora; brother and sister Dale and Odessa; and now and then a lesser-known kid who happened to walk over from the next block.

Jimmy was a year or two younger than Buzzy (whose real name was Craig), had a buzz cut and was terrified of dogs—terrified to the point of crying and screaming whenever a dog came near him. It was an oddity unaccountable and disturbing, for no one knew why he had this phobia. I assumed there was something in his childhood that caused it; but if so, no one was saying. Buzzy had close-cropped hair, not as close as some. (I had blond or light brown hair and a "regular" haircut.) He and I were only a year apart, he the younger, so we seemed to have a vague bond with one another. We almost never saw his and Jimmy's sister Sue, a shy redhead, but the family was the most like a traditional '50s family—good looking mom at home, lunchpail dad off to work in the morning (he worked at the telephone company), three kids—the only difference being their somewhat small house where the two brothers shared an attic bedroom.

Pam, Mary, and Nancy were rather different from each

other. All were brunettes of varying sizes. Pam, the eldest, a couple of years older than I, was quite heavy but not unattractive, had a wonderful spontaneous laugh, and unfortunately had to put up with a modicum of fat razzing from Ronny. Mary was the middle sister, had a good sense of humor she sometimes used to bring one's ego down a notch. She was the most thoughtful of the three, a person one enjoyed getting to know. Nancy, the younger sister, was the most attractive girl in the neighborhood, easy to get along with, and in the summer wore sweatshirts and cut-off jeans, the latter rolled into narrow cuffs just above the knee. They lived a half-block to the east up the concrete alley toward 15th Ave., the front of their house facing that arterial. Their family was Catholic, and they all attended church on Sunday, as most everyone did according to their denominations.

Ronny was my age, quick, shorter, a crew-cut mischief maker, the most athletic, a little-league baseball player; while his sister Stacey, a year or two younger, was a good looking, almost iconic '50s blond, confident, not very social but good friends with Nancy. Dale was a handsome young guy, easy to like, a couple of years younger than I, while his sister Odessa was skinny, quiet, with long stringy hair, odd enough not to quite fit in; but unlike Buzzy's and Jimmy's sister Sue, whom we barely knew existed, she usually joined in with us, even though she sometimes got razzed for being weird. In fact, weird pretty much defined her family, since her other brother was the psycho kid previously referred to, one of four siblings.

Nora was the girl whom I'd watched being chased by the psycho kid and his pal onto the top of the Hatch's garage. She was a couple of years older than I, about 5'3", good looking, wore fashionable horn-rimmed glasses, and seemed somewhat more mature than the rest of us. Her brother Ted was a couple of years older than she, medium height, combed dark hair, slightly dark complexion, brown eyes, often displaying an air of indifference but not unfriendly. His and Nora's mother was a subject of gossip, for she was almost witch-like in appearance, with a narrow face, black hair in a bun, wearing gobs of blue or black mascara. Her husband had disappeared years before down in San Francisco, so Ted and Nora had a kind of outsider profile, not having two parents at home and with a strange but not unlikable mother. Then again, my own family wasn't exactly normal, for I was living with my grandparents and aunt, dividing my time between two households and two neighborhoods. Plus my grandmother and grandfather had retained a hint of their Norwegian accents. In fact, every family was odd in one way or another, and we all knew it. None matched the Cleavers on *Leave It to Beaver* or the Nelsons on *Ozzie and Harriet,* although Buzzy's and Jimmy's family came close. Except, as noted, for their crowded house and barely existing sister.

It was rare that *all* these kids were available to play simultaneously, and of course the girls had their own activities, the boys theirs, and went off to partake in them—the girls often playing house, the boys often playing guns. These interests were real, so to speak, for there were no electronics other than record players and TVs; no computers, smart phones, video games—just hobbies of all kinds, and board games, toys (the hula hoop became that summer's big fad), records, sports, and imagination.

When a critical mass of kids, a half-dozen or more, emerged from their houses, street games were the choice, or on hot days, squirt gun fights or sometimes running through sprinklers in swim suits. There were no organized sports to which we were transported by parents: and for traditional kids' games we made up our own neighborhood rules.

After dark (no daylight savings time) we made maximum use of our freedom to run and play just about everywhere in the cool night air—usually playing kick-the-can or hide-and-seek.

At the start of summer I'd usually go down to the Red-wing shoe store on 65th St. and buy a new pair of U.S. Keds, the previous year's now being worn out and fraying. The feeling of those brand new tennis shoes was like starting life over again.

That summer of '58, a new night game was introduced that we'd never played before, and which I decided to call Body Snatchers after *Invasion of the Body Snatchers*. I hadn't even seen that movie, merely knew the story from Nora, who had. She had also seen *The Thing* and described it well enough to make me glad I'd missed it.

The Body Snatchers game was an expansion of hide-and-seek, when one person was "it" and everyone ran in different directions during a slow count of ten. Hiding wasn't necessary, just getting away. But now came a diabolical twist. When the person who was "it" found someone and tagged them, *both* became "it" and began to hunt for the others. The best tactic, if you'd been caught, was not to reveal you'd been turned into an "it" until you found someone else and made the tag. And because everyone had scattered all over the neighborhood, one could never tell who was who.

On one of these nights, I typically ran off alone. After about ten minutes of hiding out, I emerged and I saw Dale walking slowly toward me down the sidewalk on the 63rd St. side of the block.

"Phil!", he called, but not so loud as to attract the attention of anyone else, "Have you been caught?"

"No!"

"Good! Let's find a place to hide. Nancy and Stacey were caught by Buzzy and are looking for the others."

"Yeah, OK."

Except that I'd started stepping backward as Dale walked toward me. Because, of course, I didn't know if he was lying and was actually one of *Them*.

"Are you sure *you* haven't been *caught?*" I asked.

"Yeah, yeah, I'm sure. Come on, let's go hide."

It was something about his smile. . . .

I ran like hell.

He chased me, but I outran him and ducked into Mr. Brinks' back yard and over the fence into the concrete alley near the Hambly's. I hid behind the Mortlands' garage. The Mortlands were a grouchy old couple, so no one liked to go near the place, which made it a relatively good hiding place—unless the Mortlands happened to spot you.

Eventually, when most had been caught, though not necessarily everyone, those who were "it" figured they had a sufficient majority—or maybe it just got late—and started calling "Ollie Ollie All in free!" And while everyone gathered in the alley, sitting on the low bulkhead near Buzzy's and Jimmy's back door, laughing and telling of narrow escapes and hiding places, whoever hadn't been caught were considered the winners.

But on one of these nights, I had avoided getting caught for an entire half-hour and hid up in a cherry tree in the back yard of the house next to Buzzy's and Jimmy's while I listened for the other kids. No one found me, and when someone started yelling "All in free!" I decided, for some crazy reason, that I was quite comfortable up in that tree in the dark, in the cool summer air, hidden high above the ground, cozy and alone, separate from the world below. Although I was missing, the other kids wandered back home. Hey, I thought, I could have been kidnapped or knocked out, hit by a car, and no one would have known what had happened to me. Hmm. I finally climbed down and went home, too, content but mildly hurt that no one had cared to find out if I'd *already* gone home. I might still have been hiding somewhere, for all they knew, or dead!

The feeling of neglect didn't last. It was back to neighborhood games the next day.

Also, it was the first time I began going to the movies by myself, walking from my grandparents' to the Neptune Theater in the U. District, a distance of about a mile and a half. Along the way, south down "the Ave," I passed a lot of interesting places, including a couple of beatnik coffee houses, an antique store, and the Hasty Tasty hamburger joint. The first movie I went to alone was *No Time for Sergeants* with Andy Griffith, and I thought it so good that I went back a second time. After my experience with *The Curse of Frankenstein* a year earlier, I was reluctant to attend horror movies, whereas some of the other kids went that summer to see *The Blob* and *The Fly*.

As August approached (it was especially hot that summer) people began to frequently water their lawns, and one day I happened to notice the stream of water—runoff from Mrs. Mettler's parking strip a few houses to the north—running down the gutter along the curb. It was only natural to float a little stick and watch it being carried along by the stream. I made a mental connection between the water, the little stick, and the upcoming Unlimited hydroplane race the first weekend of August. So I began to make little 1.5" model hydroplanes out of flat pieces of balsa wood, with flat cowlings and tail fins, and paint them like the real ones—*Slo-mo-shun IV, Miss Thriftway, Shanty I, Miss Wahoo, Miss Bardahl*, and others, with the idea of watching them zip down the stream of water along the curb. I asked my grandmother if I could take the hose out to the street and run the water directly into the gutter. This was kind of fun, watching the little boats race along, and soon Buzzy and Jimmy and I were choosing from the boats I'd made, racing them downstream and being sure to grab them before they went into the grate at the end. Shortly, these races became an obsession, and soon all the boys wanted to join in. But the course was too short from my grandparents', so we asked Mrs. Mettler's son Stevie, to see if his mom (who looked a bit like blond actress Ann Southern) would let us use her hose for a longer run. She agreed. And every day, five or six of us, including seven-year-old Stevie, would choose one of my hydroplanes and start racing from in front of the Mettler house. We'd hold our boats next to the gushing water from the hose, release them on the word "Go!" and then walk along, watching them float down the stream as they often changed places. A woman across the street said it was puzzling to watch a group of kids, moving as a bunch, staring down at the water in the gutter, she having no idea what the hell they were doing. And then they started all over again! She finally came out to see what was going on. The gutter races went on several times each day until Mrs. Mettler almost fainted when she got her water bill. First, she stopped the water supply altogether. But Stevie, not to mention the rest of us, was so distraught, that she allowed us to race thereafter for a limit of one hour a day.

That first week in August, Seattle was again the nation's venue for the Gold Cup race for Unlimited hydroplanes, and once again KING TV would cover it "live" all day long on Sunday from Lake Washington, and all week long during qualifying as anticipation mounted. But whatever expectations developed for an exciting race, no one in Seattle was prepared for what happened that Sunday in Heat 2A as the boats raced across the starting line.

Six boats came thundering down the straightaway at 150 MPH—30-foot mahogany missiles trailing 40-foot-high roostertails in front of a crowd of several hundred thousand lining the shore and on yachts packed in around the three-mile course. Announcer Bill O'Mara was calling the race for the equally immense TV audience, including my grandparents, aunt, and me, when flares were fired over the course and the race was stopped down. Something had gone wrong.

Seconds before, as it crossed the starting line, the *Miss*

Thriftway, driven by Bill Muncey, inexplicably changed lanes directly in front of *Gale VI,* decelerating but still speeding.

Off camera, a 40-foot US Coast Guard utility boat was anchored on the *inside* of the yacht-lined log boom in the south turn, right at the end of the straightaway. Unknown to the TV audience, Muncey's hydroplane headed right for it. The crowd along the shore saw the crash a number of seconds before the KING TV cameraman found his stunning close-up of the *Miss Thriftway* torpedoed right into the side of the Coast Guard boat. Announcer O'Mara was speechless, then stammering as he tried to describe the scene. Amid the turbulent water, the Coast Guard boat and the *Miss Thriftway* were locked in a death grip, and as they began to sink, a Coast Guardsman emerged from a narrow gap in the wreck. He'd obviously been below deck, and as the water came up around him, he barely made it out alive. Other crew members had been immediately picked up by a small, nearby rescue boat.

The last thing seen was the American flag flying from the white stern of the Coast Guard boat as it sank into the lake. O'Mara announced in tone of profound shock: "The Coast Guard boat . . . the Coast Guard boat has gone down."

I imagined, correctly I was certain, several hundred thousand people with their jaws hanging open. O'Mara wondered aloud, "Where is Muncey?"

Muncey had tried to shut the motor off, but the motor continued to run, and he bailed out just before the *Thriftway* struck the Coast Guard boat. A rescue helicopter picked him up, left the scene, and after it landed at the pits, Muncey was taken to the hospital. Amazingly, no one was killed or badly injured. It was significantly noted that if the C. G. boat had not been anchored where it was, the *Thriftway* would have gone right into the floating log boom where all the yachts were anchored, perhaps killing dozens of onlookers. From that day on, no boats were allowed to park or anchor at the ends of the straightaways. I ran outside and met Buzzy and Jimmy in the street. "Did you see that!" "Yeah!" "Wow!" And then back inside to watch the rest of the race. *Hawaii Kai III* won, driven by Jack Regas.

Along with the Great Ravenna Sinkhole, Seattle had hosted another legendary event.

I built a new balsa wood kit of the *Miss Thriftway* and painted it white with persimmon red deck stripes, the colors of the new one that had sunk the Coast Guard boat and was now on the bottom of extremely deep Lake Washington. The news was that Willard Rhodes, the owner of the ill-fated craft, would build an identical *Miss Thriftway* for next year.

Soon I was pulling my new *Miss Thriftway* along the grass parking strip with Buzzy and Jimmy, doing timed runs, and also racing my little balsa wood boats down the gutter whenever we could get permission via little Stevie Mettler to use his mother's water supply.

By this time, Grandfather had built a 12-foot-long table in the basement for my Lionel train, which I transferred there from my parents' house. After all these years, I still considered my grandparents' house my real home, and over the years I had developed a deep love for Grandmother, Grandfather, and Aunt Peggy, all of them having become my real family, more or less by default.

One day, a disturbing, unexpected event was instigated by Mr. and Mrs. Brandt. That morning when I took my little box of balsa wood hydroplanes over to get Buzzy and Jimmy for some gutter racing (if Mrs. Mettler would let us use her hose again!) the two brothers met me at their back door. They had strange expressions on their faces. Jimmy, in fact, was teary-eyed, and his voice was full of despair.

"My mom and dad say we can't play with you anymore."

They looked at me from the half-closed door at the top of a small set of steps. I stood there, mute, unable to think of anything to say. I couldn't make sense of it, so I held my little box of balsa hydroplanes and remained stunned. When they didn't say anything more, I found that my voice still worked.

". . . why?" I asked.

"We just can't," said Buzzy.

"But why?"

"We just can't."

The two of them stayed in the half-closed doorway, and I didn't know what more to say or do. I was hurt. What was it all about? The thought of their parents—normal, good looking people, yet they were behind this awful thing—came to mind in a kind of wonderment. All I could think of was their objection a year before that I had told the creepy story of *The Curse of Frankenstein* to their kids. But nothing had really come of it then, it was so long ago, and it was clear that neither Buzzy nor Jimmy wanted to stop playing with me—and indeed *had* not, for they were always so enthusiastic about our gutter races and other games—but they were being forced to reject my companionship now. I just looked at them with the terrible feeling of hurt and unfairness. In a moment, not knowing what else to do, I simply walked back down the short concrete alley hill and back to my grandparents' house across the street.

I stayed indoors the rest of the day and wondered how Buzzy and Jimmy could manage to avoid me when everyone played street games, or if that counted, or if the reason for their parents' rule would be revealed. Of course I told my grandmother what had happened; and that evening she, Grandfather, and Aunt Peggy speculated during dinner about what had triggered such a thing, with questions for me. I could think of no relevant or possible answers, so there were some unkind words from my family for the Brandts.

The next day, my mother found out and was furious. She soon realized I sincerely had no idea why this had occurred, so she came over to my grandparents' house, intent on getting an answer from Mrs. Brandt across the street.

I watched from the front window as she ascended the stairs to the Brandt's front porch and rang the doorbell. In a moment or two, she was let inside. The rest of us waited, and in thirty minutes or so she came back across the street and up the front steps and back into our living room.

"Well, what happened Judy?" Grandmother asked. "What did she say?"

"We had a nice conversation," my mother said. "It seems that when the Brandt kids come back home after playing with Philip, they always ask for the same things Philip has. They want a train. They want an Erector set. They want plastic models or other toys. Mr. and Mrs. Brandt apparently can't afford to buy them these things, and of course they have two children—three, with their older girl. Mr. Brandt works as a repairman for the telephone company and doesn't make enough money to buy everything his kids pester him for."

Grandmother, Grandfather, and I just sort of looked at each other and didn't quite know how to take all this. Mother continued: "I told Mrs. Brandt—Margaret—that I was sorry to know these things, but that Philip really has no more toys than other children, that he is not a spoiled child, and that he always likes to share with others. I told her that Buzzy and Jimmy are always welcome to come over and play with Philip's train and other things, and that furthermore, neither Philip nor Buzzy and Jimmy should be punished for a few things that Mr. Brandt cannot afford to give his children right now."

"Gracious!" said Grandmother, scowling. "I've never heard of such a thing in my life!"

"I also suggested that it wasn't a very healthy thing to deny her kids friendships of their choosing."

Grandfather sat in his overstuffed chair, saying nothing—and neither did I. I had nothing to say, it was so strange. Was

I to feel pity for Mr. Brandt, or should I feel indignant, or embarrassed for having a Lionel train or a bicycle or whatever? But wait. Buzzy and Jimmy had bicycles. Or should I be mad at *them* for bugging their parents for things and not taking no for an answer? It crossed my mind that they also might have bugged their parents for a trip to Disneyland because Ronny and Stacey had been taken there that summer by *their* parents. Would the Brandt kids be unable to play with *anyone* who had been given something they did not have? I'd never been to Disneyland, either! That was a dream every kid had.

Mother continued: "I told Mrs. Brandt that it was unfair to keep our kids apart, and for another thing, it wasn't practical, given how all the neighborhood kids play together." Mother looked at me. "Margaret thought about it and finally agreed, and she admitted that her kids were terribly upset over this. I'm sure she realized she'd made a mistake."

Grandmother said, "I'll bet it was nothing more than a way to get Buzzy and Jimmy to stop asking for things."

"Maybe," said Mother. "I don't know."

I never forgot that Mother had gone to bat for me, that it took courage to walk over there and ring Mrs. Brandt's doorbell. Later, I wondered if my stepfather Larry could have negotiated with *Mr.* Brandt in the same way. I decided there was no chance that two men would have gotten together like that to solve such a conflict. It was, I decided, an example of women's natural habit of talking to each other. Having been raised mostly by women, I was aware of certain gender differences. Moreover, as I have noted, my stepfather represented "the strong, silent type," a personality (or personality disorder?) that seemed to have evolved from the Western movies of John Wayne, Gary Cooper, and other Western heroes. "Real men" don't talk much, these characters seemed to assert, they just do what needs to be done. Yet I couldn't help noticing that it was usually my mother or grandmother who did what needed to be done, at least socially. Men dealing with similar circumstance would have been cowards, I was sure, and in the present case would have rationalized inaction by trivializing children's friendships. "Work it out yourselves," they would have said. Which would have been appropriate if Buzzy and Jimmy and I were having a conflict only among ourselves. As it was, my mother came through for us.

And the summer went on as before.

§ 21

By now, more old movies for kids were being shown on Saturday or Sunday mornings on local TV stations, especially the Andy Hardy series with Mickey Rooney, Shirley Temple movies, various Tarzan films, old serials like *Flash Gordon* or *Buck Rogers*, and oddities like *The 5000 Fingers of Dr. T*. The Western shows of Roy Rogers, The Cisco Kid, The Lone Ranger, Annie Oakley, Hopalong Cassidy, had all ended as the Western fad seemed to unwind at the beginning of the Space Age.

I continued to read the Tom Swift books that Mother bought on our trips downtown to the Frederick & Nelson department store.

It was perhaps a flaw, but I think I was typical of kids my age to be mostly oblivious to news events. Our lives revolved around popular culture: play, hobbies, games, movies, television, music. The threat of nuclear war, for example, was almost always out of mind—for at that age, one expects to live forever. My exposure to the idea of personal mortality came from two sources: the movies and my grandfather Nels, who would sometimes say, "I'm getting old. I guess I won't be around much longer." Causing Grandmother Emma to scoff.

Retired from the lumber mill and with little to do, Grandfather took to walking over to the Pee Wee Tavern on Roosevelt Ave. to have a beer and play shuffleboard. He would occasionally come home slightly inebriated. Aunt Peggy eventually told me a little secret of family history: that Nels had lost his job managing the lumber mill in Montana because of his drinking habit. One day, the owner of the mill was on his way out of town but unexpectedly returned to find Nels at the tavern drinking and playing poker, having left the shop to an underling. So Grandfather was fired, and that was why he'd moved to another town and eventually out of Montana, taking his family west. I wasn't sure whether the lumber mill came before or after he and Uncle Pete owned their general store in Roy.

Uncle Pete was no less wild and undependable. He once got drunk and fired a revolver at the ceiling in the store, not taking into account the person living in the apartment above. The bullet went through the floor, narrowly missing the tenant! Nels had finally had it with his brother, so he bailed out of their general merchandise business. Alcohol had been a problem for both of them. But Aunt Peggy insisted that neither could be considered alcoholics. I didn't know what to make of it, only that one day while I was playing in the back yard, Grandfather had gotten thrown out of the Pee Wee Tavern, came home drunk, shoved me aside when I greeted him, and, cursing, not at me exactly, headed into the house. Grandmother had to clean him up and put him to bed.

From that day on, in his 70s, he never touched another drink. He became a permanent fixture in the house, walking slowly from kitchen to dining room, dining room to living room, watching TV, upstairs to bed at ten o'clock. He built a rather elaborate desk for himself, and a duplicate one for me, with a single drawer and a vertical structure of what he called "pigeon holes" at the back of the table for small objects, index cards, paperclips and such. During his projects, he taught me some carpentry, which I eventually made good use of.

Grandfather usually stayed home from church as before; and I, too, was let off the hook. My grandmother finally realized I wasn't taking religion seriously and, furthermore had begun to annoy the Sunday school teachers by joking that Bible stories were nothing more than fairy tales. My grandfather may or may not have had something to do with my attitude, but whatever had come between me and religion seemed to have been developing before Grandfather had given that little wink. Perhaps I had even prompted the expression of his skepticism with my own, because for some unaccountable reason I sincerely could not take the claims of Christian Science or the Bible seriously, never really had, and now I was apparently having an effect on the other children at Sunday school. So I was allowed to stop going. Mother likely had something to do with this decision, for she had never become a Christian Scientist and didn't regularly attend church, although most everyone in those days went to church (no street games on Sunday morning). Not partaking didn't seem odd to me, and I was perfectly happy watching Sunday morning movies on TV while Grandmother, Aunt (and indeed Grandfather, but rarely) went to church during that summer.

Regarding religion, and sometime after giving up alcohol, Grandfather developed a habit that drove Grandmother nuts. When the Jehovah's Witnesses rang our doorbell, Grandfather would answer and invite them in, feigning interest. He let them go on for a few minutes and then began a vociferous critique of their beliefs while enjoying their stunned or annoyed reactions as they realized they'd been ambushed. If they fought back, Grandfather's voice would grow louder and louder, his face turning reddish, his fist sometimes pounding on the arm of the chair, while I sat and smiled at the poor dupes who tried to maintain their dignity (such as it was) and attempt to exit the premises. Grandfather eventually let them go, taking their literature as an anemic gesture of politeness.

"Oh, I *wish* you wouldn't invite those people in," Grandmother would say.

Grandfather looked down, then up with his pale blue eyes, faintly smiling, sheepish but unconcerned.

"Don't you have anything better to do?" she said.

He gave a subtle shrug and snapped his striped suspenders.

"If you need some entertainment, turn on television."

A wry look.

In the days following the last of these incidents, Grandmother would race out of the kitchen when the doorbell rang, trying to intercept the Witnesses before Grandfather could even get out of his chair. But the doorbell was usually rung by someone else, likely one of the kids asking me to come out and play.

§ 22

Sixth grade began in 1958 with me walking up the 45th St. hill to Laurelhurst Elementary School. By then, Mother and Larry had settled into the Laurelon Terrace Apartments. My room there was much like the one on 37th NE, but on a second floor. Each apartment building contained four two-story units, and there were perhaps two dozen buildings spread out amid the landscaping.

My sixth grade classroom was in one of the wooden "portables" that had been placed near the main brick building. As was typical, one side had a row of windows, and inside at the front of the classroom was a long blackboard and the teacher's desk off to the side. The room was kept warm during fall and winter by a large floor-standing heater at the back of the room. It resembled a dark brown stove with louvers. Our desks were modern, not the old wooden ones, with "blond" Formica surfaces, tubular metal legs, and a rack underneath for books.

Most of the students had been attending Laurelhurst since first grade and were from wealthy families in Laurelhurst proper, but not all. I was a stranger from way down the hill in those weird brown apartments; but I was accepted easily enough, so it seemed. Still, this was the fourth elementary school I'd attended since first grade, and I'd developed a sense of separateness, a partly subliminal identity as an outsider. It always took awhile to get used to a new set of classmates and make friends, but I got along OK and didn't experience any consciously adverse effects from being bounced around from school to school. Yet I never felt entirely fixed within a particular group of classmates. Did others feel a separateness? Was it a common feeling? I didn't know.

Our teacher was Mr. Goertzen, a very cool guy. He wore horned-rimmed glasses, had dark hair combed like Cary Grant's but more fashionably swept back at the sides. He liked sports, obviously enjoyed teaching, never talked down to us, yet maintained a fatherly attitude and was always reserved and intelligent. You couldn't beat Mr. Goertzen as a male role model. Everyone admired him, boys and girls alike, and this was helpful because it allowed us to become more easily engaged in the new educational emphasis on science—for which all teachers, including Mr. Goertzen, were responsible since the launch of Sputnik.

One day, Mr. Goertzen brought a metal gasoline can to school and put it on a table in front of the classroom. He poured a bit of water into the can, then heated it up using a portable stove burner. The water inside the can became steam, shoving the air out of the can, all of which he explained. On the table, he had placed a pitcher of cold water.

"OK," he said, having put the cap back on the can, "What do you think will happen when I pour this cold water over the can?"

No one knew, and we all waited in anticipation.

"Here we go!"

When he poured the cold water over the can, it collapsed

fantastically with loud cracking sounds—completely crushed as if by the hands of an invisible giant. We yelled with delight! It was amazing!

"The air pressure that surrounds us," explained Mr. Goertzen, "pushes on everything, and on the can from every angle; and because the air inside had been shoved out by the heated water vapor, the actual air in the can became much less. When I poured the cold water over the can, the water vapor inside the can condensed into droplets, leaving a vacuum of air. Since there was very little air pressure inside the can at that moment, but normal pressure outside, the can was crushed inward. You can all see how powerful air pressure is."

Indeed, we were all impressed by the power of air pressure.

And so it went, with an experiment every week or so, while we worked on creating 8½ × 11 notebooks full of science subjects of our own choosing.

I drew pictures of all the planets of the solar system, copied out descriptions from my astronomy book at home, and wrote a short story about men landing on a Martian desert. My drawing of the planet Pluto was amusing—just a circle filled in with light-brown colored pencil. No one had any idea what Pluto looked like.

Aside from the science notebooks, we gave talks. I did a talk on the fire ants of South America and exaggerated their size in order to make a scary impression. I said they were six inches long and in a bunch could eat an entire cow in three minutes. Luckily for me, Mr. Goertzen did not refute this story.

Socially, I got along, made a couple of friends—a likable guy with short blond hair named Tim, a tall fellow named Jim with a somewhat narrow face, and an amusing guy, George Ruggles, from a wealthy family who lived in Laurelhurst proper—but darn it, I found no girls to fall in love with. Of some interest, though, was a girl sitting at the head of the class off to the left near the window, whose name was Kathy Morse. She was said to be the great-great-granddaughter of Samuel Morse, inventor of Morse Code—which was fairly impressive. She was very smart, too, so I had no reason to disbelieve the ancestry. Of the other kids, the boys were mostly interested in sports, as was Mr. Goertzen, who started an after-school "flag football" game every Friday. Otherwise, we played four-square and tetherball on the playground, and sometimes softball. The main sports activity was a weekly game of dodgeball in the gymnasium, with boys and girls participating separately. The inflated leather balls weren't too hard, so the game was fun, but also aggressive, and I was always sorry when we had to go back to class.

Mr. Goertzen did not teach English. For that we had a special teacher, whose name we rarely spoke of, and she was a terror—a heavy-set harridan of a woman, middle-aged, with short black hair tied in a knot at the back. She had the habit of calling out students she didn't like for whatever reason, chastising them aloud for errors on their essays or stories. More than once she brought a girl to tears. But her pinnacle of sadism came when she criticized Tim for writing a story containing a description that was *too good*.

"The class shouldn't be *surprised* at your good description of the doctor driving his wagon over the bridge, *should* they, Tim?" she said, pacing in front of the class and frightening us into silence. "Your *father* is a Professor of English at the *Uni—versity* of Washington." Her smile twisted in sarcasm, and it became clear she was accusing Tim of getting help with his story. What could he do or say but sit in embarrassed silence? And I was embarrassed for him. We all were, and we all knew that Tim was a straight-shooter who didn't seem likely to cheat. The teacher raised a suspicion that could not be proven and was not likely true.

This teacher was a tyrant, no question, and the worst one

of such caliber I'd encountered. After that incident with Tim, several of us told Mr. Goertzen. He nodded with an expression that suggested he'd heard about Miss ____ before. Might he have heard from a parent? A rumor soon arose that a parent had gone to the school's principal to complain, perhaps to threaten action, and the teacher in question, we eventually heard, wasn't coming back next year. Whatever the truth, the woman suddenly became less hostile, and it wasn't quite such a torture to enter her classroom.

Another student of interest to me in the class was named John, a tall, handsome guy with dark medium-length hair neatly combed. By coincidence, he was the son of my parents' (and my) doctor, which brought to mind the way the doctor once tried to ease my fear of getting a shot in the arm. (I was terrified of needles).

"Well," said the doc, "I guess it's time for a little ol' stick in the arm. Yup, time for a little stick in the arm."

Now, when a kid hears the word "stick," he does not think of a tiny needle or a little skin prick. He imagines a sharp wooden stick that might, at the very least, be a dangerously large sliver requiring one's mother and a stinging application of a red antiseptic called Mercurochrome.

The doctor's good intentions had failed, and I had suppressed the memory of the shot (which I assumed I had received) until I discovered the doctor's son in my classroom, and only then the doctor's words came to mind. I never mentioned to John that his father had been my doctor. Besides, John lived in an exclusive neighborhood called Windermere and was a bit conceited and unapproachable.

My friends in class became Tim, George, and Jim, while back in my own neighborhood I rode my bike on the quiet streets and sidewalks of the apartment complex. I soon met another friend my own age who lived a couple of blocks to the north and went to a different school. Bruce and I would ride our bikes up NE 45th St. to the west, to Zopf's Drug-store at the intersection of 45th and Sand Point Way. Bruce and I would go there after school and sit at the soda fountain, sipping a deliciously red cherry phosphate or a deep green Green River; but when winter came, I switched to chocolate milkshakes—the best I'd ever tasted or ever would taste. Zopf's was a haven of frozen time, an Americana throwback to traditional soda fountains. Mr. Zopf, who lived with his wife above the drugstore, coincidentally looked a great deal like Walt Disney while he dutifully filled prescriptions at the prescription counter. Tending the soda fountain were two women of middle age, Elsie and Myrtle, dressed in white jackets while they pumped the chocolate, mixed the sodas, or dished up the ice cream. Everything was hand made using chrome spigots with marble handles that pumped the choco-late or the colorful concentrates. Elsie was the nicer and bet-ter looking of the two. Myrtle was a sourpuss, always carping about how the soda fountain was losing money and would soon be gone. Mr. Zopf didn't care. His dream was the soda fountain, and he kept it going at the highest standard by stocking the best ice cream and other ingredients. The drug-store also sold a few toys, games, model kits, and paperback books from two floor-standing wire racks that rotated. There were no tables or chairs, just the fountain counter, the shelves of merchandise, and the prescription counter at the back. An oddity was an old wooden phone booth, perhaps from the 1930s, I speculated, in the back corner; and oddly enough, it worked, because now and then a customer came in, closed the folding door, and actually made a call.

Before year's end, Mother took it upon herself to explain to me "the facts of life." She managed to do this in five minutes or less, leaving me somewhat befuddled as to the exact na-ture, let alone the details, of the report she gave. Without any formal sex education, we youngsters were mostly on our own to figure it all out, and I wasn't particularly interested in the details, for I assumed it would all come naturally.

Obviously by that time, nascent sexual feelings were not new to me, and over the holidays I was appropriately spellbound, not by another real girl, but by the female star of what was to become one of my favorite movies, *The 7th Voyage of Sinbad*. The lady was Kathryn Grant, and the film was no less exceptional: an unparalleled fantasy-adventure that introduced me to the amazing stop-motion special effects of Ray Harryhausen—advertised for this film as "Dynamation!"—and the first time Harryhausen's skills (which had been mentored by Willis O'Brien with his effects for *King Kong*) were rendered in Technicolor. I'd taken the bus from my grandparents' down to the Neptune Theater in the U. District to see this movie, and it so grabbed my imagination that when I got home, I immediately went to Buzzy and Jimmy and told them they had to see it. So we three went the next day—and when the giant cyclops appeared, I looked at Jimmy next to me, and his eyes were bugging out in astonishment. Neither he nor his brother were used to seeing monster movies to begin with, but we loved this movie, and it became a big hit as well, so I went back to see it twice more before it left town. Most of us remember the highlight being Sinbad's sword fight with a skeleton, but the final scene of Sinbad's ship heading out to new adventures, underscored by Bernard Herrmann's fabulously evocative music, would reside in my young mind forever. I suspected that earlier generations must have been equally enthralled by the swashbuckler films of Douglas Fairbanks or Errol Flynn. *The 7th Voyage of Sinbad* mixed those elements with Arabian Nights fantasies—the latter used by the 1940 movie *Thief of Baghdad,* which I'd seen on Saturday morning television.

Nothing could match the big screen, and it had been clear

that a variety of movies were making a major impact on my psyche. Moreover, during these years I was getting a Hollywood film education as more and more old movies were being shown on television—most often on local stations during Saturday and Sunday mornings, but also late at night. The first movie I had seen on television, one Sunday morning, was *Mr. Peabody and the Mermaid*, a fantasy film from 1948 starring William Powell and Ann Blythe. But the favorite characters of mine were Charlie Chan played by Warner Oland, and Sherlock Holmes played by Basil Rathbone.

During weekends at my grandparents', I stayed up on Saturday nights to watch a number of the old Universal horror movies starring Bela Lugosi, Boris Karloff, Lon Chaney, Jr., and all the rest. They were shown on KTNT TV, Channel 11—not one of the big networks—and even on the small screen these old horror movies delivered thrills for my generation, as they had in theaters in the '30s and '40s for an earlier one. The first of these I saw was *The Mummy* with Boris Karloff, and I loved it. I was OK that none of these films delivered the far more shocking horror of the new Hammer Studio films that began to arrive after *The Curse of Frankenstein* made stars out of Peter Cushing and Christopher Lee. I chose not to see the second of these, *The Horror of Dracula*, which had been shown back in May. The classic Universal Studio horrors were enough for me now, and I became mesmerized by the richness and creative atmosphere of these black-and-white films, these dark fairy tales.

Coincidental to these movies, as the holidays fled and 1959 began, I was unexpectedly taken for a visit by my grandparents to a cousin's house in north Seattle near Lake Washington. The expansive brick house, custom built in the 1930s, was referred to by my grandmother as "the Chinese farmhouse" because of the circular archways in the high brick wall surrounding the front of the property, and the house's terra-cotta roof. I didn't see anything farm-like about it, other than perhaps the empty grounds behind the wall, and it was locat-ed in a high woodsy area overlooking the lake. The house, like the wall around it, was built of red brick and spread out horizontally; but the design wasn't 1930s moderne, just a unique kind of residence I might have associated with Uni-versal horror movies such as *The Black Cat* or *The Raven* with their early twentieth century settings. We were led inside by our cousin, a middle-aged woman who owned the house, and followed her down a few broad wooden steps into a sunken living room fronted by a row of tall glass windows having a view of the lake through a forest of dark green Douglas firs. The room was apparently cantilevered out over the hillside that fell away toward the lake, while above our heads was a heavily beamed ceiling. Not that I was any sort of expert, but I got the impression that the house was in some ways excep-tional for the time it was built, though the furnishings, includ-ing the floor lamps, were traditional.

An attractive girl wearing Capri pants and a boyish shirt, somewhat older than I, perhaps about 14, came into the liv-ing room. She was introduced as our cousin's daughter, and as it turned out, she was supposed to keep me company while the others sat around talking. The doorbell rang, a couple of other relatives arrived, and they were also seated in the living room. The teenage girl asked if I wanted to see the rest of the house, and she led me down a long hallway to a back room, a kind of playroom with stuffed animals, books, and games on the shelves. She was friendly and such, but I didn't know what to say or do, and apparently neither did she. We ended up sitting on the floor playing checkers.

"Our maid is making lunch," she said. "I'm getting hun-gry, are you?"

"I guess so."

"Would you like to see something really cool?"

"What is it?

She kind of shrugged, as if uncertain I'd care. "A place where I used to play with friends." My thought was that she didn't quite know how to entertain me and had come up with something to kill time.

"Sure, I guess so," I said.

She led me back down the hall the way we'd come, toward the living room and into a dining room above the sunken living room where the adults were gabbing away. Leaning over a banister, the girl asked her mother, "Is it OK if I show Philip the tunnel?"

The mother kind of shrugged. "I suppose so."

The girl motioned me to the dining room where a paneled, polished wood door was located at the end of the room. "Here," she said, turning a brass latch with a click, and like in some creepy movie the door swung open to reveal the darkness beyond.

We exited the dining room into a small space where my companion turned on a light switch that illuminated a set of stone steps leading downward. She closed the door behind us and led the way down about a dozen steps until we came to another, metal door that also had a latch, heavier than the one above. By this time I was sure this had once been Boris Karloff's house. The lower door didn't lead to a subterranean laboratory but to the aforementioned tunnel. Ah, the tunnel! We emerged at the midpoint of a damp, narrow stone passage with a rounded ceiling, apparently leading from somewhere at the front of the property and exiting at the hillside that sloped down to the lake. The light from either end of the tunnel indicated that its length was longer than the side of the house.

"Cool, huh!" said my female companion.

I said, "Chilly, too."

"The front end leads to a sunken garden, and the other

end," she said, pointing, "leads to the hill coming up from the
lake. A long time ago, ours was the only house on the hill, but
other houses were built closer to the lake, so this tunnel
doesn't really lead anywhere now, except to a neighbor's back
yard, and the garden at the front isn't cared for any longer.
My dad keeps threatening to bulldoze this old tunnel, but my
friends and I like to play in it, and in the old garden. It's really
creepy, isn't it?"

"Yeah," I said, stunned at this house complete with an
underground passageway, for I'd never seen anything like it
outside of the movies.

"Around Halloween," I said, "you could scare people to
death down here."

"And we have!" she said, giggling.

"Seen any ghosts?"

"Never seen any, but I don't come down here alone."

"I don't blame you."

I was reminded of the scary movie several kids in my
grandparents' neighborhood had gone to see: *House on Haunted Hill* with Vincent Price. Having stayed with my parents
over that weekend, I had missed joining them but was told all
about it—and that the girls had screamed during certain
frightening moments. I later learned that in some theaters, a
skeleton was flown over the audience during an appropriate
scene, but apparently our local theater wasn't one of them, or
surely the kids would have mentioned it!

From upstairs, we could hear someone calling for us.

Lunch was ready, so my guide latched the lower and upper doors behind us on our way back up and into the dining
room. The relatives sat around the dining table and we all had
lunch. What was said, or who these relatives were, I forgot
about a day later, but I never forgot what in my imagination
was Boris Karloff's secret house in north Seattle overlooking
Lake Washington.

§ 23

The next visit to a relative was closer to my emotional center—and how fascinating and terrible it was to find real life horrors that in my young mind falsified, yet somehow paralleled, the symbolic horrors on the movie screen. The visit to my father Vance was a lesson in the real-life shock of human fragility, disease, and deterioration. A year before, he'd been able to speak by slurring his words. A year before, he'd been able to point to the pieces on the checker board so that I could move for him. Now he couldn't do these things. And although he recognized me and could manage a faint smile, his head lolled to the side at a disturbing angle, and the MS had progressed to the point where he needed a live-in nurse. The nurse's name was Alice, and she was a heavy-set woman of appropriate physical strength to lift Vance in and out of his wheelchair, for Vance had lost weight along with almost all motor control, including the ability to move or turn his wheelchair or do any of the ordinary things people take for granted. As we sat in his living room along with my other grandparents, Charlie and Bessie Haldeman, he could only sit and listen to whoever was speaking. And perhaps grievously, or merely understandably for an eleven year old, I didn't know what to say to him. I did not love him, and although I knew the importance of who he was or had been, and although I'd felt some warmth toward him, as he had for me, his deteriorating condition and the gap between visits drove away any sense of his place in my life. Furthermore, my mother did not join us on these visits, only my grandmother and aunt—yet Mother wanted me to know my father and undoubtedly felt bad for him. If at any time there had been some potential for a relationship between him and me, it was now gone; and never having known him as other than badly disabled and barely able to speak, I felt no profound dismay or loss, only wonderment as to what it meant.

§ 24

The winter was passing quickly while I attended school, did homework, read, and watched TV.

In early February, the news came that Buddy Holly had died in a plane crash along with Richie Valens and "The Big Bopper." That such a tragedy could occur so unexpectedly was a dire indication for many of how quickly a vital human being, his or her existence taken for granted, could suddenly be erased from the world. Rock & roll would survive but never be quite the same. Buddy Holly's death became a somber milestone for a generation.

Later that month, during a weekend while I was at my grandparents' house, Pam Hambly reported that Annette Funicello was signing 45s of her hit song "Tall Paul" at a big downtown record store. Pam was a year or two older than I and better informed. Although Annette sang "bubble gum" rock, I was oddly impressed that a teen celebrity like her would be at a record store in provincial Seattle, although Elvis had given a concert at our minor league baseball stadium a couple of years before. Also oddly, "Tall Paul" became the first top-ten rock & roll single sung by a woman. Annette had been a "Mouseketeer" on *The Mickey Mouse Club* and had grown up to be a beautiful teenager. *The Mickey Mouse Club* had been a staple of younger kids after school, and I couldn't help noticing Annette's transformation in Disney's popular movie *The Shaggy Dog*. Disney used its TV show to advertise its movies, showing excerpts and behind-the-scenes featurettes, and it got nearly every kid in the country excited to see whatever they released. *The Mickey Mouse Club* had maintained its indispensable role on after-school TV with series like *Spin and Marty* and *The Hardy Boys*. The show came on after Dick Clark's teen influential *American Bandstand*.

In March, I escaped to the Neptune Theater on weekends. I saw *Some Like It Hot* twice, James Garner in *Up Periscope,* and of course *The Shaggy Dog.* The following month, all the girls in the neighborhood went to see *Gidget* starring the iconic cutie Sandra Dee. We fellas passed.

One weekend in my grandparents' neighborhood, Mr. Brandt across the street, placed some branches of a tree with tent caterpillars into his fireplace and lit the fire. The phone rang, he answered it, and when he returned, the caterpillars had fled and crawled out over the living room rug and up the walls. Tent caterpillars were often a spring event in Seattle.

Ted, the rather serious kid who lived with his mother and sister in a house facing onto the 65th St. arterial, was older than I, about fifteen, with an oval-shaped face and straight-combed dark hair that fell across one side of his forehead. He was science oriented, and up to that time his science reputation rested on experiments with his Gilbert chemistry set. But he was about to enhance that reputation upon hearing of Mr. Brandt's caterpillar fiasco.

One bright day I found him on his front porch fiddling with some sort of flat metal plate, about eight inches square, with wires connected to a group of flashlight batteries. Connected between the square plate and the batteries was an electrical switch—a "knife switch" to be exact—and next to that a tin can whose contents I failed to immediately notice.

"What is that thing?" I asked, pointing to the metal plate.

He looked up and smiled. "First look into the can."

I did. Inside the can, writhing around, were several yellow- and black-striped tent caterpillars.

"I don't get it," I said.

"This," said Ted with pride, "is my caterpillar electrocution machine."

"What?!"

"Yeah, watch."

He shook one of the caterpillars onto the metal plate near

the center. It started crawling. Then Ted threw the switch, and the caterpillar . . . well, I prefer not to think about it.

Ted shut off the switch and looked a little embarrassed

"This will not make it onto *Watch Mr. Wizard*," I said.

"The idea works," Ted explained, "if you place this metal plate wherever you think the caterpillars will come from, and when they crawl onto it you can throw the switch."

"Yeah, I see," I said, unable to hide my revulsion.

Although Ted was pleased with his technical success, he wasn't too happy with the practical application of his invention. Yet it wouldn't be long before he endangered himself and us kids instead of caterpillars.

My life was still divided between my parents' apartment on the outskirts of Laurelhurst and my grandparents' (and aunt's) house in Ravenna. On a Sunday evening after Aunt Peggy and a boyfriend she'd been dating dropped me back at our Laurelon Terrace apartment, I received some shocking news with at least equal antipathy to Ted's caterpillar electrocution machine. I was told that a man had died in my bed.

The death had happened the previous night. The story Mother told was that Larry had invited a potential customer, a man of about sixty, over for dinner, and that this guest had begun to feel slightly dizzy or faint later in the evening. In a cold sweat, and with some shortness of breath, he'd gone upstairs to the bathroom but was unable to come back down the stairs. Larry wanted to help him back down, but it seemed as if the man, who was heavy, might collapse, so my mother told the man to lie down on my bed, the most immediate to the bathroom. First, she removed the bedspread and then put it back over him. She went to the linen cupboard to get another blanket while Larry went downstairs to call for an ambulance. By the time the ambulance had arrived, the fellow wasn't moving, and the medics were unable to revive him. So

I'd arrived into the aftermath of this macabre situation the next day, and it had happened in my own room. I wasn't told more details, only that Mother had changed all the blankets and sheets and pillow cases, and I wasn't to worry. Yeah, right. No problem sleeping in a bed that someone had just died in—or on—or whatever.

I overheard Mother and Larry discussing how they might have acted more quickly to help the fellow, but they noted that he seemed mostly in need of lying down. At least they'd called an ambulance, but they felt they'd made a mistake by leaving him alone for a few minutes. Also, in those days, CPR wasn't well known by ordinary people, so I didn't think to ask Larry if he'd tried it. Although an echo of death hung over my family's history before I was born, death was still an abstraction to me, experienced in movies; but this man's demise had happened in my own room. Aside from the surprise of being told, what could I do? I put on my pajamas and examined the bed as best as I could, then finally got in under the covers. It took a while to get to sleep, but I eventually did, and went back to Laurelhurst Elementary the next day.

I was still absent from school more often than the average kid and therefore failed to show up for the class picture, even though Mr. Goertzen had made a personal call to my mother encouraging me to come. I just wasn't feeling well, I said.

During the day, Mother's idea of entertainment was talking on the telephone with her friend Barbara—two hours at a time, nearly every day—gossiping and discussing the trivia of daily living. She drove me nuts, for I could hear this chatter everywhere in the apartment, but it probably helped me get over whatever phony illness I had and back to school.

When not at work or watching TV, stepfather Larry sat in his chair next to the table lamp with the little cactus planter, reading a book—usually one of the Reader's Digest Condensed Books, but sometimes a popular literary novel like *The Caine Mutiny* or *The Old Man and the Sea*. Yet he himself remained a closed book and a separate entity from Mother and me. In fact, I thought of all of us as irreconcilably separate people living together, yet now and then going somewhere as a threesome—usually to a movie or once a year on vacation. My constant desire from an early age to stay at my grandparents' didn't help this feeling, either. At the same time, my mother and stepfather didn't get along well, partly because Larry kept secrets as to the health of their finances, and partly because of personality differences. I became even more acutely aware of these troubles when, for a reason I wasn't privy to, Mother had slapped Larry hard on the face, damaging his partial denture. When angry, women tended to slap men in the face in those days, at least in the movies, so I didn't react strongly when I heard about it from Mother, who declined to inform me of why she had slapped Larry. In retaliation, Larry had angrily told my mother *never* to do that again. It was the only time I'd heard of any strong emotion coming from him. He had to visit the dentist the following day and then went into his silent mode for a week afterward, sitting in his chair in the living room, not speaking. I left him alone.

To celebrate the end of the school year, one of the students, George Ruggles, held an evening party at his parents' Old English style brick house in the heart of Laurelhurst, with music and snacks and Chinese lanterns strung above the back deck. Although there was no dancing (at that age, few knew how) we played pop 45s like "Dream Lover" by Bobby Darin, "A Teenager in Love" by Dion and the Belmonts, "Charlie Brown" by The Coasters, "It's Late" by Ricky Nelson, and "I Only Have Eyes for You" by The Flamingos. Those were hit songs on the radio and on kids' record players, and of course everyone had collected earlier hits by Elvis, Little

Richard, Jerry Lee Lewis, et al.

Summer came, I had made no close friends at school or my parents' new location—nor had the token gesture of transporting Dean from the old Bryant neighborhood worked too well. So I came back to my grandparents' house on 14th Ave. in Ravenna to play kickball in the street, board games on our front porch, and whatever solo activities I could muster.

That Fourth of July, my bright idea was to stick a firecracker into an apple, light it as if it were a hand grenade, and with Buzzy standing by, toss it up onto Stevie Mettler's front porch. Did I take into account that Stevie's mother was the generous person who provided the water for our gutter hydroplane races? Obviously not. Lucky that Stevie's parents had a sense of humor—although Mrs. Mettler walked out amid the exploded apple mess wondering what had happened, and then told me not to do that ever again! Needless to say, I stupidly figured everyone could understand the fun of setting off fireworks—usually in the ordinary way, however—as part of the holiday. Dumb.

The day of the Fourth, Larry and Mother got Dean and me together for the last time, taking us to the Playland amusement park north of the city limits along the shores of Bitter Lake. Playland had a big wooden roller coaster, a variety of rides, an old-fashioned funhouse, food eateries, and best of all, a Shoot-the-Chutes that sent groups of screaming people in flat-bottom boats down a huge ramp that leveled off at the last moment, hurling them out into a big lagoon. When the boats hit the water, more often than not the spray went high into the air and got everyone wet, or at least sprayed. Dean and I went on this ride several times, for shooting down the ramp was like dropping down a long roller-coaster hill toward a lake. We were terrified and delighted.

Mother and Larry had spread a picnic blanket out on the large lawn in the center of the park. After going on rides, we had sandwiches and soft drinks while waiting for the evening fireworks display. Nothing, I thought, was quite like a warm summer night at a great amusement park on the Fourth.

In mid-August, my stepfather, mother, and I were off on a road trip to Montana, stopping at motels and restaurants. Larry had purchased a new Plymouth Savoy with the huge tail fins that were an icon of car design for 1959. Although it was a basic model with the old three-speed transmission, we were enjoying the spaciousness of the interior. Cars had gotten much bigger in general. I saw a new Lincoln Continental convertible—a stunning red one—parked at a motel. The trunk lid was so long it looked like you could land an airplane on it.

Larry and mother had a nasty fight, a yelling match, in Kalispell, MT, the subject of which I quickly forgot. The next night we were staying at Yellowstone Lodge. Not for long, however, inasmuch as my mother was afraid because she'd heard the park was prone to earthquakes.

The highlight of the trip was a visit to the Lewis & Clark Caverns. No one with claustrophobia was allowed inside, not because of the caverns themselves, but because one literally had to slide on one's back through a narrow passage to gain entrance. My mother remained outside. The caves were spectacular, and I took flash photographs with my Kodak Brownie camera, not thinking I might be bothering the other tourists. The tour guide said nothing to dissuade me, and the photos I got back later were wonderful.

Starting around late August, street kickball on 14th Ave. gave way to touch football. The Ravenna neighborhood kids began to play it every weekend before the coldest fall weather; and since this possibility didn't exist at my parents' apartment complex, I had another excuse to stay at my grandparents' on weekends. We created our football field by designating the sidewalks as out of bounds, the telephone pole at the south as one goal line, and a tree on the parking strip at the other end as the northern goal. The lines of the big concrete squares that made the street were used as first-down markers. When a team could get across the next line, it was a first down. The football itself was an official leather ball, and it got pretty well scraped up. The few parked cars (most were parked in garages behind the houses) were considered natural obstacles over which the ball could be passed or the runner could zigzag around using the grass parking strips. Now and then a player would be looking to catch a pass and smack his or herself into a parked car. ("Jimmy, are you OK?!") As usual, everyone played—girls and boys of any age who could. If we got six people into the street, we'd have a game. This went on right through fall "football weather," often picking up again the following spring. It became the favorite neighborhood activity, and to me, a greater blast than school sports. A benefit was that everyone got to know one another; we settled our own arguments, sometimes having to make compromises if someone may (or may not) have stepped out of bounds, got touched with one hand or two ("I got ya!" "Only one hand!"); and all the rest of what it took to play. Sometimes, we'd simply have a "do over." As in our games of kickball, no one ever took the ball and went home. Actually, we forgot who even owned the ball. The danger was retrieving the ball if it landed in Mr. Entrup's front yard; for at least twice he'd rushed out and taken the ball into his house. The cliché of our lives was Mr. Entrup yelling, "You kids stay off my lawn!" But the next day the ball would appear in front of his house on the parking strip next to the sidewalk. And the game would begin again. Sometimes during a kickoff, the ball would fly up into the Mortlands' garden above their rockery. Mrs. Mortland would kick the ball back down into the street and yell at us, ala Mr. Entrup, scolding us for crushing her flowers. The ball didn't go astray all that often, we figured, and we weren't nasty about it, we just didn't know how to control everywhere the ball went. Several times, it fell with a thud on the hood or top of someone's car.

So Aunt Peggy began to more routinely park her Ford in our back alley garage. Nobody ever complained about our ball hitting their car, so I guessed it didn't leave any marks.

Ronny (the kid who locked me in the garage) and I usually played quarterbacks on opposite teams. A couple of times, the psycho kid who'd trapped Nora on the roof came to play—and as a result of something he did, our street football game made the newspaper. It started with the line, "Kids on 14th Ave. . . ." and went on to describe what happened when a car came down the street. As the car passed, our psycho kid struck the back fender with his fist, then grabbed his knee and started hopping around as if he'd been hit. The driver of the car might stop, jump out, and walk back to see if the kid was hurt. But the psycho kid just ran away, leaving us to make excuses to the concerned (or infuriated) driver. This trick happened several times until one of the drivers reported it to the police, and so it was picked up by *The Seattle Times*.

I later wished that the psycho was the only one of us who did this. But I couldn't tell a lie. Ronny did it once, and I did it once. Neither of us ran away, but tried to smile and joke our way out of it. What Buzzy and Jimmy or the girls thought I had no idea, but they seemed amused and didn't protest. This was my second mischievous act that summer and fall, the former being the exploding apple on the Mettlers' porch.

I counted Buzzy (Craig) and Jimmy, and also Ted, as best friends. (From the end of summer forward, we were instructed to call Buzzy by his real name Craig. His mother insisted, and so we were told.) Minor differences in age matter a lot at age eleven or twelve; I was now twelve, Craig was a year younger than I, Jimmy was a year younger still, and Ted was a few years older. Only Dean from my old neighborhood was my same age; but after that Fourth at Playland, he, as well as the time we played guns, went trick-or-treating on Halloween, or built spaceships out of refrigerator boxes in summer, had faded irretrievably into the past.

The cataclysm of junior high was about to begin.

§ 25

Nathan Eckstein Junior High was an icon of architectural modernism, built in 1950 to accommodate the baby-boom generation. Although two-stories tall, it was horizontally conceived—an immoderate, sprawling layout with a huge, curving panorama of tall, upper-story glass that connected long wings that went off into directions east and south. The entrance and interior were Deco influenced. All of it contrasted rather preposterously with the population of intended inhabitants that wandered or lingered in the hallways—something like 900 adolescent seventh, eighth, and ninth graders. I immediately became aware of the disparity in the ages of the students, for the ninth graders seemed far older and more mature than I and my fellow seventh graders. Rumor had it that in earlier years, the ninth graders would have attended high school. Did the concept of junior high exist before planning committees panicked to accommodate the baby boom? I had no idea, but a feeling of intimidation greeted us seventh graders, at least the males, who had only last year been at the top of the heap in elementary school.

I rode the bus to school with what seemed like a hierarchy of wild delinquents. I struggled with anxiety, trying to make sure none of the bullies grabbed my notebook and threw it out the window. Junior high society was punctuated with bullies, occasional fights after school, intolerance for "wimps," or anyone with non-conforming shoes, pants, shirts, or haircuts. It was a jungle.

Classroom desks were modern, and we were instructed to write with fountain pens on normal blue-lined paper. The pen that almost everyone used could be purchased at any drug or stationary store and had become iconic in junior high. Made by Sheaffer, it had a stainless steel tip and was refilled with little cylindrical, transparent cartridges of blue ink inserted into the body of the pen that was also transparent to monitor ink supply. We wrote our essays and book reports in longhand (later known as cursive) and our penmanship was noted, but not graded, by the English teacher. Of some frustration was a tall fellow named William, sitting next to me in class, who had superior handwriting that was broad, confident, somewhat feminine perhaps, and that constantly garnered "Good penmanship!" notes on his papers. I was not able to improve to his level. Ahead of me sat a rotund fellow named Stuart who liked to draw at the top of his papers old cars with bullet holes in them. This habit lasted for several weeks due to the popularity of *The Untouchables* on TV. The series starred Robert Stack as Eliot Ness fighting the Chicago mob starting in 1929. The pilot episode was a TV movie with Neville Brand as Al Capone, and aside from praise, the series drew a lot of criticism, not only for its extreme violence, but among Italian Americans for constantly portraying Italians as mobsters. The Al Capone family actually tried to sue ABC, Desilu Productions, and the show's sponsor Westinghouse for portraying Capone as a gangster! (The suit failed.)

My mother pointed me to another TV show that fall of '59 that offered first-rate dramas with imaginative viewpoints and weird, alternate realities that sometimes ripped the veneer off of society. *The Twilight Zone* became one of those must-see shows shared by many in school. "Did you see *The Twilight Zone* last night?!" The show and its creator Rod Serling became an iconic part of the shared imagination. But *The Twilight Zone* had a predecessor from earlier that year called *One Step Beyond*. The earlier show had a similar anthology format that delved exclusively into the supernatural, with an authoritative, silver-haired gentleman named John Newland who introduced each *true* episode. That was the grabber—that the supernatural stories of ESP, ghosts, pre-cognition, impossible coincidences, and other things in these dramas were supposedly taken from true events. Even the eerie music for the show could cause one's hair to stand on end. These shows helped draw my maps of reality as I tried to understand a world full of possibilities.

The degree of influence *One Step Beyond* had on my psyche was reinforced by my reading of a popular book of supposedly true supernatural events. *Stranger than Science* was offered as "A fantastic collection of fascinating stories taken from life." Its presumed authenticity was given legitimacy by its author, the well-known, respected news commentator Frank Edwards. The jacket blurb continued: "These fabulous occurrences have been studied, documented, checked and double-checked—and still offer *no* plausible explanation." The first sentence in the book was: "Is it possible for a human being to literally walk off the earth in full view of witnesses?"

The answer to the reader, of course, was yes. The story, as I read it wide-eyed, was of one David Lang, who, in broad daylight while walking back toward his farmhouse near Gallatin, Tennessee on September 23, 1880, vanished in full view of his family and a local Judge named Peck. Lang was never seen again. The grass turned yellow and refused to grow in a fifteen-foot circle where he had disappeared. Months later, his children decided to go to the circle of dead grass and call to him. They were astonished to hear their father's voice . . . "calling faintly for help . . . over and over . . . until it faded away forever." End of Chapter.

I fell for this and other such stories "hook, line, and sinker," as they used to say—stories, in the case of Edwards, that had mostly been culled from the pages of *FATE* magazine.

Unfortunately, later research proved there was no such person as David Lang or his family, no Lang farm, no Judge Peck, or any substantiation whatsoever of the event, such as a missing persons report or any other trace of evidence.

Maybe they'd all disappeared from the record books, including the farm, the family, and the judge, and ended up in The Twilight Zone.

Or the story's author, Stuart Palmer, in *FATE* had lifted the tale from an Ambrose Bierce short story, "The Difficulty of Crossing a Field" from his collection *Can Such Things Be?* (An affidavit supposedly by Lang's daughter published in *FATE* was later shown to be in Palmer's hand writing.)

I did not know any of this, or the sources of the other legends in *Stranger Than Science,* or of the veracity or otherwise of *One Step Beyond.* It was a matter of youthful fascination and gullibility. The stories seemed so authoritative, and so the landscape of my reality was shaped by such tales. I knew, of course, that *The Twilight Zone* was pure fiction, for it was presented as such, but *might* similar things happen? I did not know. One day I asked my mother if she thought such things might be true. She said, simply, "People make things up."

Also contrary to the seductions of the supernatural, my feet were kept planted on the ground by a mild-mannered science teacher who, during the first day of school, went to the blackboard and signed his name "T. Smith." Eventually we pestered him about his first name, and eventually he revealed the old fashioned name of Tobias. In both appearance and personality, Mr. Smith was much like the character actor William Shallert who played the high school English teacher in the TV show *The Many Loves of Dobie Gillis;* he, too, wore tweed sport coats. Perhaps our junior high had called up Central Casting. But in any case, Mr. Smith continued the mandate of more science education, and he balanced my attraction to the weird tales of Frank Edwards by teaching basic scientific principles such as the importance of experimental rather than anecdotal evidence.

Never was I to forget his lecture one day on superstition. He went to the blackboard with a thick piece of chalk and drew a simple building. He then drew a ladder leaning against the building wall from across a sidewalk.

"I'm not a very good artist," he said bemusedly, "but as you can see, here is a ladder leaning up against a building. OK, now here is a fellow coming down the sidewalk." He drew a stick figure supposedly approaching the ladder. "If he's very superstitious, he won't walk under the ladder, right? That is supposed to be bad luck. But let's say there's a big truck parked at the curb and cans of paint near the ladder, blocking him. So he says, what the heck and walks quickly under the ladder to be on his way."

He turned to the class. "Let's now suppose that our mildly superstitious—I say mild, because he walked under the ladder anyway—fellow has some bad luck during the day, or even the next day. Maybe he falls down and sprains his ankle, or maybe he loses his wallet. What will he think? Anyone have the answer?"

Hands raised.

"Emily?"

"He'll blame his bad luck on the ladder."

"Exactly."

I understood the concept. It wasn't quite new to me (kids sometimes carried "lucky rabbit's foot" key chains that most realized did no good whatsoever), but for some reason Mr. Smith made a big impression because he clearly and authoritatively demonstrated it. I was not superstitious other than having a lucky number, which I'd decided a long time ago was 5. How I came by this number I'd long forgotten.

"What we have is a common coincidence," continued Mr. Smith. "The man connected two separate incidents because he'd always heard that walking under a ladder would bring bad luck. There are other such superstitions, such as breaking a mirror—that would bring *seven years* of bad luck! But these things aren't proven, and they don't make sense, because there is no theory as to how one would cause the other. There's a phrase you should all remember: 'Correlation does not imply causation.' Our man walked under a ladder and shortly afterward had some bad luck; so in his mind he connected the two things—they correlated." Mr. Smith wrote the phrase on the blackboard and had us write it in our notebooks. "The one thing did not *cause* the other. Walking under ladders do not cause lost wallets or sprained ankles—unless you trip because you tried to duck under the ladder."

One difficulty of childhood was the plethora of mixed messages received from various sources—parents, teachers, books, movies, television, other kids, sheer rumor. In the latter department for example, just after school the previous summer, a rumor went around our neighborhood that George Reeves, the actor who played Superman on TV, thought he *was* Superman and tried to fly out of a 50-story window. Reeves was in fact reported to have committed suicide, so this neighborhood rumor of how he died was more than slightly false. He had died by a gunshot to the head. In any case, it was a disappointment to those of us who'd become fans of the show. More than that, it had been a rude awakening—for how little we knew of the lives of those we saw on the screen.

Or for that matter, of the life and death of many thousands or millions of human beings that no super hero, *not even God*, ever rescued. For in contrast with Mr. Smith's rationality at the blackboard, history revealed a dreadful aspect of human behavior with the first broadcast on television of a grim documentary about Hitler's concentration camps. That special broadcast one night jolted my perspective again, for it appeared to be an unedited depiction of the horrors of Auschwitz, Dachau, Buchenwald, and others, with shocking scenes of conditions in the camps—and of thousands of cadaverous dead bodies bulldozed into huge pits. And scenes of starving, emaciated human beings. And the mountains of shoes, glasses, or watches taken from those who were exterminated. And the lampshades made from human skin. I sat with my stepfather and mother watching these unspeakable horrors with a sickening revulsion I had never experienced. The scenes lingered in my mind for days and weeks, even film of Eisenhower touring one of the camps during its liberation, not to mention Germans from a nearby town who were forced to visit a nearby death camp they'd willingly or unwillingly allowed to exist. I had to incorporate this terrible truth of human cruelty—and *very* recent history—into my view of the human species of which I was a part. Yet I also had to set it aside. I had to believe that it was remote from my own surroundings. Again, it was the shared experience of television in those days that meant other kids had seen the show. Not all. But with a friend or two who acknowledged it, a kind of silent abstention of comment was the reaction. Nothing much could be said. Only a nod and "Yeah, I saw it. Wow." And so a lot of us were introduced to true horror, not the Hollywood variety.

So too did the underlying themes of racial hatred and bigotry more fully enter my awareness. Of course I had experienced the attack on the Negro kid in the industrial south end, and now, by way of television, the results of Nazi extermination of Jews. These things were not covered in school except perhaps in a few passing remarks. Our textbooks relayed such things in the context of dry historical facts. Contrarily, in stepped our science teacher Mr. Smith again with a documentary film about prejudice and tribalism. It was a stylized, avant-garde animated film demonstrating both the power and the dangers of racial or tribal identity. *"They* are not one of *us,"* said one of the brightly colored figures, pointing at a differently colored figure threateningly. I forgot the name of the film, but its message stayed.

Theatrical movies were still on my list of activities. Grandfather Nels hadn't been to a movie in perhaps thirty years, but he and I and Aunt Peggy went to the must-see movie of the year, *Ben-Hur.* I both recognized and appreciated the greatness of that film, while my tastes also continued along familiar lines with *The Angry Red Planet, The Atomic Submarine,* and *The Battle of the Coral Sea.* More popular in general was the first of the Doris Day sex comedies, *Pillow Talk,* with Rock Hudson. Not much sex, plenty of talk. Yet this movie was entertaining as I was beginning to form ideas of romance between men and women. I expected to enter into such enjoyable capers in the not too distant future.

In the meantime, seventh grade was totally lacking in opportunities for sophisticated behavior. At lunchtime, we ate at long tables amid the cacophony of a hundred kids talking, yelling, laughing, and sometimes throwing food at one another. When Mr. Moffatt, a teacher who had drawn this years' dreaded lunchroom duty, had his back turned, some rowdy might throw a glop of food against the wall just for mischief. Mr. Moffatt would also rush around trying to keep the worst ninth graders from bullying the vulnerable seventh graders. We seventh graders sat in tight knit groups for protection. Once, when Mr. Moffatt was turned the other way, he got hit in the back with a jelly sandwich. My reaction to this was one of dislike and embarrassment, which was the majority's reaction. But it took only a few idiots to ruin, now and then, what was normally a simple break to eat lunch. Nevertheless, as the year rolled on and Mr. Moffatt sent a kid or two to the principal's office, things improved.

My English teacher, a middle-aged woman named Miss

Bland, had us read a paperback of Shakespeare's *Julius Caesar.* The language was difficult, to say the least, but I liked the story, and Miss Bland wasn't bad at explaining what was going on while we read it over a week or two. What was unusual about Miss Bland was that she dressed like Sherlock Holmes. Her normal attire was a thick wool, full-length plaid suit with a waist-length cape that she removed with a flourish after entering the classroom. No deer stalker hat, but I thought she was very cool, if slightly odd.

At home, I wrote an extra-curricular science fiction story about explorers on the moon called "Moonquake" and handed it in. To my embarrassment the next day, Miss Bland read it aloud to the class. I wanted to hide under my desk, for she seemed more amused than impressed. At least the class didn't laugh, and Miss Bland was doing her duty to encourage a young writer.

An uncomfortable feature of junior high was gym class, when, after each session, thirty or forty naked boys crowded into glazed terracotta shower stalls, then lined up soaking wet, bumping and shoving, until the whistle blew to signal our return to the locker-room benches to towel off and get dressed. The procedure was distasteful to almost everyone, and I understood it as a necessary part of sports—at which I was average at everything. I liked flag football, when instead of tackling, one would pull off a hanging rag, i.e., flag, from the runner's back waistband. I also enjoyed tumbling lessons on the long, thick, gray mats. I was tall enough to play basketball pretty well, but organized sports didn't interest me enough to be involved after school. If we'd had the option to race go-karts, I'd have been first in line.

At home that fall of '59, television remained the center of family togetherness. My grandparents and aunt were addicted to *The Lawrence Welk Show* every Saturday night, the pop music of which I found bland after being exposed to rock & roll. My mother never missed the courtroom drama *Perry Mason.* On Monday night I was a big fan of one of the less-watched but great TV detective shows, *Bourbon Street Beat,* starring Richard Long and Andrew Duggan. It was a spinoff of the Warner Bros. big hit *77 Sunset Strip,* but it had a unique New Orleans setting that leaned toward Southern Gothic. One episode called "The Golden Beetle" was a take-off on Edgar Allan Poe's "The Gold Bug," so of course I was captivated. The show lasted only one season (although there were 39 episodes that allowed it to run halfway through the summer without reruns) and because the show got canceled I learned that my own tastes didn't always match those of the public. *77 Sunset Strip* was the most popular of the Warner Bros. detective shows (which included *Hawaiian Eye* and later, *Surfside Six*), but I liked that show, as well. I preferred the dapper Efrem Zimbalist, Jr. character, but the girls mostly liked Edd "Kookie" Byrnes, a blond surfer-type dude who played a car hop and spoke cool '50s slang like "squaresville" (boring) or "antsville" (a place too crowded). He also kept combing his hair, which led to a hit song, "Kookie, Kookie, Lend Me Your Comb." This was the continuing heyday of so-called novelty songs like "Witch Doctor," "Purple People Eater," and "Itsy Bitsy Teenie Weenie Yellow Polkadot Bikini."

Guys my age didn't merely *like* TV detectives such as Efrem Zimbalist, Jr. or Roger Smith (*77 Sunset Strip*), Craig Stevens (*Peter Gunn),* Richard Long (*Bourbon Street Beat*) and others; we wanted to *be* those guys! It was the era of "cool," and TV detectives were the coolest—dated the coolest chicks and drove the coolest cars. What more could a man want out of life?

Another cool aspect of these shows was the introduction of mainstream jazz to the mass TV audience. Henry Mancini's theme for *Peter Gunn* became a top-40 hit, climbing to #8, which was an amazing accomplishment for a TV theme; but most of the music for that show was pure jazz. A great deal of jazz or jazz-influenced music elevated the style of many TV shows of the genre. For example, music for *The Naked City* and *The Untouchables* sometimes echoed Elmer Bernstein's breakthrough "big city" music for motion pictures like *The Man with the Golden Arm, The Rat Race,* and *Walk on the Wild Side* (Elmer Bernstein not to be confused with Leonard Bernstein). So along with rock & roll, baby boomers' tastes in music were influenced by television because the soundtrack music was taken seriously by the studios. TV soundtrack LPs were sold, as well. The first few times I could afford to buy an LP, I bought *Peter Gunn, Mr. Lucky* (also by Mancini), and *Bourbon Street Beat,* orchestrated by Don Ralke that included jazz standards "Blues in the Night," "I Cover the Waterfront," and "I Gotta Right to Sing the Blues." This music, along with most other TV detective music, was essentially big band jazz made for mass market entertainment; but it had a unique quality that was new and attractive. Mancini in particular was a "pop" genius who went on to write film music such as *The Pink Panther, Charade,* and *Hatari,* and whose records sold in the millions. His TV music was at my level of sophistication then, and I remained a fan.

Other music that made an impression on me was Bernard Herrmann's film music for *Journey to the Center of the Earth* starring James Mason. That film, coming out near the holidays, continued a series of movies based on the works of Jules Verne; *Around the World in Eighty Days* had won five Oscars including Best Picture back in '56.

Movies, books, music, school, and street football were at the center of my life, but I had also become fond of chess, having acquired a plastic chess set and a paperback copy of *Chess in a Nutshell* by Fred Reinfeld. Other boys were ecstatic about receiving new baseball mitts for Christmas (indeed, I had received a first baseman's glove the year before) but this Christmas my mother gave me a gift I came to prize second only to the Lionel train. A few weeks before the holidays I'd seen a large *wooden* chess set at Frederick & Nelson and asked for it for Christmas. The set, with its traditional Staunton pieces, came with a board of maple and mahogany squares. The white pieces were of maple, the black pieces painted glossy black, and so the set combined beauty with the promise of table-top strategy. Most games I'd learned depended on luck by rolling dice or drawing cards. Chess was different. It promised brainy adventure—strategy and tactics—with castles, knights, bishops, kings and queens. Wow. My problem would be finding another player. In the meantime, I studied the game and moved the weighted pieces on their green felt bottoms across the hardwood squares. No denying the aesthetics. I didn't quite know why it was so compelling. Maybe the set *and* the game itself was symbolic of some quality of adulthood, perhaps even of manhood. The obvious answer was that it was symbolic of warfare. Girls did not play chess. But there was also a gentlemanly aspect—the challenge of engaging in battle while sitting at a table having tea (or a Coke and cookies).

I may have been studying at the chessboard that week after Christmas when Aunt Peggy came home from work in hysterics. She had been taking the bus from her job at the Federal Reserve downtown and had been dropped off a couple of blocks away from home. It was dark by that time, and she came into the house, upset and crying. Grandfather sat in his usual chair looking up at Peggy while Grandmother and I came into the living room to find out what was wrong. Peggy removed her round glasses, sat on the sofa still with her coat on, found a Kleenex in her purse and started to dry her eyes. "Oh, we have to call the police!" she said. "Someone grabbed my purse and ran!"

"Oh, honey!" said Grandmother. "I'll call them."

Peggy sat, trying to compose herself, finally standing up to take off her long wool coat. In a little while a policeman arrived and took Peggy's description of what had happened, but of course he couldn't do anything except make a report. I registered a powerful impression of his blue uniform, black holster and gun while his more than conspicuous presence filled the living room. I'd never been near a policeman.

Nothing further came of Peggy being mugged, but from that day forward she would no longer walk home in the dark from the bus stop. She drove her car to work throughout the winter months.

The downside of human behavior was accentuated in a far more general way via a terrifying adult movie I'd seen which summarized the ongoing fear of nuclear holocaust. *On the Beach* was a post nuclear war movie intended as a warning by producer/director Stanley Kramer. After World War III, human beings who survived the initial conflict were killed by radioactive fallout, with only a few enclaves of population in the southern hemisphere, mainly Australia, as the deadly radioactive clouds move toward them. It was one of several big production black and white films dealing with "the bomb" and the possibility of nuclear war. *On the Beach* was such a powerful statement (near the end, it was the first time I'd heard people in an audience sniffling and trying to hold back tears) that I came to believe such a movie might spur politicians to see reason and stop building nuclear weapons. How could anyone, I thought, not be affected after seeing such a film? This was the beginning of my *belief* that powerful movies could influence culture and behavior in important ways.

I'd not been alone in thinking so. In previous decades it was thought that movies would encourage *immoral* behavior just as they would encourage the opposite. The industry, fear-

ing censorship by Congress, started The Motion Picture Production Code, an infamous but not entirely detrimental self-
censorship eventually known as the Hayes Office. Although
Hayes Office decisions were often preposterous, some of the
standards provided directorial discipline that made films less
dependent upon graphic violence, overt sex, or unnecessary
obscenity. Parents could usually send their children—at least
their older children—to the movies without fear of them being corrupted or overly distressed. And so at age twelve I
started going to movies intended for adults.

During this time, as well, before the end of seventh grade, I
had discovered the first major author that not surprisingly
captured my dark imagination fostered by horror movies and
Halloween—and was there another factor? The author was
Edgar Allan Poe, and over the next couple of years fervently
and repeatedly devoured his most famous short stories. Here
were horrors of a deep psychological nature, cast in moody
settings that created an atmosphere of melancholy fascination. I was particularly enthralled by the opening paragraph of
"The Fall of the House of Usher," the beginning of which
was the following:

> During the whole of a dull, dark, and soundless day in the au-
> tumn of the year, when the clouds hung oppressively low in the
> heavens, I had been passing alone, on horseback, through a sin-
> gularly dreary tract of country; and at length found myself, as
> the shades of the evening drew on, within view of the melan-
> choly House of Usher. I know not how it was—but, with the
> first glimpse of the building, a sense of insufferable gloom per-
> vaded my spirit. . . .

I found myself alone among my acquaintances in appreci-
ation of this kind of literature—and later, of science fiction,
as well—for it was rare to run into another kid at that time
who shared an interest in either. Nevertheless, it was the

gruesome, often grisly tales of Poe that kept me in my room reading on a high literary level.

The last month of seventh grade became a blur, with one notable exception. For the second time in my life, I almost lost an eye. I was standing at the bottom of Eckstein's west stairwell when I heard someone yelling my name from above.

"Hey, Phil!"

I looked up and saw a black-haired, moon-faced guy who sometimes pestered me in one of my classes. He was leaning over the railing, raised his arm, and threw something down at me as hard as he could. It struck me on the bridge of my nose just to the left of my right eye. I felt a sharp pain and started to bleed as I put my hand up to my eye. I bent my head down, dripping spots of blood on the floor. Next to my right shoe was a penny. He had hurled a penny at me down the stairwell, and the result could have turned into a catastrophe instead of a prank. But it seemed as if my eye was OK. I went into the nearest classroom to hunt for a Kleenex to staunch the wound. A woman teacher was there, saw the blood oozing out between the fingers I held at my face, and in a panic asked, "Is it your eye?!" To which I answered, "I don't think so. I think I can see OK." She rushed to her desk, got some Kleenex from a drawer, and asked me what had happened.

Now in those days, it wasn't good to "tell" on anyone. But at the moment, given the potential of losing an eye, I decided not to give a damn, so I told this teacher exactly what and who. She told me to get over to the nurse's office. For years afterward, it was possible to see the little white scar right near my eye—another reminder of how luck plays a part in one's life. I never found out what had happened, if anything, to the bully who'd thrown the penny, but he was back sitting next to me in class the next day. He made a dull apology and never bothered me again. I felt no need for revenge, and no self-righteous anger. By his hesitant behavior toward me afterward, I figured he must have known he'd been an idiot who hadn't thought what might have resulted from throwing a penny at someone. No real harm done. . . .

§ 26

My birthday had come and gone in May, I had turned thirteen, had graduated from seventh grade and moved back to my grandparent's house in the Ravenna neighborhood.

June of 1960 brought more adult movies to the Neptune Theater in the U. District—one of which caused me further certainty that the movies would change the world. Walking out of the theater after seeing *Inherit the Wind,* I knew that fundamentalist Christianity was dead! How could anyone see that film and reject the scientific reality of evolution and believe in a literal interpretation of the Bible? *Inherit the Wind* was a fictionalized account of the famous Scopes Monkey Trial of 1925, with Spencer Tracy playing the Clarence Darrow part, Frederick March standing in for William Jennings Bryan, and Gene Kelley as H. L. Mencken. I strongly believed that producer Stanley Kramer had done it again. He was changing the world with movies that made people *think*.

On another plane of adulthood, the loopy romances of Doris Day and Rock Hudson were overthrown in my maturing brain by Jack Lemon and Shirley MacLaine in the widescreen black and white movie *The Apartment*. This was what adult life was like, and I fully expected to meet a young woman like MacLaine's character, a cute elevator operator, and someday fall in love. A tentative sense of what my future would be like was forming.

Then came Alfred Hitchcock's *Psycho*.

Ah, no surprise there! I would not go to see it. Neither would any of the neighborhood kids, because the film's reputation was enough to scare away even some teenagers. Adults, too. Mr. Mettler, Stevie's dad, mentioned specifically that he would not go to that movie, either. But he relented when it hit the drive-ins, and he and Mrs. Mettler made Stevie, age 9, lie down in the back seat and not watch. Even so, Stevie reported being frightened by the music and his parents' reactions to the scary parts.

For most of us, *House on Haunted Hill* and other William Castle produced movies were scary enough. But I avoided those, as well, and wondered if my cowardice was because I saw *The Curse of Frankenstein* at too young an age—age ten.

Yet at the very time I was considering this, I saw an ad in the movie section of the paper for *House of Usher* starring Vincent Price. This ultimate haunted house tale (but without ghosts) was the first of director Roger Corman's widescreen color adaptations based on the stories of Edgar Allan Poe. So I rushed down to the Neptune theater again and was thrilled to the core of my Poe-esque soul. At the very least, the gloomy setting and design of this film—the mansion permeated with dark passageways, and the reliance on atmosphere more than shock and gore—was something I could immerse myself in. I still didn't know what attracted me so thoroughly to this genre (as indeed I'd been attracted to the trappings of Halloween) but I was not alone, for *House of Usher* became a big hit for American International, was the most vividly atmospheric horror film up to that time, and made a major star out of Vincent Price. In the final scene, when the mansion is burning and the hero escapes back across the grim landscape, and the eerie, wordless choral music reaches a crescendo, I was in Poe ecstasy. What was it that so thoroughly stirred my wide-eyed emotions amid all this dream-like terror? Would I ever understand it? Captivated, I came back to the neighborhood and told everyone I could find that they had to go see this movie! The Hambly sisters did, *and* they agreed it was the best scary movie they'd ever seen. That others could share in what seemed like my private Gothic modality was very satisfying. The public was now treated to first class horror films alternating between the Hammer Studio monster remakes and American International's "Poe pictures." More than ever, movies had become a meaningful part of my life, and I began to pay regular attention to the movie section of the newspaper.

In the month following the dark fantasy of *Usher* (the separation of a few weeks seemed like forever at my age) an ad came on TV for a movie in another favorite genre. Science fiction films were still hugely popular, and nothing was better that summer than George Pal's *The Time Machine*. I had recently read H. G. Wells's short novel and found it deeply thought provoking, so this was another "must see" film adaptation. Near the end of the novella, the Time Traveller journeys farther onward to stand on a lonely, desolate beach to witness the dying Earth while the sun had become a red giant. This was the most elaborately written scene in the book. So a minor disappointment was that this particular scene wasn't used in the film. But the movie did capture the essence of Wells's vision. My emotions were unexpectedly touched when the Time Traveller stops in the *near* future and finds England engaged in war, and that his good friend Filby had been killed. H. G. Wells hated war—and because Rod Taylor was perfectly cast as Wells's Time Traveller, I had found another dynamic Englishman (Taylor was actually Australian) whose persona I admired and identified with. I went back to see the movie twice more. I could not get it out of my head. Films that emphasized the passing of time, such as the final scene in *The Egyptian*, or Rod Serling's *Twilight Zone* TV episode "Walking Distance," profoundly affected my awareness of impermanence, time, and change.

*   *   *

Yet the summer of 1960 in the small-town atmosphere of the Ravenna district did seem timeless. Not only did we play the old games, we came up with two new ones of a more intellectual bent. Occasionally tiring of street football, a few of us, girls and boys close to the same age, gathered at the base of the steps leading up the "rockery" embankment to the Brandt's house—to play charades. We acted out the names of books, movies, and TV shows for our team to guess, having learned a complex set of hand signals for little words such as "the" and "a", or to indicate syllables, etc. Most of us learned these ancillary signals from a TV show called *Stump the Stars*. The show, basically charades played by teams of TV and movie stars, paralleled the popular party game throughout the '50s, so among us we were able to put together the rules and various signals. One of the most amusing turns came when I got the secret slip of paper giving the name of the TV show *One Step Beyond*. I gave the hand signal for "TV show," then the signal for "the whole idea," stood for a moment, and took a big step forward. My team got it immediately. A huge laugh.

We soon devised an original game exclusively our own. It was a collective neighborhood invention, the idea taken from the hugely popular *Perry Mason* TV show. We called it "Court." A half-dozen of us got together in the Hambly's empty garage when Mr. Hambly had driven to work, opened the big doors for light, and used various boxes or things to sit on. Two people were chosen as attorneys, and the rest of us went outside to make up a story, usually involving a murder, with all the clues necessary for the attorneys to guess who did it. Each person in the story had to know their role and be prepared to answer questions or make up things on the spur of the moment in the courtroom—which could be very funny, because of course not all the details could be invented beforehand. Each witness (or "witless" as we sometimes called them) took the stand, and each would have to take into ac-

count what the previous witness had sometimes created out
of thin air. This could be challenging! The attorneys would
win the game if they correctly identified the culprit. The rest
won if the attorneys guessed wrong. Sometimes the whole
thing broke down into complete nonsense, but it was amazing how often the story retained the logic necessary for the
attorneys to guess correctly. The players were usually myself,
Pam, Mary, and Nancy, Craig and Jimmy, and a nice young
guy named Dale whose family lived in a tall old house with a
fenced back yard across from the Hambly's garage. We played
"Court" infrequently, it didn't last, but it was another instance
of how our neighborhood defaulted to include girls and boys
alike, in street sports or otherwise. How unusual this was I
didn't know, but as time passed, we began to think of our
neighborhood as special in trying to include everyone—not
to mention using our imaginations.

There was no question of individuality and little of the
notorious '50s conformity other than basic clothing (jeans
mainly)—and too many family peculiarities, as I often noted,
to qualify for the '50s TV family model. Certainly my own
family situation was odd. The three Hambly sisters (Pam,
Mary, and Nancy) came from a Catholic family, as I mentioned, their mother being both religious and an active Democrat, while their father worked in some unknown capacity
"for the railroad." Pam and Mary, short-haired brunettes,
were considered to have a weight problem—Mary far less—
and were reportedly made to stand on a scale every morning.
Pam had a good sense of humor, and it was easy to elicit her
delightful laugh during whatever silliness arose. Pam was the
sort of person everyone liked, and she developed a friendship
with Ted's sister Nora, although they had quite different per-
sonalities. Nora, slightly less than medium height, long-
waisted but not thin, with medium length brown hair and
those 1950s horn-rimmed glasses, was an observer more than a

participant, though I guess it counted that she had often baby-sat for little Stevie. Mary Hambly was a bit like her sister Pam but more thoughtful and with a biting sense of humor that made her more interesting as time went on. Sister Nancy was the more typical young girl of the three sisters, a very good looking brunette. I would have been romantically attracted to "Nan" had she been a bit older, for she was easy going, pretty, and easy to be fond of. The rascal Ronny I'd gotten to know better because of being locked in his garage. His sister Stacey was an enigma, an attractive blond with an aloof attitude, difficult to get to know, good friends with Nancy because they were the same age. She and her brother Ronny were raised as Mormons. Craig and Jimmy were typical young boys interested in sports; but it was their neighbor Ronny who participated in Little League with his baseball uniform and equipment. Ronny was the most athletic of us and was always up for a game of street football. Craig and Jimmy's older sister Sue continued to remain mostly out of sight and didn't partake in the neighborhood games. No one seemed to know why.

Other than sports, we played board games: these included offerings by Parker Brothers (*Monopoly, Clue, Careers*) and Milton Bradley (*The Game of Life, Yahtzee, Stratego*).

Ted (boy genius inventor of the caterpillar electrocution machine) was more interested in science experiments, and it was sometime in August that he decided to make a rocket. . . .

Ted being several years older than I, it was natural for me to take interest in what he was up to, so one day I went over to his house where he invited me down into the dark, musty basement to help him.

In those days, it was possible to simply walk into a drug store and buy all the ingredients necessary to make gunpowder. This Ted had done. And his rocket was rather crude. It consisted of about 5" of a ¾" diameter lead pipe.

My contribution was to hold the pipe while Ted heavily squeezed one end closed in his workbench vice. He then inserted about a two-foot fuse and firmly packed the pipe full of gunpowder.

I didn't know at the time (presumably, neither did Ted) that this might as easily be a pipe bomb as a pipe rocket. Ted, however, was older, so I figured he knew what he was doing.

The next step, he said, was to make a launching chute out of aluminum rain gutter. So we nailed together some wood to support one end of a three-foot section of rain gutter at about a 45-degree angle. The rocket would be lit off at the bottom of the chute and, if all went as planned, take off into the heavens. One problem, however, was how high, how far, and where it would land. Ted wasn't bothered by such details and suggested we take the whole thing up to the empty Roosevelt High School playfield.

First I had to get Craig and Jimmy to witness the launch. Ted waited while I ran down to the Brandt's house, and then we four walked the two blocks to Roosevelt High, carrying the rocket, launch chute, and matches to light the fuse.

The big playfield was indeed empty, for it was summer, and we went to the baseball diamond at the near end, with the west side of the huge brick high school building at our right. Ted set up the launch chute and rocket about ten feet out from home plate. The rest of us went behind the wooden backstop for safety.

Ted, in his usual plain brown shirt and gray slacks, stood confidently at the launch site, having pointed the rocket toward the other end of the big field. He hesitated as we peeked out through cracks and knotholes in the wood. I was glad the wood was thick.

"Hey, you guys!" Ted yelled.

"What?!"

"How about one of you go to the other end of the field and be a spotter?"

We looked at each other. A grass embankment rose up near the far end of the track where athletes ran the 220 and 440. The distance was well beyond the outfield.

"OK," said Jimmy, volunteering, and he left the backstop while we waited for him to run to the far embankment. Once there, he went up the embankment and waved at us.

Ted waved back, turned to make sure we were still behind the backstop. He then knelt down to light the fuse. It caught immediately, and he ran back to join us.

Sometime later . . . as the summer passed . . . we realized how utterly insane this "rocket" was. But the realization *began* to occur as I wondered if the backstop was thick enough. I fully conceded in that moment—perhaps we all did—that the rocket might EXPLODE! taking out all the windows in Roosevelt High and perhaps us.

YET, believe it or not, the damn thing sizzled with flame shooting out the back and took off!

In an instant, it was gone!

Jimmy, on the embankment at the other end of the playfield, didn't see it coming. He heard it, though, because by an incredible circumstance of trajectory physics, the rocket landed with a thump twenty feet away from him into the turf of the embankment. The result could not have been planned more perfectly. Jimmy was waving at us and pointing. We ran. Ran to where Jimmy had heard it thump into the grass. We found it and were glad Jimmy hadn't been struck dead. We should have yelled and shouted at Ted's success, but we were too stunned with awe at the odds of the rocket landing where it did. Any farther and it would have gone into the row of houses across the street. Ted seemed to take it all in stride. But I suspected, even as he had waited with us behind the backstop with a pale look, that he might have had second thoughts. He never made another one.

Ted seemed content from that time on to read science books and science fiction instead of doing experiments. Likely it was necessary. His mother was single and supported him and his sister Nora by working downtown at Skyway Luggage. His father had disappeared years ago. Little money remained in the household for science equipment beyond normal childhood curiosities.

Ted's abandonment of crazy experiments in favor of reading sci-fi gave us something in common as I expanded my reading to include works such as Ray Bradbury's *The Martian Chronicles* and Arthur C. Clarke's *Childhood's End*. In the '50s and early '60s, such novels were little known in school outside of a small number of presumed eccentrics. One could go through an entire grade of junior high or, in Ted's case, high school without meeting a fellow science fiction fan. Worse yet, English teachers turned their noses up at that kind of literature.

As the summer of 1960 was on the wane, my stepfather passed along an Ace paperback of the best-selling *The Report on Unidentified Flying Objects* by Capt. Edward J. Ruppelt (former head of the Air Force's UFO investigation unit Project Blue Book). Ruppelt's meticulously objective descriptions taken from the testimony of pilots, military personnel, scientists, and ordinary folks witnessing extraordinary things in the sky was another confirmation for me that our map of reality was incomplete. UFOs had not only been observed by credible witnesses, but tracked on radar, flying in ways that defied known laws of physics, at speeds not possible with current technology. Ruppelt's book also recounted the details of the Washington D.C. events of July, 1952, and his clear-eyed, official investigations impressed me like nothing I'd read before. Although my fascination would later be tempered by a more questioning attitude, Ruppelt seemed like a contemporary hero on a quest for truth, and I began to wonder if this greatest twentieth century mystery would be solved before I reached adulthood. The last sentence of his book was: "Only time will tell."

§ 27

I had few chores at my grandparents' or my parents' other than mowing the lawn. Responsibilities for kids were based on an allowance of 50 cents a week, increased to a dollar by my age of thirteen, and few took on jobs outside their house other than the usual lawn mowing, perhaps for an elderly neighbor. I was alone most of the time. I loved my grandparents and aunt. My mother was good-hearted. I could have done without my laconic stepfather, but he more or less became part of the furniture in our Laurelhurst apartment, as did Grandfather in our Ravenna house. Both of them did a lot of reading. Stepfather still sold fire-extinguishing sprinkler systems. Aunt Peggy continued her job at the Federal Reserve Bank and took up photography on weekends, having purchased an Argus C-4 35mm camera. She and a couple of girlfriends went on country expeditions to photograph scenery and show their slides on a home screen. Slide shows were a popular family pastime. Grandmother cooked, cleaned, did the laundry, and watched TV soap operas. I didn't receive much individual attention.

I had begun to reflect more on my extended family. For example, as fall approached I became somewhat interested in the 1960 presidential election, favoring neither candidate but discovering that my family preferred Nixon and were Republicans. From what little I cared about politics, this didn't make a lot of sense to me, since Grandfather had a working class background and I understood that the Democrats were the party of the working class, something that Mrs. Hambly made aggressively clear to me one day out on her back porch. Furthermore, Pam, Mary, Nancy, and other kids in the neighborhood liked Kennedy, and so I was prompted to ask Grandmother why she and Grandfather were Republicans.

"When your Grandfather came to America," she said, "he asked which party Abraham Lincoln belonged to, and when he learned he was a Republican, he said 'That's good enough for me.'"

Case closed.

Forever.

So I, too, decided to prefer Nixon over Kennedy. As did my mother and aunt—while Larry remained silent on the subject, as he usually did on every subject. No big political discussions took place among us, though Mother decided Kennedy was most handsome.

The superficiality of all this infringed upon cognizance of my family's politics. After the first presidential debate in late September, I liked Kennedy and was particularly interested in the part of the debate involving two small islands named Quemoy and Matsu. Nixon claimed the islands were included in a treaty of protection the United States had signed with the Nationalist Chinese in Taiwan, and he accused Kennedy of weakness towards Communist aggression. It became clear that Kennedy was not prepared to go to war with China over Quemoy and Matsu, which I thought sensible, although the majority of the country agreed with Nixon about not backing down.

The election that fall coincided with my entry into eighth grade at Nathan Eckstein, and it was cool to wear small political buttons on shirts and blouses. Insofar as campaign issues, no one seemed to know much. If one's family was a Democrat, one was a Democrat; Republicans, a Republican.

I put my Nixon button in the drawer and decided to remain neutral. Neither Grandfather nor Grandmother could precisely explain why Nixon *should* be president (other than Lincoln was a Republican and "that's good enough for me"). I learned from Mary Hambly that "if Lincoln were alive today, he'd be a Democrat." When I submitted this astonishing fact to Grandfather, he just looked at me. I did not have an explanation, being ignorant, so he just shrugged and turned his attention back to a book he was reading. I figured he hadn't rejected what I'd said, he just didn't know the answer and wasn't going to change. He'd made up his mind what party to support when young, given a bit of reflection along the way, and that decision was sacrosanct. Whatever issues came up in the debates would be shoehorned into that decision. I understood that when it came to my family's politics, any claim by a Republican would be construed as belonging to the correct side (because Lincoln was a Republican and "that's good enough for me"). No other consideration need be made. It was religion. As was Christian Science to Grandmother's life, as well as Aunt Peggy's.

Even after school started again, I spent weekends with my grandparents and aunt, the neighborhood attraction still being street football.

I don't recall if Grandfather had put little wheels under the Zenith TV or if it came with them, but at some point he began to move the TV on its wheels around the corner of the archway between the living and dining rooms so that during dinner he could watch the six o'clock news with Walter Cronkite. He began to hush our table conversation so he could hear; then Grandmother began to serve dinner a little earlier than six.

It must have been a Friday evening that fall when Aunt Peggy's narrative trailed into Walter Cronkite's, for she was in an indignant, emotional state about how she was again being treated at the bank by her boss, one appropriately named Mr. Quarrells. These narratives had become fairly routine, especially at the end of a long week at work for Aunt Peggy. She was a single woman working her way up in the Auditing Department, and over the years, although she was promoted little by little, a new man who knew less than she would often be hired as her boss. As I came to realize, there was very little a "career gal" (as Peggy referred to herself) could do about being treated as an underling, or passed over for promotion. Grandmother, Grandfather, and I listened to her at the dinner table with sympathy while she expressed consternation between bites of potatoes and gravy. Mr. Quarrells, a petty autocrat, brought out the most anger in Aunt Peggy, the details of which changed from week to week and faded quickly from my memory. What could she do? What could *we* do? What could Walter Cronkite do? wondered Grandfather who kept glancing at the TV. Nothing. So Peggy put her thick round glasses back on after airing her resentment at the latest horrors from work and watched the election news with Grandfather and the rest of us.

On one of these early fall weekends at my grandparents', I was in my bedroom when Grandmother called upstairs to say my mother was on the phone and wanted to talk to me. I went into Peggy's bedroom where the phone sat on a small table in front of a side window. I picked it up, and Mother told me the news that my father Vance had died.

He had finally succumbed to the multiple sclerosis, and yet the news was unexpected. Vance's existence was a suddenly empty piece of my life whose importance I had always had trouble relating to. Now my mother was on the phone saying how much he had loved me. She mainly referred, I assumed, to the first two years of my life when he and she were still married, though her voice revealed none of the emotion I might have expected, only sympathy for me. I felt she was waiting for my reaction. I was merely dazed and didn't know what to say.

"I wanted to let you know," she said.

I searched for something to say other than "Oh, that's sad," and failed. We said goodbye.

I wasn't especially sad. I just didn't know what to think. My father had been a peculiar figure in my life, which might have been a cause for unhappiness; yet I accepted the news of his death without sorrow, perhaps by not comprehending the gravity of losing a father without having known him as he might have been.

Sunday evening I was driven back to my parents' apartment to start another day at school in the morning.

Mother's secretarial skills (fast typing, the ability to take shorthand, and a beginner's knowledge of medications because of her various dietary and digestive maladies) had been rewarded with a job at Harborview Hospital. She was able to drop me off at school in the morning so I didn't have to take that hellish bus ride. Larry bought her a tiny used car—a '58 Fiat 1100 sedan, to drive to the hospital on Seattle's First Hill. Uncharacteristically, Larry had been reading a couple of magazines about the practicality of foreign cars and the joys of small British and Italian sports cars; but all that ever came of it was the little Fiat 1100, essentially a motorized tin can with seats.

§ 28

John Kennedy won the election! After his inaugural address in January, the very atmosphere of the country seemed to change. Renewal and youthful energy was in the air. Kennedy's "New Frontier" meant something, the space race had begun, and rock & roll was still in its prime. That fall before the inauguration, "The Twist" became a hit by Chubby

Checker, and although its initial release reached #1 on *Billboard*, it was for just a week. The dance craze was in its early stages and hadn't really caught on yet. We eighth graders were still learning "the swing," still the standard pop dance in the '50s, and there was an upcoming school dance in the Nathan Eckstein gym. Elvis was still cranking out hit after hit, a number of pop singers all named Bobby (Bobby Darin, Bobby Rydell, Bobby Vee) had become the rock mainstream, The Shirelles were paving the way for The Supremes and other Black girl harmony groups, Kathy Young sang "A Thousand Stars," and I bought a 45 of "Poetry in Motion" by Johnny Tillotson on the Cadence label. It was almost impossible to keep up with all the music, pop and rock, whose intentions seemed to be to make everyone feel good and glad to be alive. Optimism was everywhere.

Nathan Eckstein Junior High was a big school with hundreds of students, I was thirteen, and my attraction toward lovely girls was augmented by more sensual emotions. This was not a mystery to me by this time. Nor had these more libidinous feelings supplanted my captivation of the primary attractions of beauty, intelligence, and charm. Yet I was exposed to the more primitive revelations shared by my male classmates, including knowledge of *Playboy* magazine foldouts and the sharing of certain bookmarked passages in paperback novels being sneakily passed around. Language played a role, too. But an amusing incident regarding the onset of puberty had occurred at the end of the summer when Ronny, my sometimes neighborhood nemesis, said he had something to show me.

Now, the last time he had something to show me, you'll recall, was when he'd locked me in his garage. No way was I going to fall for one of his tricks again. But instead of raising that sort of suspicion, he simply led me down to Cowen Park a couple of blocks away from my grandparents' house. What was he up to?

We went down the slope into the park and walked along the trail at the bottom of the ravine. The hard dirt trail led under the 15th Ave. Bridge and eastward at the bottom of the ravine between steep embankments of trees. After a couple of minutes, Ronny left the trail and found a particular tree he pointed to, then proceeded to climb it. Lifting himself up on the first large branch, he reached into a natural hole in the tree trunk and removed a wrinkled brown paper bag. I stood mystified below while he climbed back down and motioned me off to the side.

Pausing for effect, he withdrew from inside the limp bag a "girlie" magazine by the name of *Nugget*, and looked at me with a how-about-that (!) kind of expression. He began flipping pages to show me photos of very sexy naked women. This was truly amazing, I thought, not because of the taboo, or that I was attracted and fascinated by the steamy photos (which I was) but because Ronny had actually hidden this magazine *inside a tree trunk in Cowen Park*. It may have been the nuttiest thing I'd witnessed in my entire life up to that point.

After we gawked at the photos, one page at a time, Ronny carefully put the magazine back in the paper bag and climbed back up the tree. He replaced the bag, peered into the hole to see if it was secure, then climbed back down. He seemed so proud of himself that I did not thank him. As we walked home, I considered the length to which he'd gone to hide his sin and knew that he couldn't take any chance whatsoever that his Mormon parents, let alone his younger sister, might discover a *Nugget* magazine, even in the best hiding place at home. I guess I felt embarrassed for him that he had to go to all this trouble. Perhaps a bit chagrined myself, too, for I had as yet no such desirable magazine to ogle. Finding ways to look at beautiful naked women in 1960 was a daunting task for a teenager. Even *Playboy* was kept off the magazine racks and behind the counter at most places, and you had to be an adult to buy one. Embarrassment would have prevented me anyway.

Investigating one's feelings about sex was a struggle. Having sex on one's mind, though quite infrequent at my age, was supposed to be bad, and there was no "sex ed" in junior high.

Within this dubious context, the first girl I was ambiguously attracted to in the eighth grade happened to be sitting next to me in Washington State History class in the back row of a portable behind the school. I normally didn't choose to sit in the back row of a class, but here I was, and in the seat to my left was a pretty, petite blond, hair pulled tightly around the sides of her head into a short ponytail, with a nice heart-shaped face, a slightly v-shaped chin, and an attitude that might be described as, well . . . spicy. I was later informed by some guy that the young lady I was next to had been intimate with a college man. (He did not use the word intimate.) In any case, how it started I didn't know, but for about a week she and I began to whisper a certain taboo word (the most notorious word) to one another while in class. Well, not exactly *to* one another. More like the idea that the word could *be said* by a boy and a girl. It was nothing more than shared mischief. Neither of us developed an attraction to each other, or if so, vaguely, although I found her intriguing. She seemed cool and inaccessible, and I had no idea if what I'd heard about her was true. I frankly doubted it. I suspected that her diminutive, fetching looks and subtle hauteur caused unfounded speculation among idiots. After all, she was thirteen. . . . Then again, one of the great pioneers of rock & roll, Jerry Lee Lewis, had nearly destroyed his career by marrying his thirteen-year-old cousin when he was twenty-two. What did *I* know about such things? In any case, the girl in question and I stopped swearing for fun after a week or so. The incident was totally out of character for me, an anomaly that allowed her and me to simply flaunt a taboo; for I didn't like swearing—didn't like to hear it even among friends. What had come over me—over us?—I couldn't say. Apparently a release from inhibition.

Around that time, one of the first "adult" TV dramas premiered that fall (no swearing on TV then). *Route 66* became a favorite of mine as its two lead characters, Tod and Buzz, drove a Chevy Corvette convertible around the country in search of adventure—although they never seemed to actually drive on US Route 66! These young male characters, played by Martin Milner and George Maharis, made pretty good role models for me as they got jobs here and there, bantered intelligently with one another, saved girls in distress, and dealt with a variety of dramatic adult situations. And that car was so cool!

Two other TV shows came along that fall that engaged my attention: *Checkmate* turned out to be one of the best TV detective shows, with the interesting premise of a detective agency (Checkmate Inc.) that specialized in preventing crimes before they occurred. The other show was one of the great comedies of TV history: *The Andy Griffith Show*. As noted, I'd seen Griffith as a country bumpkin in the film *No Time for Sergeants*. He'd also done a serious movie, *A Face in the Crowd*, about the rise of a corrupt know-nothing country bumpkin politician. His primary fame came from a couple of hilarious comedy records wherein—in that same country bumpkin persona—he described sporting events and the plots of Shakespeare plays. On *The Andy Griffith Show*, however, he had a relatively mediocre role as a sheriff and straight man to comedian Don Knotts who played his skinny, high-strung deputy, Barney Fife, a character that became a TV and cultural icon. This was a show I never missed, and neither did my parents or grandparents.

Back in school during the day, my favorite class was Mechanical Drawing. I learned how to use a T-square, triangle, compass, and three-sided wooden ruler with various scale markings to draw cubes, rectangles, wedges, and various geometrical objects. We were graded on neatness and the completion of tasks that got more complicated as the semester rolled on. Sitting at a drafting table near me was my friend Bruce from the Laurelon Terrace neighborhood. After school, we sometimes met at Zopf's Drug Store soda fountain for our usual Green Rivers, cherry phosphates, or chocolate milkshakes to die for. Why were the latter so good? "It's the quality of the vanilla ice cream," said Elsie (the good looking middle-aged woman I could hardly call a soda jerk).

Mr. Smith was once again my science teacher, and sometime after the first of the year I decided to design, and possibly build, a submarine. I had been reading about David Bushnell's Revolutionary War submersible *Turtle*, the first submersible to be used in combat. The year was 1775, and the idea was for the *Turtle* to go underwater and attach bombs to the hulls of British warships. No ships were sunk or damaged by the *Turtle*, but in looking at the diagrams of the craft, I figured it wouldn't be too hard to build a small submarine of a different design out of wood framing, plywood, electric motor, batteries, and a surplus bomber aircraft canopy for the nose. I studied all the aspects, including how to calculate water pressure per square inch, how to achieve neutral buoyancy, and how to drop a weight to enable the thing to surface if the pumps failed.

I made a detailed drawing and one day placed it on Mr. Smith's desk as I left class, expecting admiration the following day for the work I'd done, which was considerable. During the process my grandmother and Aunt were frightened that I might actually try to build the damn thing. I told them I planned to launch it down at Green Lake. My stepfather, in one of his rare attentions to something intellectual of mine, seemed a bit proud of my mathematical calculations, although he doubted the frame and plywood construction.

The next day, after the bell when class was dismissed, I came up to Mr. Smith's desk. He smiled and reached into his drawer for my design drawing.

"Phil, this is very interesting."

"Thanks!"

He looked at it. "What do you want me to do with this?"

"Uh, well . . ."

He examined the design without commenting about anything specific. "It's certainly very interesting, but it doesn't fit into any of the assignments."

I wasn't sure how to respond, but my mind instantly went to the idea of what was known as "extra credit"—something pertaining to the class generally, although not specific classwork. But I defaulted to Mr. Smith and couldn't bring myself to suggest it.

"Thanks for showing this to me, Phil." He handed it back to me.

"Sure."

That was it.

I rolled up my design, slightly perplexed, left the classroom, and put it back into my hall locker.

For a while, I continued to dream of building the little submarine, but I finally felt foolish and realized I had no way to actually accomplish this. It was also clear I would not get any credit or encouragement from my teacher for studying the problem further, or from gaining more knowledge. So I put the drawing and a notebook of calculations in my desk at home and did not look at them again until they were finally discarded.

§ 29

My English teacher was sixtyish, dark haired, solidly built, be-spectacled Mr. Abbey who delighted in describing comedy scenes, in detail, from Charlie Chaplin movies. We had to memorize "The Village Blacksmith" by Henry Wadsworth Longfellow:

> Under a spreading chestnut-tree
>   The village smithy stands;
> The smith, a mighty man is he,
>   With large and sinewy hands,
> And the muscles of his brawny arms
>   Are strong as iron bands.
>
> His hair is crisp, and black, and long;
>   His face is like the tan;
> His brow is wet with honest sweat,
>   He earns what e'er he can,
> And looks the whole world in the face,
>   For he owes not any man.
>
> (Etc.)

What the purpose of this assignment was I couldn't quite figure. Maybe it was merely the task of memorization. Mr. Abbey also enjoyed reciting "A Fence or an Ambulance" by Joseph Malins (1895).

> 'Twas a dangerous cliff, as they freely confessed,
> Though to walk near its crest was so pleasant;
> But over its terrible edge there had slipped
> A duke, and full many a peasant;
>
> So the people said something would have to be done,
> But their projects did not all tally.
> Some said, "Put a fence around the edge of the cliff;"
> Some, "An ambulance down in the valley."
>
> (Etc.)

Oddly enough, I would always remember the lesson of this poem, its metaphorical depiction of an aspect of human nature, and its conclusion.

More so, my attention was captured by a girl in Mr. Abbey's class. It took only a while before I was in love with her. She sat in the far left row near the windows, about three seats back. She had long, raven black hair with the unusual combination of blue eyes—what I later understood to derive from Irish ancestry—and matched to a soft, white complexion and warm smile. She often wore white blouses with those iconic Chantilly lace collars, along with tight skirts, and she had a somewhat more mature figure than her equally young peers.

But there was something even more striking, personal to me alone, as I attempted to understand the intensity of my attraction to her. By degrees, as I saw her out of the corner of my eye, or as she came and went before or after class, I was struck by the vague but nonetheless discernible resemblance to the actress Myrna Fahey, the beautiful black-haired, white-complexioned Madeline Usher of my favorite Edgar Allan Poe movie. A Gothic heroine, the reminder of which must have touched something erotic deep within my subconscious was unavoidable; yet the image was allayed by the young lady's bright smile, not to mention a subtle cluster of light freckles about her nose and cheeks. She was an Irish beauty. Her name was Candice, and the nickname Candy was incongruous to the persona my mind created for her. Perhaps the most endearing feature of her personality was a seeming lack of self-awareness as to her obvious attractiveness. She did not seem to socialize with other popular girls who clustered here and there, and when I saw her in the hall, she was often with a very plain-looking girl I eventually took to be her best friend. To me, this embellished her beauty with an element of virtue. How might I plan to get to know her? The enterprise seemed impossible. Eighth grade boys barely spoke to girls, let alone asked them for dates. Whatever thoughts—daydreams?—I had along these lines would have to wait until an appropriate circumstance or simple opportunity.

I became aware of an interesting trait among the good looking girls: Some seemed to understand the effect or influence they had on boys as the result of their feminine charms, while others, equally pretty, seemed naive or even puzzled by it. The latter were all the more attractive—I daresay sweeter—for being unselfconscious about their looks. I suspected that the object of my new infatuation was of the latter type, but one could never really tell for sure.

All such thoughts came and went, replaced by ordinary activities. Sometime over that winter my Aunt Peggy took me bowling. She and a couple of her girlfriends were league bowlers. And on most Saturday mornings she and I watched *Championship Bowling* on television at my grandparents' house. Over the course of the show I had watched with fascination the likes of Ned Day, Andy Varipapa, Steve Nagy, and other professional bowlers competing against each other for the top prize. Bowling was hugely popular, for it provided family and friends a unique social venue. More than a half-dozen bowling alleys shared the north Seattle area alone: Sunset Bowl, Green Lake Bowl, Village Lanes, Kenmore Lanes, Leilani Lanes, Lake City Bowl, Robin Hood Lanes (in Edmonds), and others. I quickly learned how to score the game, so I was able to go bowling with friends as well as my aunt. After school, Bruce and I walked from Laurelon Terrace down 45th to the Village Lanes near the U.W. Neither of us had our own bowling balls or shoes, but we did OK with what the alley provided. Between users, rental shoes were put inside some sort of box with a glowing purple light that was supposed to kill germs. It was weird.

I read *A Tale of Two Cities* by Charles Dickens. The opening sentence was: "It was the best of times, it was the worst of times, it was the age of wisdom, it was the age of foolishness, it was the epoch of belief, it was the epoch of incredulity, it was the season of light, it was the season of darkness, it was the spring of hope, it was the winter of despair." I memorized the famous first part of that sentence, the part everyone knew.

It was true.

In April, *Vostok I* carried Yuri Gagarin around the earth in a single orbit; he was the first person to do so; and about a month later, America sent Alan Shepard via a Mercury space capsule into sub-orbital space for fifteen-minutes. We were still behind the Russians but starting to catch up. A month earlier, most of the kids in my grandparents' neighborhood happily went to see Disney's latest comedy, *The Absent-Minded Professor* starring Fred MacMurray. *The Guns of Navarone* was the year's biggest hit, and my mother, stepfather, and I went to see it at the Northgate Theater after dinner out. On the radio, Del Shannon sang "Runaway," The Highwaymen sang their one-hit precursor to the folk music era, "Michael Row the Boat Ashore," and The Tokens did "The Lion Sleeps Tonight," while Ricky Nelson sang "Travelin' Man" on *The Ozzie and Harriet Show*.

Half of the world I experienced never seemed to really change. It was variations on a theme, and it was the best of times—the records, movies, TV shows, board games, outdoor sports, and sharing it all with neighborhood friends. Also, President Kennedy had begun to give history-making live TV press conferences, displaying a sophisticated wit and charisma that did much to bring about the fanciful notion of "Camelot."

On a personal level, especially while with my grandparents on weekends, I was cognizant of the special love I had for my grandmother Emma who had cared for me as much as had my mother. She had been through so much in her life, having lost two children, yet retained a loving resilience and kindness as she went about her job as chief homemaker—a job she took seriously and with remarkable stamina. Her hands were neither particularly soft nor calloused after decades of housework, including daily dishwashing, and when she placed her hand on my forehead to check for fever during a cold or flu, it was remarkably comforting. If she spent any time outdoors during winter, her fingers would turn white for lack of circulation, even in the mittens she wore. Indoors again, I would sometimes hold or rub them for a minute to warm them up, wondering if the blood might decide to vacate them permanently. She always put on her brown-plaid overcoat when taking a sack of garbage out to the garbage cans near the short back fence next to the garage. We all tried to take turns with this, but she usually did it spontaneously herself. As for the kitchen, she would mostly chase us out, though Peggy often helped with washing the dishes. I rarely did. Before and after meals, Grandfather and I pretty much stayed out of the way. Grandmother taught me how to cook my breakfast. I sometimes helped her make cookies, as well, but she never considered any of us responsible for such things. Even Aunt Peggy never took much part in the cooking and never became a good cook herself. I always thought that was a little odd. Grandmother was in charge, and her busy routines around the house left the rest of us feeling slightly useless at times, which at my age of self-absorption was not unwelcome. I just went with it. Nothing much was routinely expected of me other than my usual mowing the lawn most of the year and keeping my room in order.

That's not to say the family wasn't always busy with one thing or another, and there was time to appreciate each other's individuality, sometimes argue with each other, or sympathize when things went awry. The unusual nature of my

upbringing wasn't entirely lost on me. The boomer generation was rarely blessed with such an extended family household. Here was my grandfather Nels, thinning white hair,
sitting in his flocked velvet chair with a book in his hand
while my grandmother went about her daily routine including
her TV soap operas in the afternoon ("Time for my programs," she would say), and then my aunt coming home from
work before dinner with stories of her day at the bank. We
were all close to one another other. So while I was in junior
high, I continued to shuttle back and forth between my parents' apartment on weekdays and my grandparents' house on
most weekends. My upbringing was odd, I guess I knew it,
but I never thought much about it.

I should describe something about the bedroom I kept at
my grandparents', since it became my primary refuge. It was
located on the upstairs northwest back corner of the house,
with a side window facing toward the house next door. My
double bed was against the wall longways by the side window,
while over the foot of the bed, the ceiling formed a sloping
wedge that conformed to the roof-line next to the room's
wide central bay. The bay was of one large double-hung window in the middle with a view facing west across the city. On
the south side of the room, a dresser was placed against the
wall, and to its right was the door to a deep closet tucked under the opposite slope of the roof. The hardwood floors were
made of fir, not untypical of old Seattle houses (this one built
in 1906). The solid paneled bedroom door had a large glass
doorknob that was fashioned to look like a big diamond. An
old-fashioned glass ceiling light illuminated the room and was
turned off and on by antiquated push-button plungers to the
left of the door. My desk, the duplicate one with the "pigeon
holes" Grandfather had built, resided to the right of the central window, and another bureau and small table were opposite, the table being next to the bed. My model ships and

planes took up every available horizontal surface. From the bed, I could reach a '50s-style radio placed near me on the table. My initial disappointment was that the room had been painted a dull lavender by some previous owner. My grandparents never took the time to repaint, and I never bothered to ask permission; I barely noticed it after a few months. It was my own room, and that was enough.

Outside of this refuge, as well as the comforting zone of my extended family, the other half of the world involved my increasing awareness of the worst of times, starting with the dark history of World War II just before my birth. The segregation and racism in the South was increasingly coming onto the six-o'clock news, therefore a reminder of the incident I'd witnessed in south Seattle—but it was still the best of times for those of us who were white and middle class. We never saw a Negro in person in north Seattle. We were mostly unaware, but of particular note that spring were the Freedom Riders who went on a bus tour in protest against southern segregation. Their bus was firebombed in Alabama, and they were viciously attacked by the KKK with the *complicity* of the police. Arriving in Birmingham, many were beaten nearly to death by a white mob who particularly targeted other whites who were riding with the Negros. I was shocked to learn that the police were on the side of the mob, and this represented a loss of innocence for me. We were taught to respect the police ("officer friendly" and all that when we were very young) but this created a dissonance I carried with me from then on. The Kennedy Administration intervened on the side of the Riders, but it was an ongoing situation that was quickly becoming the most intense period of the civil rights movement and a test for the new president. My grandparents, mother, and stepfather watched the crisis unfold on the six-o'clock news with little comment; although because of television, this harrowing struggle was coming into living rooms in graphic detail and could not fail to elicit emotions, stated or not. I figured that my family's reluctance to discuss it was that, after all, these things were happening quite far away. Or were their feelings mixed? My family had come from Montana, my step-father from Kansas. I didn't know their exact feelings and didn't press it. Eventually my aunt expressed sympathy for the Negros ("What they are doing to them is terrible") and I knew by my previous experience in the industrial district that my stepfather was in some significant way anti-racist. His atti-tude, or what I knew of it, along with the shock of the TV news, was the one I chose as my own. I knew that in such in-stances I had to take sides, and it was becoming clear from what I'd learned of the US Constitution, which side I must take.

§ 30

On a Friday, my mother picked me up in her little Fiat after school to take me, as usual, to my grandparents' for the weekend. I plopped my books and notebook into the back seat as we crested the 75th St. hill and began to descend steeply down to the west.

The brakes failed.

Mother screamed, clung desperately onto the wheel and began rapidly pumping the brakes. I could do nothing but sit in paralyzed terror. The car gathered momentum, the hill was steep and long, and it was clear the outcome would be very bad. But Mother didn't lose her head. She took a gamble and turned the car to the right into the next side street, going way too fast, but we didn't roll over, and came to a halt halfway along the residential block. We sat catching our breaths. I then got out and pushed the car on the level street over to the curb. Mother was in a state of near collapse, but she got hold of herself, opened the door, got out, then walked to the nearest house and found a resident who let her use the phone. Larry came to get us, the little Fiat was towed away, and Mother refused to drive that car ever again. It was the end of my stepfather's infatuation with small foreign cars. He and Judy would find a way to share the big Plymouth until another car could be found for her.

The next "automobile" incident we had was on a day I rode my bike up to Zopf's Drug Store. (By that time, I had a new black Raleigh three-speed made in England) and when I got home I put the bike into the common cellar of our apartment building. I walked cheerfully up the back steps into our kitchen and was greeted by my mother—who was nearly hysterical. She tearfully grabbed and hugged me. "What happened?! What happened?! Are you all right?!"

I had no idea what she was talking about.

"I called the police three times!"

I looked at her with amazed perplexity while she stepped back, staring as if uncertain it was me. "I got a call," she said, "from a boy who told me you'd been hit by a car!"

I was stunned.

"No, it's a lie," I countered. "Someone was playing a practical joke."

"Oh, God, who would call me to make a joke like *that*?"

"I don't know."

I was furious, for it was no joke at all. But certain kids my age thought differently and were probably snickering at the terror they'd caused. I couldn't guess and never found out who'd made the call. Mother called the school the next day to report the incident, but what could they do?

§ 31

In April, our new President, with the help of hundreds of Cuban exiles, tried to invade the island of Cuba in order to depose the communist dictator Fidel Castro. The attempt, known as The Bay of Pigs Invasion, was bungled, and hundreds of lives were lost. Kennedy took full responsibility, but the US was chastised and embarrassed. I and others were impressed by Kennedy's public apology for his failure. Although he'd been misled by his generals, he took full responsibility, and since he was a young and charismatic president, most of the country forgave him, and he never again trusted his military advisers as completely as he did when making the decision to invade Cuba. No one knew, of course, how this experience would affect future developments between the communist world—especially the powerful Soviet Union—and the US.

But for someone like me, just turning fourteen, world events were still distant, abstract, and primarily news on television.

While in Mr. Abbey's English class, I noticed that the girl of my dreams had been absent for several days. At the end of class, Mr. Abbey asked if anyone lived near her, and if so, could they take some make-up assignments to her so she wouldn't fall too far behind.

My hand shot up like a rocket. I had no idea where she lived, but no way was I going to miss this opportunity that had unexpectedly fallen into my lap. I went to Mr. Abbey's desk where, with what I took to be a knowing smile, he handed me her assignments along with her address. (Having her address in my hand seemed like a small miracle.) She lived only a few blocks from school, eastward down the 75th St. hill, and the address had an apartment number.

I left the classroom and put her assignments into my locker while waiting for school to let out. Watching the clock until the final bell seemed endless—as did the half-mile or so walk down 75th to the apartment complex where she lived. The complex of pitched-roof buildings was in the same 1940s style as my own. I might tell her we had something in common. I might start a conversation. But how would that lead anywhere? No, maybe I could talk about English class. Or school. Or . . . nothing came to mind that could lead to anything. Besides, she'd probably be recovering from the flu or something. Still as I walked toward the apartments, I hoped that some hint of attraction might be initiated because of my gallant delivery of her make-up assignments.

In a mild state of mental paralysis, I rang the doorbell. And it was she who opened the door. It opened only part way, yet there she was, beautiful with her pale, lightly freckled face and long black hair, standing in the narrowly open doorway and wearing a long flannel nightgown. She continued to hold the door open only a foot or so, and then I heard a woman's voice in the background: "Who is it?"

"Just a boy from school."

I smiled without trying to look dumb and handed her the folder. "Mr. Abbey asked for someone to bring these make-up assignments to you, so I volunteered."

She took the folder. "Oh, thanks."

"I guess those are some assignments you can work on until you come back to class—so you don't get too far behind."

The voice in the background sounded impatiently: "What does he want?"

Candy turned her head. "He brought some homework." Then looked back at me.

"I hope you aren't too ill," I said.

"I don't think so," she said.

"Is it the flu?" I asked. Nothing else came to mind now

that the circumstances had become slightly awkward.

"I don't know," she answered as if kind of puzzled by the question.

The conversation had turned a bit odd. My mind went blank.

"Well, thanks," she said.

"No problem."

She closed the door.

I went to catch a bus back to Laurelon Terrace.

When I told my mother about my encounter with the girl I liked, and that the girl didn't seem to know why she was ill, Mother thought for a moment, then said, "She's probably having her period."

§ 32

Spring had me looking toward the end of the school year, but this destination was a bit far off. My birthday arrived on May 11, and Mother and Stepfather gave me what I had asked for: an Aurora Model Motoring set with HO scale cars (a blue convertible Jaguar and a black convertible Mercedes) that ran on two-lane black plastic track and was the ecstatic beginning of my enthusiasm for slot car racing. The set was designed to use as a realistic roadway along with an HO scale train layout, but of course everyone used the speed controllers to race the two cars. From that time on, one didn't merely have to watch a train go around a track, but could race a car in miniature against an opponent. The early Aurora cars had fussy motors with a thin metal tab that vibrated against the downside of a horizontal cylindrical gear driving the rear wheels. It was weird, but the cars worked well, at least most of the time, and provided hours of fun while one developed racing skills. The controllers were beige-colored plastic cases with chrome plastic "steering" wheels operating an internal rheostat that controlled speed. The steering wheels had a tendency to break because they weren't designed for the heavy use of slam-bang acceleration and braking. Nevertheless, my Lionel train was boxed away in favor of expanding the Model Motoring set downstairs on the big, long table my grandfather had built for me in the basement of my grandparents' house. My most enthusiastic opponent turned out to be Stevie Mettler (now about ten), and we spent hours racing each other around a track I began to design and decorate with multi-level terrain, scenery, and other items that created a table-top reality.

Boys' or girls' lives often revolved around miniature worlds—toys, games, model planes and ships, trains, dolls, doll houses, and other hobbies that in the mind simulated reality and a figurative participation in the adult world—or what seemed to be that world. And the closer such things could be made realistic appearing, the better. The 1950s version of the game Clue, for example, had a board which appeared to look down into a real mansion with realistically designed rooms and hallways. My Aurora Model Motoring cars were beautifully done renditions of actual cars, and the design allowed the cars to "drift" while taking the curves, spin out if the driver failed to slow down, and respond to occasional cleaning and maintenance. Girls' dollhouses (aside from the "Barbie" sets boys made fun of) were sometimes like works of art rather than toys. Model ships, planes, and cars were praised for the most detail. Although these things depended on one's imagination for engagement, they were nonetheless real things rather than ephemeral images on a screen.

Another eighth-grade dance in the Eckstein gym was scheduled for near the end of the school year. I had missed the earlier one, but in the meantime I'd taken "swing" lessons in a Laurelhurst church basement near the top of NE 45th and so decided to attend the dance. Eckstein hired a local disc jockey to play records, and almost everyone came to the dance alone, girls hanging out together in clumps, boys like-wise. I was on the lookout for Candy, who had returned to class some time ago, but how was I to get the nerve to approach her for a dance? In fact, no one was dancing. None of us boys wanted to be the first to "break the ice," so to speak, ask a girl to dance, and go out on the gym floor. But soon, the problem was solved by the music teacher, Mr. Budelman, who had the girls line up on one side of the gym, the boys line up on the opposite side. As the music began, we boys were supposed to cross the floor and ask a girl to dance. Once the girls lined up, I spotted Candy! She was standing next to the friend I'd seen her with in the hall a few times. I didn't know if she saw me. I doubted it. Of course, we'd known each other from class long before I'd delivered her homework; I meant nothing to her insofar as I could tell, though she had never been other than normal and friendly.

The music began, Mr. Budelman's instructions took hold, and us guys walked across the polished wood floor to choose a partner. I headed toward Candy but was beaten out by a crew-cut athlete who'd been better positioned and was faster. I ended up choosing Candy's friend, next to her, which was OK, since none of the other boys seemed likely to ask her.

Everyone could do the swing, and the top-40 hits played over the loud speaker system were, of course, danceable—recent hits like "New Orleans" by Gary U.S. Bonds, "Blue Moon" by the Marcels, and even Henry Mancini's "Peter Gunn Theme," the latter of which was requested a second time. After the first dance, the boys and girls returned to their sides of the gym, lined up, and the routine was repeated, this time a "girl's choice."

I stood there awkwardly, anticipating the next dance, and when the record started, the girls walked toward us and (was it possible?) I saw Candy coming across toward me. She reached out her hand, I took it, and we went out on the floor and did the swing together. I held her around the waist during the first steps of the dance, the feeling being indescribable, and then twirled her under my arm as the dance progressed. We danced apart, then back together again, and finally apart as the song ended.

After a couple of minutes I was able to zip across the floor and choose her for the next dance. I don't think we said a word to one another. She chose me the next time, too, and as she came toward me I quietly counted down "3 . . . 2 . . .1" which she apparently heard as she took my hand and said curiously with a smile, "What was *that* about?"

I didn't know, I was slightly embarrassed, and I guess I'd spontaneously needed to reassure myself that it was I she really intended to choose, that it was a kind of inevitability, and that I wasn't dreaming this. We did a slow dance. The song was "Sleepwalk" by Santo and Johnny. I again held her, not too tightly, but having my arm around her and holding her hand, this unforgettable Irish brunette with blue eyes. How simple it was, yet how unique to feel her presence under my arm and hand. I believed she had picked me those two or three times because, as I'd noticed before, she was not particularly social and wasn't much familiar with other boys at the dance. I was a good choice because we'd sort of already met. I did not suppose that she felt much toward me. But it was enough that she was dancing with me just before the end of the school year.

On one of the last days, I happened to see her walking down the sidewalk just as she'd begun to walk home. I decided to catch up, but casually, of course, as if I was going in the same direction.

"Hi."

"Oh, hi," she said.

We walked together for a couple of minutes.

"What will you be doing this summer?" I asked.

"Nothing much, I think."

"You live in an apartment like the one I live in. But I stay with my grandparents during the summer." I struggled to find something else to say. "I have this idea that your family is Irish. Mine are Norwegian."

"Yes, that's right. How did you know? My ancestors came here because of the Irish potato famine."

"Potato famine? That sounds weird."

"I guess it does."

"Well, ah . . ."

"People were starving in Ireland at that time."

"Because there weren't enough potatoes?"

"I guess so."

"Well, how about that."

She smiled at me.

"Are you going home now?"

"Yes. I have some things to do."

"I see. Well then . . . take it easy." (I love you! I love you! Can I see you this summer!)

"Bye now."

"Bye," I said, giving her a little wave as I jaywalked across the street. I went back the other way to catch the bus, my heart pounding because I didn't have the nerve to ask if I could see her over the summer. It was too early for me. Too early, and I was too shy at fourteen, to ask a girl such a thing.

§ 33

Another opportunity I let go by about that time was learning to play the clarinet. I had struggled and struggled to play at least one page of music and not blow a squeaky note through that black funnel of terror. I just couldn't seem to get my fingers to press hard enough, consistently enough, quickly

enough, to completely cover the holes without a little air leak-
ing through. The struggle and practice time wasn't worth the
effort to me, so I finally gave up. What I learned was a big
chunk of respect for musicians who did summon the patience
and motivation to overcome the difficulties. My mother was
undaunted, however, and decided to schedule me for piano
lessons.

Eighth grade was over with at last, and I was back at my
grandparents' in the Ravenna district for the summer. On one
of the first warm days, I walked over to Ted's house where
we began our occasional custom of sitting on his concrete
front steps—four or five steps facing busy 65th St.—to ob-
serve passersby in cars and on the sidewalk and, among intellectual things, discuss the science fiction we'd read. Although
Ted was three or four years my senior, we developed a
friendship based on the relative rarity, as I mentioned, of
meeting another person who'd read the classic authors of the
genre: Arthur C. Clarke (*Childhood's End*), Isaac Asimov (*I,
Robot*), Ray Bradbury (*The Martian Chronicles*), and Robert
Heinlein (*Starship Troopers*), and of course H. G. Wells and
Jules Verne. Our reading was limited pretty much to key
works, but we'd also read a few authors not in common and
were able to describe them. Ted was more familiar with Robert Heinlein than I, for example, and with A. E. Van Vogt,
the latter of which had written a novel, *The Voyage of the Space
Beagle* (named after the ship Darwin sailed on) that would
eventually open my mind to a key theme of science fiction—
interstellar exploration and potential encounters with hostile
alien life and the boundlessness of space.

That summer, but for a couple of unexpected events, was
much like the others I've described. Although it was now
1961, the change of decade did not engender an equal change
in culture. A hot rod would sometimes appear driving down

65th, people still went to drive-in movies and restaurants, cafes were independent and unique, gas stations still had guys who filled your tank, cleaned your windshield, checked your oil, and adjusted your tire pressure if you asked. News on TV paced itself along the timeline of current events, but neither I nor the kids in the neighborhood experienced much change in everyday life or in the overall mood. Certainly I was growing older, more aware of the adult world, and was becoming more adult myself, but that particular summer seemed forever idyllic and easy-going. When not watching favorite reruns on TV, the younger of us still played kick-the-can or hide-and-seek on those late summer nights, the last year I was young enough to play them. I was getting taller and starting to feel a bit conspicuous running along the sidewalks, through the alleys, and over the fences. Not, however, for street football during the daytime hours; but those games would begin closer to fall. We still played charades.

The first of the two interesting events of that spring or summer was my Aunt Peggy's purchase of a new Magnavox stereo console, she having decided to accept the stereo LPs that began selling in record stores back in 1958. Peggy had foregone LPs altogether while depending on her large collection of 78s. The walnut "lowboy" Magnavox was fairly wide, but not too much so, with cloth-covered speaker panels on each end, bass drivers facing outward at the sides, tweeters facing front. The left-hand top cover slid back to reveal the record changer and AM/FM radio, and on the right was a bin for storing records. She placed this new stereo diagonally across the southeast corner of the living room, while the 1949 Magnavox remained just to the left of the fireplace. This fireplace, incidentally, I had once used (to the consternation of my grandmother) by pretending that a cardboard box was a house (cut out windows and doors) and my squirt gun a fire hose. I would set the "house" on fire, wait until it was well ablaze, then try to put it out. I was about the age of nine. (Sorry for the digression.)

Anyway, Aunt Peggy's new stereo got my spellbound attention, for it was a marvel of audio progress in which differing musical instruments or parts of an orchestra could come separately from either the left or right loudspeakers, creating a greater illusion of reality. The Magnavox came with its own "demo" record making use of the technology, mainly for some odd reason with bongo drums and percussion that someone figured would be impressive. And it was! Soon, we were buying stereo LPs at Standard Records on 65th St. Peggy bought a Doris Day album on Columbia, while my first was Henry Mancini's *Music from Peter Gunn* on RCA. On the cover of this album, the promise of stereo magic was delivered with a colorful band across of the top saying *"LIVING STEREO."* This was very cool, as was the music—my first ownership of recorded jazz outside of my "Twelfth Street Rag" 45 and "Sweet Georgia Brown" 78. I didn't have much money to spend, so 45 singles were still the way to go for hit songs.

I knew that the Hatch family had some mono LPs of "exotica" by Les Baxter—a musical fad of the '50s—with colorful album covers of ersatz Polynesian scenes and tiki statues. Stereophonic LPs were an irresistible advancement over those records, and by some form of coincidence, Les Baxter had also written the music for Roger Corman's movie *House of Usher*—though no soundtrack LP existed. Movie soundtracks were still relatively rare on records. Ted and Nora had an LP of Elmer Bernstein's *The Man with the Golden Arm*. (They also had the only rock LP of anyone in the neighborhood: Elvis Presley's 1956 debut album, with a raucous black-and-white photo of Elvis on the cover and his name in large pink and green letters—a classic album.)

Nevertheless, coincidence came full circle, and my second

stereo LP managed to mingle jazz with Edgar Allan Poe sans Les Baxter. I saw the album on display at Standard Records, and of course I could not resist Buddy Morrow and His Orchestra doing big-band "jazz impressions" of E.A.P. poems and short stories—another RCA *"LIVING STEREO"* LP—titled *Poe for Moderns.* I appreciated Standard Records more and more, for like all record stores at the time, it had listening booths for customers to try out records before they decided what to buy. The era of shrink wrap would end that. But owners Kay and Millard Smith kept their booths open throughout my youth by re-sealing records only played in their store. Because of the Smiths' listening booths, as I grew older I was able to eventually expand my musical horizons into classical music. For the present, I just played what caught my eye. And the third album that caught my eye was the TV soundtrack music for *Checkmate* by a new composer, Johnny Williams (yes, later John Williams), where in the listening booth I was taken with his music for a TV show I liked. I'd never heard anything quite like his synthesis of big-band jazz, pop, and the use of French horns on several tracks. Television music? Yes, but the TV studios in those days competed to find something new, different, well composed, potentially popular—and *Checkmate* was as uniquely enjoyable as Mancini's music for *Peter Gunn.*

§ 34

The second unusual event of the summer happened at about 3 AM one night when I was awakened in my upstairs back bedroom of my grandparents' house by the sound of rocks hitting the roof. It lasted only a moment, but I sat up in bed. What the hell? Was that psycho kid throwing rocks on the roof? In fact, he and Ronny had not long ago pestered my grandparents by ringing the front and back doorbells at the same time, over and over, until the two ran off. This led to another complaint to Ronny's father.

So here I am, sitting up in bed, alert in the late night, listening and wondering about the sound of rocks on the roof. Two or three strikes? Three or four? It didn't make sense. Neither my aunt, grandmother, or grandfather seemed to have been awakened, so I just kept listening. But no further sound was heard, so I went back to sleep.

"Did you hear rocks on the roof last night?" I asked at breakfast in the morning.

"No," said Aunt Peggy.

"What did you hear?" asked Grandmother, taking a bite of bacon.

"It was weird. I heard rocks hitting the roof."

"What time?" asked Grandfather sitting at the head of the table.

"The clock said about 3 AM."

"We must have all been sound asleep," said Peggy.

"Sure," I said.

"You weren't dreaming?" asked Grandmother.

"The sound woke me up."

"Hmm."

So it was one of those mysteries I assumed would go unexplained. Nevertheless, after breakfast I went back upstairs to my room and did something I'd been told not to do, which was to climb out of the rear window onto the small flat area of red composition roofing directly in front of the window, a kind of pocket area before the roof sloped steeply away. However, I slid down the slope to have a look in the back gutter. No rocks. Not surprising, since they might have rolled off anywhere. And I didn't want to take any more chances of falling.

I climbed back inside, closed and locked the window. Mystery unsolved.

Until later that morning. I went out the front door, down the front porch steps, not yet down the concrete steps to the sidewalk, and happened to glance over to my right because of an oddity in an area of green lawn—the level part near the southeast front corner of the house above the embankment slope.

A large hump of grass seemed to have formed there—a mound about eight inches high and two feet long. What was I looking at? Not a mole hole for sure. Much too large, no pile of dirt, and the turf was intact as if it had just bulged up. It was my sudden awareness of something perplexing, abnormal, unexpected, and vaguely disturbing for the lack of explanation. Was I seeing what I thought I saw? I stepped close to get a better look. Yes, this was a pretty damn big bulge in the lawn, and at the end of the hump facing toward the house, or rather to the narrow yard at the side, was a small hole, maybe two inches in diameter, as if a small object had punched or been shot into the turf with great force and shoved the very earth up from under the grass to form the big elongated hump.

While I stood there trying to understand what I was seeing, my mind quickly referred back to the strange sound of rocks during the night. Was it logical to connect these two strange incidents? I now raced to the conclusion, amazing though it was, that *I was looking at the result of a meteor impact.* A small meteor must have punched into the ground right here, and the rocks on the roof were trailing fragments that had slowed down in the atmosphere, falling at just that moment, while the core slammed into the ground at terrific speed.

Excited, I went back into the house, through the living room, dining room, into the kitchen, then down into the basement to get a shovel. I should have carried the shovel out through the back, but I went back through the living room.

"What are you doing?" asked Peggy as I cruised quickly

back through the living room toward the front door.

"Oh, uh, nothing."

Outside again, I went to the punched-in end of the hump and started to dig. My head was spinning with planets, stars, galaxies, and the unprecedented yet somehow natural intrusion of outer space. Of course these things happen, I thought. Why not here? Now? To us?

I struck the shovel into the dirt at the end of the hump and pried up the turf. Then, the first shovel-full of dirt showed only a few ordinary rocks. I pushed the shovel in again, but nothing unusual came up with it. I figured the meteor—technically now a meteorite—must be fairly deep. My grandmother appeared on the front porch, looking down at me from over the shingled siding, as if from the deck of a ship.

"Philip, for heaven's sake, what are you doing?"

I paused. "Those rocks on the roof last night . . . look at the grass here . . . I think a meteor came down!"

"A what?"

"You know. A meteor. This hump of grass was bulged up. By something."

She looked, but only a frown came over her face.

"What have you done there?"

"I haven't done anything. We have to dig down."

"Nothing doing."

"But I think a meteor . . ."

"Now Philip, I can't have you digging up my lawn."

"But do you understand? This is important."

"Do I have to get your grandfather out here?"

"But . . ."

"Now you put that shovel back, come on inside and stop that digging."

I leaned on the shovel using two hands and considered the consequences of disobeying. Nothing had emerged in two shovels full, and I didn't know how deep I'd have to dig. What if I found nothing? What if there was an alternative explanation? A big rodent of some kind? I began to lose confidence. Nothing in my grandmother's voice indicated a millimeter of flexibility, and I knew the pride she took in her lawn. So I gave in. I stopped.

Later, Grandfather came outside and with effort stomped down the turf and smoothed over the hole where I'd started to dig. In time, the grass grew back. The meteorite remained undiscovered and would continue to remain undiscovered. Eventually, the memory retreated into a remote corner of my mind.

Yet it was another episode in a web of experiences having to do with the *presence* of outer space in my life during those years, from the movie *This Island Earth* when I was eight, to building refrigerator-box spaceships, to *Science Fiction Theater*, to UFOs, to *Forbidden Planet*, to Sputnik, to the stories of H. G. Wells, Ray Bradbury, and Arthur C. Clarke; to a 50× Tasco telescope I'd been given at age twelve, and to an ever-increasing awareness of the unfathomable multitude of stars in the night sky.

§ 35

Yet the summer was also earthbound, with more music and the release of Chubby Checker's "Let's Twist Again." One could say that the twist craze had a checkered career (sorry!) since Checker's earlier single "The Twist" was from the year before but hadn't evolved into the ubiquitous craze of '61 forward. That original song was actually a "cover" of the B side of a 1959 Hank Ballard record (poor Hank could not convince his label, King, to flip the A side, "Teardrops on Your Letter," to the B side). Sure, "The Twist" was a big hit the previous year but had caught on mainly with high school teenagers. No one could have predicted, certainly not I at the time (even though I'd started watching Dick Clark's *American Bandstand*) that the dance would become a wild defining aspect of pop culture around the world, lasting far into the decade.

Adults increasingly began to do the twist. Prudish conservatives condemned it as indecent (if not the end of civilization as we knew it). Even Eisenhower, our former President, disapproved. It wasn't hard to understand a bit of shock at the sexy gyrations, especially those of young women, especially those with a callipygian physique (you are welcome to look it up). No matter, the dance caught on in a big way. It was easy to do, as Checker said, and everyone could do it. So from kids to grandparents, the dance caught on, and I found it downright fun to see everyone doing a crazy thing all together, boys and girls, young and old, to the rhythms of rock & roll.

Later, celebrities began doing the twist to the music of Joey Dee and the Starliters in New York's Peppermint Lounge. That notable phenomenon began one night with a middle-aged actress, Merle Oberon and her escort, Prince something-or-other, being seen doing the twist at that club. The very next night, after a note in the newspaper about the actress doing the twist, the police had to start erecting barricades to control the crowds that wanted into the suddenly famous Lounge. More celebrities began to show up night after night, people such as Judy Garland, Tennessee Williams, Audrey Hepburn, Truman Capote, Shirley MacLaine, Nat King Cole, Marilyn Monroe, Liberace, Noël Coward, Frank Sinatra, Norman Mailer, Annette Funicello, even John Wayne, and the reclusive Greta Garbo. (Joey Dee noted that Western superstar John "Duke" Wayne did not dance, however). Then, First Lady Jackie Kennedy brought the twist to the White House where she managed to get distinguished ambassadors and such, even a cabinet member or two, and the President himself, to do the twist at parties. The twist had now been everywhere. What a time.

In July of '61, I ran into my old friend Dean in front of a movie theater after we'd coincidentally been in the same audience watching *Voyage to the Bottom of the Sea*. It was a moment when I spontaneously wanted to revive a friendship, for of all the kids I'd grown up with in the Bryant neighborhood, Dean and I had shared the most fun. We agreed that the movie was pretty good and that we should get together again. But how? When? Driving was still in the future, meeting somewhere by bus was inconvenient, parents would likely have to shuttle us, and although we might call one another, we really didn't have much to say. As we parted, I realized that making and maintaining friendships could be complicated. Although I was close to most of the kids in my Ravenna neighborhood, the only one I decided might make a "best" friend was Ted, since we shared an interest in science fiction and the future. Yet there is a big difference in ages between a fourteen-year-old, me, and a seventeen- or eighteen-year old, Ted. So I was still left to myself most of the time and was also beginning to develop a melancholy sensibility. My daily world still consisted mainly of books, music, movies, HO slot cars and an occasional neighborhood game of football.

I played board games, but if I could not connect with anyone for that, or if the street was empty and no one was around, Hollywood was happy to indulge my tastes in movies, and I was content to go to movies alone. I now had a favorite row in the Neptune theater, an anomalous row down at the left with extra space in front to make a path for people coming through a side entrance. There I could stretch my legs out a bit. My favorite time was a late afternoon showing on Sundays. In August, the second of Roger Corman's "Poe Pictures" arrived, *The Pit and the Pendulum*, again with Vincent Price, who had become most associated with the horror genre. The new Poe movie was the equal of *House of Usher*, with exactly the right level of horror for yours truly.

Because I thought that going to movies was as natural as breathing, I wasn't cognizant, per se, of the confidence my mother had of me choosing whatever movies I wanted to see. That silent permission wasn't necessarily true of other parents. Or for that matter, of theater managers. I was turned away from the Varsity around the corner from the Neptune by the manager who decided that the picture being shown wasn't suitable for someone my age. The Varsity specialized in bringing in British films, old and new, and apparently *The Key* was too adult for me to see, according to the manager who happened to be standing at the door. I wasn't offended and went around the corner to the Neptune where, ironically, I watched *The Hustler* with Paul Newman, George C. Scott, and Piper Laurie. It was, to say the least, a very adult film and very dark. Nevertheless, a young person of fourteen could see any adult movie without being subjected to overt sex or gory violence (Hammer horror films a tolerable exception). The Motion Picture Production Code was in effect, which meant that I could learn something about adult behavior, adult morality (often the lack thereof) and adult situations in general. I thought *The Hustler*—Paul Newman as a pool hustler and Piper Laurie as his tragic girlfriend—was one of the best movies I'd ever seen, and I went back to see it the following weekend. Another adult movie I saw around that time was *Judgment at Nuremberg* about the Nazi war crime trials. Also a light, presumably sophisticated comedy with Bob Hope called *Bachelor in Paradise,* the only good thing about which was an infectiously tuneful score by who else: Henry Mancini.

I might apologize for writing too much about movies, since I haven't room to adequately describe them or my reactions to them in detail; but that they were an important influence on my development, most of it wishful thinking, must be noted beyond doubt. Not having the benefit of a father—

at least one with whom to identify—I sought out the desirable characteristics of male movie stars, ranging from those I've mentioned to others, such as Cary Grant and James Stewart, but not so much to Paul Newman or John Wayne, however much I enjoyed their films. Still influential was the attraction to the fantasy lives of TV detectives, I having graduated from the colorful Western heroes of my younger days.

Other heroes of mine were race drivers—not of automobiles, but of Unlimited hydroplanes, the one major league sport Seattle had acquired in the 1950s. The history of the sport went back to nearly turn of the century New York, Detroit, and elsewhere alongside motor racing in general. The Seattle race was no less spectacular than the Indy 500, and the huge crowd along the miles of shoreline at the southern end of Lake Washington would again be optimistically estimated at nearly a half-million. With hundreds of yachts lining the long backstretch, the atmosphere on race day was like the Monaco Grand Prix and Indy 500 rolled into one, and television coverage had grown to national stature.

Steve Mettler and I would attend our first race this year, but it was on a weekday a couple of years earlier that Aunt Peggy drove Craig and Jimmy and me down to Lake Washington to see a real Unlimited hydroplane running on the water for the first time and watch a couple of hours of qualifying for the Sunday race. She had parked on the street at the top of a hill near the southern end of the race course, and we kids jumped out of the car and started down toward the shoreline park at the water's edge. We ran down the long street of the hill, for we heard the unmistakable roar of an Allison aircraft engine, meaning a boat was on the course. Previously, I'd watched the qualifying and the races on Aunt Peggy's 21" black and white television. Exciting. But here I was—here *we* were, the three of us kids, with Aunt Peggy trailing—hearing one of the big Unlimited hydroplanes for the first time in "real life."

As we reached the bottom of the long hill, out on the beautiful blue water came the twin-engine *Gale VI,* the largest boat in the fleet, a rocket-shaped, varnished mahogany hull and green-trimmed raceboat throwing up a tall white roostertail as it hurtled by in front of us. The sheer sound of its tandem 2000 horsepower Allison aircraft engines could not only be heard, but felt as the sound waves bounced off our chests. The rest of the boats with their single engines—Rolls Merlins or Allisons that had powered World War II fighters—thundered with equivalent intensity; but this first experience of witnessing one of these streamlined craft in person was unforgettable.

That was a couple of years earlier, and this year, Steve and I saw our first race—and the first start of a race as *seven* boats came thundering down the main straightaway and past us into the south turn. In all of sports, there was nothing like this awesome spectacle while the crowd was on its feet yelling for the Seattle favorites to beat the wealthy easterners from Detroit. At the end of the day, Steve's favorite Seattle boat, the *Miss Bardahl,* won, driven by one of the best, Ron Musson. It was a glorious day in Seattle.

At about this time at the beginning of August, I began to find a modicum of glamour in being a city kid. My stepfather, having become an independent contractor selling fire-prevention sprinkler systems, took us on a summer trip to Spokane in eastern Washington where he had some business. We could have made the trip across the state uninterrupted, but we stopped about halfway at a motel in some semi-desert town. The modern one-level motel was classic 1950s with a beautiful outdoor swimming pool that we had plenty of time to enjoy. The main attraction for me, though, was a girl about my age who, with her mother, manned the small lobby where we checked in. She reminded me—in retrospect because I had yet to see *The Hustler* at that point—of Piper Laurie, Paul Newman's movie girlfriend. She had short-cropped blond hair that slightly swept over her forehead, a pleasant and rather weary smile not immediately engaging, and an efficient use of her feminine hands as she handed us the key to our room. She was not an ideal beauty; but some girls, I'd begun to note, could be quite sexy while looking like a fairly ordinary girl from next door—something about attitude, personality. Later, she appeared in a one-piece bathing suit at the side of the swimming pool. I had a brief conversation, and she asked where we were from—which was where the big-city kid, me, found a grain of imagined sophistication. She'd never been to Seattle, just to Spokane, and that was when she was eight years old, she said. My role of cool guy from the big city made zero impression on her insofar as I could tell, but I began to wonder if I might have connected with her anyway. I began to think of how I might continue in this regard. I swam in the pool, she remained in her lounge chair and eventually went back to her duties in the motel office.

I stopped by there later, pretending to look at the post-cards in a revolving rack, glancing now and then at her while she and her mother went about their business. What causes such attractions is beyond reason, and I was waiting for an opening. When her mother went into the back somewhere, I got up the nerve to more formally introduce myself: "Hi again, uh, my name is Phil, incidentally." I then asked the young lady her name and made sure I got both first and last. We chatted a little about junior high, and I found that she, too, was about to enter the ninth grade that fall. "Well, bye," I said, and went back to our room. There I told my mother and stepfather that I'd met the girl in the motel office. My mother, having instant understanding of these matters, suggested I write down the address of the motel and perhaps write to the girl after I got home. If there was one thing my mother understood, it was a young girl's interest in boys, and why shouldn't this particular young girl be interested in my mother's particularly outstanding, not to mention handsome, son? This was slightly embarrassing, yet her advice seemed sound.

When we got back to Seattle, I walked up to Zopf's Drugstore from Laurelon Terrace to see if I could find a postcard to send to "Piper" at her motel. The card I found fit the image of myself as the cool-guy fantasy detective from the big city: an extra wide panorama of the Seattle skyline at night. I imagined myself, like Rex Randolph in *Bourbon Street Beat*, cruising the city in my white Oldsmobile Super 88 convertible, heading for my detective office and another adventure.

Now, Seattle in 1961 wasn't exactly New York or L.A. (let alone New Orleans), but plans were afoot to hold the World's Fair there the following year, which would be a really big deal. Our level of city, if not as worldly as Paris, New York, or even Chicago, would surely increase in sophistication and was vastly more cosmopolitan compared to anything in eastern Washington—thoughts of which gave me the kind of confidence I observed in TV detectives. I was oblivious to my general idiocy.

I addressed the postcard, and with my Sheaffer cartridge fountain pen's blue ink wrote a few sentences, identifying myself again, saying something about my summer thus far, asking about hers, and saying that "I'd very much enjoy hearing from you sometime."

Mr. Cool never received a reply.

§ 36

As I was about to enter the ninth grade in September, I began
to notice, with the exception of an attraction to pretty girls,
that my life had acquired a non-conformist contour. Whereas
other guys' interests gravitated toward sports, mainly through
participation at school, I was content with street football and
watching the UW Huskies on TV leading up to the Rose
Bowl. (My step father and I attended one "live" Husky game,
and I found it tremendously exciting.) Interest in science fiction was considered nerdy, as was chess (I had still found no
one to compete with). I loved racing my Aurora Model Motoring cars with ten-year-old Stevie Mettler and designing
track layouts with HO scale scenery—while we all still played
Monopoly and other board games.

A board game company called Avalon Hill revolutionized
the market with several interesting wargames. Their new
game, a historically researched game called *Gettysburg*, depart-
ed from the traditional chessboard squares and used instead a
grid of small hexes on a map recreating the actual terrain of
the Battle of Gettysburg. Small printed counters represented
the actual army units of the North and South, while battles
were resolved by rolling dice and referring to an odds table
to calculate outcomes based on the forces involved in individual battles. For me, this game was impossible to ignore.
The box shouted, "Now YOU fight the Civil War Battle in
this REALISTIC GAME by Avalon Hill."

Clearly, this wasn't *Monopoly*. Opponents took on the
Southern commands of Lee and Longstreet, or the North's
Meade and Reynolds, with battles along Cemetery Ridge or
Little Round Top. Combating players poured over the map,
the scheduled arrival and potential movement of various
forces, the odds of winning battles and taking or defending
the high ground. This game and the Avalon Hill games that

followed encouraged participants to take on the role of generals and learn the real strategy and tactics of war.

Yes, realism! That was the thing we craved in toys and games of whatever kind we chose. This new kind of game was something different but nonetheless a continuation of the miniature worlds—trains, planes, automobiles, buildings, roads, forts, and the rest—that enveloped the lives of boys. I kept *Gettysburg* at my grandparents' and set it up on a flat wooden table in my upstairs bedroom. I invited a new kid on the block to come over and play.

Dave Dickey was only a year younger than I. His family had moved in on our side of the block, second house down from 65th. Dave was short, quick, fast at street football, and began to compete with me, Ronny, the Brandts, and the rest of us. With Dave added, and with us boys and girls getting older, our football games increased in speed and capability. But I also got to know Dave while playing *Gettysburg*. (Luckily for Stevie, Dave wasn't interested in racing HO slot cars.) He and I got along well, but he was also an example of how friends touched certain interests but not others. Finding a friend who shared all or most of one's interests and hobbies seemed impossible. Plus, my interests were so varied.

§ 37

September arrived, and I was back at Laurelon Terrace weekdays with Mother and Larry, starting ninth grade at Nathan Eckstein.

I joined the boys' choir. I was classed as a tenor. Our enthusiastic director, Mr. Budelman, looked a bit like Paul Newman, so the girls in the girls choir were smitten. I liked him, too, for he took the music and us seriously.

I saw Candy distantly in the hallway one day. But it was a big school and she was not in any of my classes. I met a girl named Barbara who was in Mr. Budelman's girls choir. She was the first girl I regularly socialized with at school and whom I considered a friend or girlfriend. She had a pleasant, oval face, an attractive figure, and luxurious reddish-brown hair. We bowled together in an after-school league at the Village Lanes. Mixed teams of younger teenagers, each with two boys and two girls, competed. Barbara wore culottes—a somewhat stiff skirt divided in two sections that gave her freedom of movement, and she swayed nicely when stepping forward to throw the ball.

The problem with having an unofficial girlfriend at age fourteen was being unable to drive a car, such as to a movie, without depending on parents (or worse, the bus). The formality of planning and being driven was all too obvious and embarrassing. So Barbara and I merely saw each other now and then—until one day a guy named Jeff asked what I was doing on a particular Saturday night that winter. He had a good-looking girlfriend, Lisa, who was a friend of Barbara, and they all decided to get together at Barbara's tall brick house on a hill at the eastern end of 65th in Sand Point. Unknown to me, it was to be a make-out party, two by two, in Barbara's parents' basement rec room.

Now, it is one thing at age fourteen to be romantically attracted to beautiful girls, and quite another to physically indulge. The only females I had ever kissed, and lightly, were my mother and grandmother—and only on the cheek after about age seven. So here were Barbara and the sensuous, slim, dark-haired Lisa, and this guy Jeff whom I barely knew, sitting around on a couple of sofas in "the castle" (Barbara's house having acquired the nick-name because of a tall brick turret) in the basement rec room playing records and joking around. Soon, Jeff and Lisa were beginning to "make out," as they say, while I wondered what was expected of me while Barbara and I sat quietly on our opposite sofa. Then Barbara suddenly

lay down with her head on a pillow and wedged her legs behind me. I moved to sit on the edge of the sofa at her waist.

Why I'd been invited was now unmistakable. She looked
good, somewhat flushed, I thought, but with feigned relaxa-
tion, waiting for me to make a move. I was unsure and certainly flushed myself; then I leaned forward, close to her face,
closer, and almost to her lips; but I hesitated. Kissing her
right then, while she looked at me with a kind of plastic anticipation, triggered a paralytic onslaught of shyness and hesi-
tancy I had never known. I stared at her, she at me, eyeballs
to eyeballs, and I went no further. Simple as a kiss may have
seemed, it was something I realized I was not ready for.

Whatever Jeff and Lisa were up to I wasn't aware of right
then, but after a few moments of Barbara and I looking at
each other like opposing magnets about to repel, Jeff jumped
up from the opposite sofa and motioned me over to the corner of the room. I quickly obeyed.

He whispered to me, "Hey, man, you got to get with it,
you know?"

"Yeah, ah, OK."

"What do you think we're doing?"

"I know."

"Then . . ."

"You might have mentioned what it was about," I intoned.

Jeff sighed impatiently.

I looked at him.

"OK, well . . ." he said.

"Well . . ."

"Well . . ."

"OK."

We returned to our respective sofas.

Barbara once again lay back down, I once again came
forward to kiss her. And under that social pressure, I sat

looking at her oval lovely face, but I could not complete the action I was to contribute to our evening of lust. Put simply, I failed my test at making out. Luckily, Barbara took it in stride, finally got up and put on another record. Jeff and Lisa stopped kissing. Jeff got up, went to a small fridge and got a Coke. I did the same. We sat around talking as we'd done earlier, and our evening came to an end when Barbara's father called down to say it was getting late. So my first physical encounter with a girl involved unpreparedness, insufficient lustful motivation, a heavy dose of shyness, and in general a situation for which I was not ready.

Going over it later, as we all do under such circumstances, I supposed that if Barbara had taken and pulled me to her (I was only a couple of inches away!) everything would have gone better. But this was merely rationalization. The man was supposed to be the aggressor. Still, in my embarrassment of having failed a test, I didn't take into account that she might have been as shy as I. Another thing that entered my mind— more so a question—was that I wasn't sufficiently attracted to her. Had she been someone else (and I knew who, having seen her walking away in the distance again) the result *might* have been different. I just didn't know. The mind can rationalize. To be honest with myself, I'd likely been overcome with the typical shyness of a fourteen-year-old.

Barbara and I continued our casual relationship, but there was nowhere to go with it—literally—as I began to daydream about learning to drive.

Speaking of which, Larry bought my mother a '61 Chevy Corvair in dark metallic red. It was an interesting rear-engine car with an automatic transmission that was activated by a short lever under the dash to the right of the steering wheel. I liked this car a great deal and hoped to drive it someday. You had to be sixteen to drive in Washington State. I didn't think I could wait that long, but of course I had to.

§ 38

At Nathan Eckstein, I began to notice that a number of ninth graders were carrying new paperback books along with their normal text books and three-ring binders. In English class that year, we did oral book reports once a month, reading books of our choice. A kind of status seemed to evolve regarding the reading of recent mass market paperbacks of Biblical length. Two popular ones were *Hawaii* by James Michener and *The Rise and Fall of the Third Reich* by William L. Shirer. For the latter author, I settled for *Berlin Diary*, Shirer's account leading to the start of the war. At one point, I tried to tackle *Hawaii* but gave up for lack of interest after three or four chapters. Another book that made the rounds was Orwell's *1984*, and I was fascinated (and horrified) enough to pass it along to my grandfather Nels. He read it just after I did but was shocked at certain sexual references in the book, and with considerable irritation told me I shouldn't be reading such things. Nothing more along those lines was said as he finished it and admitted it was like nothing he'd ever read before. Whether that meant he fully appreciated it or not I didn't know. After that, I handed him my Ballantine paperback of *Childhood's End* by Arthur C. Clarke, which he also read. I then passed that copy along to my stepfather Larry, who, as I mentioned, was a voracious reader of whatever fiction happened to come along. I was glad that the two men in my life actually finished a couple of my recommendations, however little discussion was involved afterward. My complaint was they each had an annoying habit regarding paperbacks (considered by the older generation to be disposable). Grandfather would mark his place by bending a page corner instead of using a bookmark, while Larry would often curl the covers completely back around while he read, as if it were a comic book. I had been taught by my mother to care for books. Oh, well.

One day, a girl in my class gave a book report on *To Kill a Mockingbird* by Harper Lee, a favorite novel of the girls, it seemed, although I was interested as well. As she went back to her desk, I was called upon and gave my report on *The Time Machine*, a book I'd read previously (a fair enough ploy, I figured), with my vivid oral rendering of the latter paragraphs when the Time Traveller journeys to the distant future of the dying Earth. Perhaps, along with my laziness of reporting a book I'd read before, I was trying to make up for the missing scene in George Pal's excellent movie; but whatever the case, I genuinely wanted to share this amazing work and put my best effort into it. Furthermore, ever since those illustrations of Earth's birth and death from *Life* magazine's *The World We Live In*, part of my mind had been occupied by the crushing aggregate of time and the catastrophic themes from science fiction. I could see that I shared these perceptions with an author, H. G. Wells (who had died one year before I was born). His ideas revealed him as the author to whom I could most relate. Finding an author who seems to speak directly to you is a priceless gift.

On a more humdrum, earthbound level, my friend Bruce showed up at our apartment door one evening and announced he was quitting his Wednesday paper route in a week and wondered if I wanted it.

It would be my first job. So I jumped at the chance, and the next day I went around with Bruce while he delivered his last batch of *The Shopping News*—a one day per week quota of fifty or sixty papers, one to each door of the many quadraplex apartment buildings. It took about an hour. Bruce was bored to death of doing this every Wednesday, and as a result he'd gotten into the habit of cutting down the time by simply throwing away a couple of dozen papers into a dumpster—

papers he should have delivered to the farther end of the route.

"No one actually subscribes to this rag," he told me. "It's free, and hardly anyone misses it."

Hmm. I did not take this at face value, so I aimed to be responsible and not miss a delivery. The manager of the paperboys gave me a brief interview at our apartment, signed me up, and gave me a gray canvas kangaroo bag to hang heavily over my shoulders from which I would toss the newspapers to those shoppers presumed eager to get a paper containing almost nothing but advertising.

The first Wednesday, I found a bundled ton of *The Shopping News* on our doorstep. I hadn't taken into account that Bruce had pre-folded quite a number of papers before going on the route. All of them had to be folded a certain way, and this took an extra half hour, although one could fold quite a few during the walk. No big deal, I thought, the job was only one day a week, and the minimal pay was better than nothing. I had my first job, and that was a rite of passage.

That fall, the twist craze was still going strong, and in January "The Twist"—the original recording by Chubby Checker— made a surprising, unprecedented comeback, rising to #1 over a year after its initial release. The twist seemed to enjoy never-ending popularity. The whole country—young, old, middle-aged, rich, poor, smart, stupid, liberal, conservative— was doing the twist, a togetherness of the multitude.

In the meantime, in common with most every other American male, I had fallen in love with Mary Tyler Moore on the *Dick Van Dyke Show*; the show itself being the best sitcom ever on television, never to be entirely surpassed because of its attractive, funny, believable, unforced characters and situations that arose out of the real lives of the writers, including its creator, Carl Reiner.

Saturday Night at the Movies was the first to air relatively recent feature films on television, i.e., from the previous decade. The telecasts were hugely popular. One particular movie became a special event on television. *The Wizard of Oz* ended up a family tradition around Xmas time, and I was quite spellbound the first time I saw it, even though we had yet to buy a color television! Speaking of which, Walt Disney's prime time show on Friday nights, originally called *Disneyland*, then *Walt Disney Presents*, switching to Sunday nights a year earlier, now became *Walt Disney's Wonderful World of Color*. Disney was now able to repeat a large archive of previously aired material, but in color. The first Western to be broadcast in color was *Bonanza* with its quartet of a father and three sons, the Cartwrights (Ben, Adam, Hoss, and Little Joe) adventuring from their prosperous Ponderosa Ranch near Virginia City. The era of color television had begun.

In February, John Glenn became the first American to orbit Earth in his Mercury capsule *Friendship 7*. The flight included three orbits and lasted nearly five hours. Everyone watching TV was spellbound as Glenn described the blackness of space above the blue curvature of the Earth, of the myriad lights of cities far below, and of the twilight sunsets he witnessed as he orbited. But the flight was not without drama. Glenn's automatic control system began to fail and he had to use manual control. Then it appeared as if his re-entry heat shield was loose. People prayed that he wouldn't just burn up on re-entry. After some frightening minutes, the capsule held together, the parachutes deployed, and Glenn splashed down in the Atlantic. In March, he was given a huge ticker-tape parade of the kind Charles Lindbergh had received many decades earlier for his flight across the same ocean in the airplane *Spirit of St. Louis*. How quickly had we advanced because of aviation. It had been less than a century since the days of the covered wagons crossing the North American plains, an era

I'd watched so many times in the movies and on TV Westerns. On the one hand, this recognition was an intellectual milestone, on the other a suggestion of how quickly one could become used to the continuing progress. It was my mother, more than I, who remained fully engaged during the following three Mercury flights. "Aren't you excited, Philip?!" she would say. And I'd say, "Sure, Mom." But not *quite* as entranced as she. After all, I'd grown up with books and movies about outer space and was absolutely confident in the inevitability and future of space travel. Yet television itself was changing our lives, maybe more than we knew, because along with entertainment, it brought history into our homes in real time.

The earthbound texture of life went on, too. I had taken clarinet lessons, but as mentioned, played too many honks and squeaks. I'd gotten better, but I wasn't motivated enough. Piano lessons came next, taught by one Bernard B. Brin who had written a boogie-woogie treatment of *St. Louis Blues* that I learned to play with near perfection. I liked boogie-woogie and learned more, but in my lessons overall I became too lazy to practice the standard tunes in the designated "swing method" using syncopated chords for the left hand. ("You'll be playing songs after the very first lesson!" said the ads.) And although Mr. Brin seemed OK with teaching me boogie-woogie, my mother decided she wasn't getting her money's worth, which was true because of my lack of practicing the standard songs, so we decided I could quit. (To impress friends, I did keep in practice the three boogie-woogie numbers I'd learned. Too bad we didn't just continue along those lines. But children's lives have a lot of dead ends.)

Sometime in early '62 my friend Bruce and I took the bus into downtown Seattle to explore the seamier side of the big city. We walked along 1st Ave. where sailors would hang out while on leave. Brazenly taking advantage of our height as budding teenagers, we lowered our heads and slipped into shops selling girlie magazines and other "adult" paraphernalia, getting quite an eyeful. These rare expeditions—two or three at most—were on Saturday mornings. Once, after exploring the Pike Place Market and delighting in the magic shop on the lower level, we walked a few blocks up to a strange place on 4th Ave.—Ben Paris Recreation and Sporting Goods. It was entered down a dark set of stairs across from the Bon Marche department store. The 1930s oeuvre with its dark woodwork, shoeshine stands (complete with a shoeshine boy at the ready), lunch counter, vacant card room, and pool hall was a throwback in time, right out of the era of *The Untouchables*. I imagined Al Capone strolling in.

Bruce and I sauntered past the wall of cigar displays and cases of fishing gear (how very Seattle was this place, regardless) and went to shoot some pool. We entered a room with four pool tables, keeping our distance from some raffish-looking young men at other tables who seemed to know each other. I wasn't entirely comfortable in there. But nobody bothered us, so we pretended to be cool guys who did this all the time. We spent a couple of Saturday mornings there.

On another day, we happened along 2nd Ave., and at Union St. we noticed a pool hall named "211" up on the second story of an old brick building. We entered the big door and went upstairs to check it out. No question: *This* was the real thing—a dozen starkly lit tables in a serious pool room like the one in *The Hustler*. We stood on the wooden floor looking around a bit nervously as the manager eyed us from behind a counter cash register. Only two other people were shooting pool on that early Saturday morning; I noticed two long rows of elevated, empty wooden seats just across from the center tables, apparently a gallery for watching serious competition. A sign on the wall said:

211 Club Billiard Hall
Rules
No Bullshit
No Noise
Just Pool

Bruce and I were slightly intimidated by the atmosphere and weren't quite in the mood to partake of a game, especially under the eyes of the manager as he now stood by the cash register sizing us up. We kind of looked around from our spot near the door, then quietly left.

§ 39

I can't say it was my forays down to those 1st Ave. magazine shops that created an interest in photos of sexy nude women. I might have reported by now that I was likely in a stage of post-pubescence and was experiencing the biological subtleties of lust. It seemed to me a natural attraction, but because such desires at age fourteen were basically a cultural taboo, I was led to commit a crime. I suppose I had been exposed to just enough erotica to want a little for myself. And so, one day after school I decided to muster the courage to buy a *Playboy* magazine from Craigen's Pharmacy. Moreover, unlike Ronny, I was not about to hide a magazine of naked unrestrained females in a hollow tree. Hiding it in the house would suffice.

First, I had to consider the acute discomfort and embarrassment of trying to actually buy, at my age, a *Playboy* magazine. Assuming I'd be allowed to in the first place. And making it all the more embarrassing was that I'd been a customer of Craigen's Pharmacy for years and didn't wish to be seen as having "inappropriate" tastes, even though it would come as no surprise to anyone that a normal kid would love to have a *Playboy* magazine. I also knew that going to another store someplace wouldn't matter at the point of purchase. I might go to that inconvenience and find, impossible to antic-ipate, that a *woman* was tending the cash register, a situation unbearable to even contemplate. At least at Craigen's, I could assess the situation at a place only a few blocks from home. I knew that the magazine was kept on the flat shelf below the normal magazine rack and not behind the cashier's counter as was often the case elsewhere.

Still, I briefly thought of taking the bus by myself down-town to First Ave. where they sold far more pornographic magazines than *Playboy*, but it seemed clear I wasn't ready to go into one of those places and actually *buy* something—likely from a cigar-chomping cashier of the kind I'd seen when Bruce and I were exploring there. No, that was unimaginable. Better to try my luck at the local drugstore with a potential spur-of-the-moment act of courage. After all, I'd paged through the magazine there when no one was looking or standing nearby.

That at least was a simple act. The purchase could be a simple act, too. So I walked down there at night, after dinner, opened the glass door and went inside.

I figured I could just go home without the magazine if a woman was tending the register, no big deal. If a man was on duty, I might be able to act casual and try to make the pur-chase. It was at least plausible.

I decided to walk around the store first, pretending to look at things. I had begun to sweat as I thought about just going to the magazine rack, picking up the *Playboy*, walking over, plopping it down on the counter and making the pur-chase. In the meantime, I cruised by the short length of check-out counter framed on one side with rows of cigarettes and on the other with chewing gum and . . . something I'd never noticed before. It was a small sign. Was it new? I could barely believe my eyes.

You must be 18 years of age to purchase *Playboy* magazine.

Oh, no! That ended my plan! How could it be? I could not carry out a deception of the magnitude necessary. On the other hand, my fear of embarrassment drained away. The sign was actually a relief. So I merely walked back over to the magazine rack and hung around, looking at *Sports Car Graphic* and thinking about flipping through the magazine I'd wanted, since the store was nearly empty at the moment, with one customer, not nearby. I put the car magazine back, drifted to my left and waited for the right moment to bend down and lift a *Playboy* from the left of the bottom shelf. The cashier was now busy ringing up a sale to the one customer.

My decision was instant. I reached down and spontaneously put the magazine up under my jacket, then held it to my side. Quickly, but not too quickly, I walked out of the store. The heat of fear rose into my head. I half expected to hear someone yelling after me, chasing me, or calling for the police. But after a minute, I realized I'd gotten away with the crime. The farther I walked, the more relieved I became. My racing heart slowed. I hurried home in the dark, down the 14th Ave. sidewalk, up our front steps, and into the house, still pinching the magazine under my coat and, not unusual for me, passed through the living room and immediately went down into the basement. I supposed no one noticed I hadn't removed my coat. I was often in a single-minded frame of mind to get something done in the basement with my HO scale slot cars or some other thing. Down in the depths of my presumed degradation, I hid the magazine in a dark gap between beams in the ceiling near the furnace—my version of a hollow tree—later to ogle its wonderful color fold-out and other exposures of feminine beauty.

§ 40

The Seattle World's Fair (formally the Century 21 Exposition) opened on April 21, 1962, about a month before my fifteenth birthday. Aunt Peggy was the first of our family to attend. She stayed on into the evening with her friends and came home with praise and excitement, one of her phrases being, "It's just like a fairyland!"—something I tried rather unsuccessfully to equate with the Space Needle, Coliseum, and other featured places at the fair; furthermore, the phrase seemed to echo something I'd heard previously. Ah, yes, it was the very thing Judy Garland said about the 1904 St. Louis World's Fair at the end of *Meet Me in St. Louis*. I didn't fault Aunt Peggy for lack of originality.

In a couple of days, I and a school acquaintance named John attended and were equally impressed, though in a different way than Aunt Peggy. We partook of most of the exhibits housing the presumably glorious future of the 21st century, and went on carnival rides in the colorful Gayway (a name lacking its later associations). Most impressive was the United States Science Pavilion designed by Minoru Yamasaki, with its lacy cathedral-like towers and exhibits by NASA— including Alan Shephard's Mercury space capsule and other space-oriented exhibits—but most impressively a 750-seat, 360-degree "Spacearium" dome taking visitors across the galaxy into the universe. More down to earth, amid the concourse was the Belgian Waffle House, temporarily becoming the most famous eatery in the city outside of Ivar's on the Seattle waterfront. The world-class scope and size of the fair was equaled by an A-list of entertainment, including *The Ed Sullivan Show, The Roy Rogers and Dale Evans Western Show,* comedian Victor Borge, and Hal Holbrook performing *Mark Twain Tonight*; classical musicians such as Isaac Stern, Van Cliburn, Eugene Ormandy and the Philadelphia Orchestra;

jazz greats Benny Goodman and his Orchestra, Count Basie and his Orchestra, Ella Fitzgerald, Nat King Cole; and a number of visiting movie stars. Elvis Presley made a movie, *It Happened at the World's Fair*, shooting scenes on the Monorail and up in the Space Needle. The Old Vic gave performances of Shakespeare, while Rod Serling and Ray Bradbury gave a panel discussion on science fiction. On my first visit, my friend and I did go to the top of the Space Needle. It was breathtaking indeed, and (being a Seattle native taking it all for granted) would be the only time I did so for many years. Yet I revisited the fair twice more over the summer.

My Aunt Peggy, who at forty was becoming more like an older sister to me, had started to teach me photography. She took me to the fair one night after dark to teach time-exposures. I didn't yet have a 35mm camera, but she loaned me her Argus C-4 and tripod, which allowed me to get beautiful Kodachrome shots of the Space Needle, Science Pavilion, Gayway rides, and various art such as the big International Fountain and twin tiki statues outside of the Hawaiian pavilion. It was a memorable evening for which I was ever grateful to my new "big sister." Many of the resulting slides (formally called transparencies) looked totally professional. I decided I had to get a good camera like my aunt's.

The Fair became a huge success as millions of people came to town from all over the world, and it brought Seattle out of its ostensible provincialism. Beyond that, it created a permanent civic center with an opera house and symphony hall, multi-use buildings, new works of art, a sports and rock-concert arena (the aforementioned Coliseum) and much else. The Science Pavilion would become known as the Pacific Science Center. This splendid place, dazzling at night with its opulent lighting and high fountains, did seem, notwithstanding its intended reverence to science, "like a fairyland."

§ 41

Back in the Ravenna neighborhood after graduation from junior high, I happily welcomed another summer. Little Stevie Mettler was now Steve, and he and I continued to race Aurora HO-scale slot cars in my basement. He lived near the north end of the block on my side of the street next door to the Dickeys. The Mettlers owned the oldest house in the neighborhood, high above a rockery wall, supposedly built by a sea captain in 1900. Inside and out, it definitely had that look about it—not a particularly large house at all, but with fancy woodwork and "pocket" sliding doors between the entry hall, parlor, and dining room with a fireplace. I was beginning to take a further interest in old houses, undoubtedly the result of my childhood in the old house on Ravenna Boulevard.

Back at the movies, I twice witnessed what I thought was the most terrifying of all monsters. These monsters weren't created in a lab or arrived from outer space or from under the sea, but were of a more ordinary form: that of psychopathic human beings. The first was a classic black-and-white movie near the end of the classic Western era, *The Man Who Shot Liberty Valance*—the villainous character of Liberty played by Lee Marvin, with James Stewart and John Wayne playing disparate good guys. But it was a modern-day black-and-white film that reached into the disturbing depths by way of the character Max Cady, played to repellent perfection by Robert Mitchum. Here was a type one might, with bad luck, encounter in real life—a roving psychopath without conscience or empathy. I sat watching *Cape Fear* with increasing anguish as Cady sought revenge on an attorney (Gregory Peck as the prosecutor who'd sent him to jail years before) and his family. Leaving the theater, I was satisfied that I'd seen a great film about evil, reminded again that the worst monsters are human monsters. I recalled *The Bad Seed*. How could it be that a func-

tioning mind could become so altered, twisted, and dangerous—willingly so, it seemed. I knew it wasn't just in the movies, for there was enough murder and mayhem in the news to
convince anyone otherwise. At the end of 1957, *Life* magazine
had run a horrific story about a psychopathic killer and grave
robber named Ed Gein, the story of which inspired Robert
Block to write his novel *Psycho*, which in turn became the film
by Alfred Hitchcock. All this fostered a suspicion in me that
the human brain—perhaps the human species—was funda-
mentally flawed in a biologically indisputable way, destined
for murder and destruction in some inevitable proportion. In
Cape Fear these idle thoughts were brought into broad daylight, with a more personal threat than in war or horror movies. There was no reassurance, only vexatious doubts
triggered by certain kinds of human beings.

Back in the neighborhood, Ted said that Mitchum had
played a similar character in *Night of the Hunter*. Mitchum
played a psychopathic Reverend, a character based on the
true story of West Virginia serial killer Harry Powell (who was
hanged in 1932). On the knuckles of one of the character's
hands was spelled out L O V E, on the other was H A T E.
This detail of the film Ted was interested to supply, for I had
neither seen nor read about it.

Movies influenced me from all over the emotional map.
Happily, the next movie I saw was the comedy *That Touch of
Mink* with Doris Day and Cary Grant. I think it was critic
Pauline Kael who said that in this Doris Day movie, Cary
Grant finally played the Cary Grant part. Needless to say, I
admired the Cary Grant part. In fact, I wanted to *be* Cary
Grant. Every man, it was said, wanted to be Cary Grant.
Even Cary Grant said he wanted to be Cary Grant. Like so
many role models, Grant's movie persona was another one I
could not (and likely no one) could live up to. Unfortunately,
it was in films that I was seeking the role model I was missing

in real life. By a quirk of imagination, I would come out of a theater *feeling* like the hero, being possessed by that persona for a while afterwards. It was spooky to attain that much identification, though it always wore off in an hour or two. Luckily for whatever authentic *me* was hiding in my brain.

But who was this *me*? I wasn't sure. The mirror did not tell me. My thoughts or feelings did not tell me. Or did they? These things, therefore my identity, were formed by my experiences. But was that all? Surely I'd been born *me* in some way. Surely that little kid back in the big house on Ravenna Boulevard, the one whose grandmother walked with him in the snow under the street lamp, was a special child. Was it not I who had those experiences, and not the *experiences* that created "I"? Or was it a combination of these things, including all the influences?

Did the movies, so important in those days, count as formative experiences? Did they provide portraits of the world, including mental associations, to the young who were by nature impressionable? Certainly they did to me, as these memoirs show. *Cape Fear*, but no less *The Music Man* with its iconic American small town, no less *Mr. Hobbs Takes a Vacation* with its befuddled family portrait. All those came along that spring.

And so, it was about this time I mentioned to my mother that I wanted to be a film director. I had little idea of the difficulties. All I knew, parallel in thought to the movies I'd seen lately, was that they had yet to film the best of the science fiction novels I'd read. That would be my emphasis—movies of the novels of Arthur C. Clarke, Ray Bradbury, and Isaac Asimov, not to mention A. E. Van Vogt's epic *The Voyage of the Space Beagle*. That these works had yet to be done, let alone well, and should be done, wasn't in doubt. Thus my fantasy film career.

I also wanted to write. I'd cranked out several short stories on the bright blue Olympia portable typewriter my mother had bought for me during ninth grade. I could type using hunt-and-peck but found out that Roosevelt High had a daily typing class during summer school. The class lasted only a couple of weeks, so I signed up, even though I wasn't yet a high school student; and with a dozen other kids, clicking and clacking, learned to type with correct fingering on an office model Remington. I got up to about fifty words per minute (bing! went the manual carriage returns) with minimal error, and the skill transferred to my little Olympia portable. I sure wasn't up to an experienced secretary's level (e.g., my mother's) but from then on I could write professional-looking copy for my forthcoming high school assignments and, if I remained motivated, extracurricular fiction.

Early that summer, starting at 11:30 PM, I began watching *The Steve Allen Show* almost every weeknight while living once again at my grandparents' house. Years before, Allen, a tall, dark-haired, multi-talented comedian/musician/intellectual with black horn-rimmed glasses, had essentially invented "late night" television with *The Tonight Show* in 1954. His new show, known informally as the "Westinghouse" show (to identify it apart from his earlier Steve Allen shows) became a nearly indescribable potpourri of celebrity chit-chat, comedy (with regulars Louis Nye, Don Knotts, Tom Poston, Bill Dana, and Pat Harrington), satire (often elaborate send-ups of popular movies), wild stunts done by Allen, such as dropping into a huge vat of Jell-O, joking wittily with the audience while cruising with his microphone, prank phone calls, a hidden camera on Vine St. watching people stroll by while Allen made hilarious off-the-cuff remarks, and the music—great jazz artists such as Bill Evans, Gerry Mulligan, Oscar Peterson, Mel Tormé, Joe Williams, and others rarely seen by a national TV audience—not to mention Allen's own piano playing and his habit of introducing new talent in every area of entertainment, such as the earliest TV appearances on his previous shows of rockers Elvis Presley, Jerry Lee Lewis, and The Supremes.

I also enjoyed Allen's sporadic parade of eccentrics and entrepreneurs who seemed to just wander in and become guests, including health food nut Gypsy Boots, physics professor Julius Sumner Miller doing science experiments, a then unknown Frank Zappa using a bicycle as a musical instrument, and Miss Measure Your Mattress Month, a beautiful young blond representing bedding manufacturers. When Allen found out the latter was also an aspiring singer, he spontaneously turned the show over to her for a song with the band. It was that kind of confident spontaneity—unplanned moments sometimes involving the crew, the band, the audience, and the scheduled or unscheduled guests—that made the show addictive, while holding it all together was Allen's unfailing wit and intelligence. Aside from spontaneous verbal exchanges with audience members, he enjoyed wordplay and invented his own slang such as the word "fern"—as in, "How's your fern?"—a greeting (although the word was originally coined by Louis Nye), "fink" (a bad person), "kreel" (referring to almost anything) and the ultimate bird cry, "Schmock! Schmock!" which was soon heard coming from teenagers all over the country. Not to mention "little black things," those tiny specks that Allen noted would inexplicably appear on surfaces.

Now and then the producers would fool Allen by bringing on a phony guest, such as a famous table tennis champion. In this case, Allen found out while playing the game on stage—that the national champ, jumping around and swinging the paddle, rarely could hit the ball over the net. These practical jokes never failed to break up audience and crew alike.

Sometimes they went a bit too far. During a jungle comedy sketch, Allen was lying flat on the ground, and, by surprise, a man came over to him with a bag, and, without

further ado dumped a dozen live tarantulas onto Allen's lap.
"Oh . . . yeah?!" Allen yelled, and after a paralytic moment of
horror (for everyone), one of the creatures started to run up
toward his neck. Allen jumped up in panic, desperately brush-
ing the creatures off. The tarantulas ran away in all directions
while the crew frantically tried to find them!

As wacky as the show could be, it also had a certain sophistication because of Allen's intelligent persona and comic
sensibility. I almost felt a part of the goings on. It was like attending a great party full of fascinating people—so during
that entire summer of the first season of the show, I never
got to bed before 1:00 AM. on a weeknight.

On July 10, the communications satellite Telstar was
launched, and later that month the rock band The Tornadoes
released an instrumental of the same name. I'd already been
taken with rock instrumentals "Walk Don't Run" by The
Ventures and "Apache" by Jørgen Ingmann; but the uniquely
inspired "Telstar" brought the space race onto AM radio, and
everyone in a prime geographical location was looking up at
night to watch for the orbiting satellite. The future in space
was once again at the forefront of my mind; it prompted me
to read Arthur C. Clarke's *Profiles of the Future*, a mind-
expanding non-fiction book of science and speculation that,
like Loren Eisley's *The Immense Journey*, was capable of changing a reader's perspective on the planet, the universe, and the
depths of geologic time.

We seemed to be moving ahead toward a future of infinite possibilities while the bulk of the news remained bogged
down in societal difficulties, the cold war, politics, air pollu-
tion, and racism. I found myself turning away from these latter issues to stay on the path that had inspired my intellect
and elevated emotions.

But I was pulled from every direction as the incipient

start of political '60s activism began to make itself known in popular culture. I could easily be drawn into a more earthbound mindset upon hearing "Where Have All the Flowers Gone?" sung by The Kingston Trio, having been written and sung by Pete Seeger years before. Could *war* ever be ended? It was the questioning negative of optimistic futurism.

That summer my stepfather and mother decided to go on vacation to California, stopping in San Francisco; Reno, Nevada; then Hollywood; and ending up at Disneyland. Unlike most kids my age, I had never been to Disneyland, a neglect that was nearly considered child abuse in those times. Wisely, my parents offered to bring my friend Bruce along on the trip so I'd have a good companion at Disneyland and elsewhere.

It would be superfluous to describe my time at Disneyland, for it was undoubtedly like anyone else's time at that remarkable place. On the way, I loved San Francisco and its Victorian-style houses. Reno was fascinating, although I could not gamble.

The most memorable experience, aside from Disneyland, took place in Hollywood when I escaped alone, without Bruce or my parents, from our hotel and began to walk east down Hollywood Boulevard that evening. I walked past Grauman's Chinese Theater and examined the famous handprints of movie stars pressed into the concrete slabs in front. I walked past endless blocks of boutiques, coffee shops, restaurants, clothing stores, a bookstore or two. The fascination of simply *being* there led me on until I'd walked perhaps a mile all the way down to Vine St., gazing at the Hollywood Walk of Fame with its five-pointed brass-and-terrazzo stars implanted in the sidewalk, with the names of movie stars on them.

Standing at the corner of Hollywood and Vine, it suddenly struck me that it might be a night *The Steve Allen Show* was

MEMOIRS OF A BABY BOOMER

being taped at a theater somewhere down Vine St. From the show, I knew that the theater was at the intersection of Vine and La Mirada, so I asked a passerby which way to go. I then headed south along Vine.

It was now sometime after 8:00 PM, I'd already been gone a long time, but eventually I saw a group of people gathered on the sidewalk in front of what was the theater I sought, since it displayed *The Steve Allen Show* on the marquee and was across from the famous Hollywood Ranch Market that sometimes played a role in Allen's outdoor shenanigans (the most notorious being a satire on the war movie *The Longest Day*, when Allen's cast and crew, dressed in army fatigues, made a fake attack across the street into the Ranch Market and began impaling fruits and vegetables with bayonets—the grocery customers having no idea what was going on or why!).

After a summer of watching the show on TV, I was actually there! I walked to the group of people who seemed to be gathered around someone or something on the sidewalk just past the intersection in front of the theater. I kind of nudged my way in, although there weren't too many people, maybe a couple of dozen, to see what was going on. And there, sitting on a high stool with a mike in her hand, with a big TV camera pointed at her, was Joanie Sommers, whom I'd thought of as Allen's most attractive guest singer. Sommers was indeed cute and attractive, her voice unmistakably jazzy, feminine, and expressive, and here she was, waiting to do a song outdoors on a warm August night. She was chatting with the impromptu gathering surrounding her at about ten feet away. I kept my position while she was waiting for her cue. The camera was opposite my side of the gathering, pointing at her but also in my direction, and she hadn't turned to face it yet. About ten minutes went by as the floor director asked everyone to please not wave or make faces, etc. He then gave Joanie a one-minute signal, and everybody got quiet.

Certain moments are recalled forever in one's life, often having little to do with overall importance. Waiting there to hear Joanie sing, it was clear that I would be seen behind her on camera, for she was now turned away but not *in* the way, so to speak. My situation was kind of miraculous, and because I knew the show was taped two weeks in advance, I could call my friends and tell them to watch for when Joanie Sommers sang and see if they recognized this tall, lanky kid in the background!

But it didn't happen.

Suddenly, without warning, someone grabbed me by the collar.

I was yanked backward, almost fell down while being jerked away out of the gathering. I was being violently removed by someone. *Why? What was happening?!*

I was spun around by a powerful hand to see the angry face of my stepfather Larry.

Saying not a word, he firmly escorted me by the arm to our car by the curb on the other side of the intersection from the direction I'd come. My mind was racing, more in shock than in anger or frustration. How did he find me? Had I actually said something about *The Steve Allen Show* before I left our hotel? Or because I'd been gone for over two hours, had he set out randomly to look for me? Or was it because he knew I liked Steve Allen, he had intuited where I might have gone? I didn't know, I didn't ask, and he remained silent all the way back to the hotel.

By the time we got to our room, my mother was distraught. Or *still* distraught. Bruce stood with a blank look on his face, and Larry said nothing.

"Where have you been?!" Mother asked. "I was worried sick!"

"I walked down to *The Steve Allen Show* on Vine St. I didn't think I was gone that long."

"We didn't know what had happened to you!"

"Nothing . . ."

"What were you *doing* down there? Yes, I was worried sick!"

"Waiting to hear Joanie Sommers sing. She was outdoors."

"Outdoors?"

"Yes, they were taping the show with a camera outdoors," I said in exasperation. "I was standing behind her, holding my place and waiting for her to sing. I would have been behind her right on camera. A minute before she began to sing, Larry yanked me away."

My stepfather sat silently in a chair, triumphant.

Mother had a slight change of heart.

"I'm sorry it happened like that."

My mind went into missed-opportunity-of-a-lifetime mode, which evolved into anger . . . that if Larry had shown an ounce of understanding, he might have seen the situation and left me alone for just a few minutes while Sommers sang. But he was now Mr. Murdstone from *David Copperfield* again.

Mother's voice was somewhat sympathetic. "Larry, I guess you could have let him stay there for a few minutes." But I figured her usual overprotectiveness was to blame. She'd sent Larry out to find me. He'd been inconvenienced and was glad to have taken control of me.

Two weeks later, I happened to be at my parents' apartment, not at my grandparents', watching *The Steve Allen Show* late at night on the black-and-white TV. Mother had gone to bed, but Larry had stayed up, sitting in his usual easy chair.

Then, there it was, the very part of the show in which I'd almost appeared on camera. The show went out to the sidewalk with Joanie Sommers. She sang beautifully in front of the little gathering in which, but for my stepfather and bad timing, I'd have been seen by my friends—and me, too. The feeling of watching, and knowing what might have been, was a terrible letdown. I knew how trivial it would seem in the span of my life, but that didn't matter. Although tempted, I did not turn to look at Larry. The song finished. Larry said nothing. But the scene was obvious. He must have known. Did he feel any sense of guilt at all? I wondered. I could not imagine it. Before the show ended, he rose from his chair and went upstairs to bed.

§ 42

Although it opened in 1922, Roosevelt High School was one of those classic, massive three-story brick buildings often used in 1950s and '60s movies to depict big city high schools. Luckily for me, the main entrance of the school was three blocks directly north of my grandparents' house. So, in September of my fifteenth year, I settled permanently into my upstairs room at the back of the house on 14th Ave. and prepared for my next step up the ladder of being a teenager.

This coincided with a clean break from my mother Judy and stepfather Larry. They had purchased their first house, a single-story, three-bedroom rambler in the north Seattle suburb of Shoreline. It was a standard house of the time, built in 1959, with a large picture window; and although I visited many times and maintained good contact, I was never to stay another night with my parents.

Because I'd already taken a typing class at the high school that summer, Roosevelt's rectangular maze of hallways, stairs, and rooms were not unfamiliar. Less familiar was the large population of students, about 2500, crowding along those hallways and into classrooms that included the ubiquitous portables handling the overflow. Nothing much had really changed other than I was aware of how close I was to being able to drive a car (but didn't need to, at least to get to school and back). A number of juniors and seniors had their own cars. Sometimes a hot rod would appear in front of the school, but that was rare, and the ducktail haircuts and black leather jackets so often depicted in the movies were by that time passé. Those people were generally thought of as creeps, anyway, and as the first few weeks went by, I doubted there were more than a dozen of that ilk in the entire school. In fact, Roosevelt, being dead center in Seattle's north end, had the reputation of being "preppy." Students were drawn from a wide variety of socio-economic neighborhoods, including the wealthy areas of Laurelhurst and Windermere, some of whom I was friendly with because of my parents' apartment on the outskirts of Laurelhurst and of my attending Laurelhurst Elementary and then Nathan Eckstein. Some rich kids went to private schools, of course, but very few. The north end of Seattle was almost entirely white, and there was little intermingling with any of the schools in more blue-collar or Black neighborhoods in south Seattle. Although there were well-defined Black areas of the city, most of the south end was middle-class, with poor sections but no real ghettos. Racism, per se, was a far greater problem in the deep southern US and other places. Yet not a single Black student attended Roosevelt High when I started there in '62. I assumed it was the natural order of things due to socio-economics. I gave almost no thought to any of it at the time, at least insofar as Seattle was concerned.

My thoughts had more to do with girls, the number of good looking ones having increased generously. Yet as a mere sophomore, I was at the low end of the age group and had little time to consider socializing once classes began. Math, social studies (i.e., sociology, political science, and economics), English, and US History, kept me busy, not only with homework but in study hall during one of the six periods into which the day was divided. Gym was mandated during the week, as well, mainly for physical exercise—push-ups, sit-ups, pull-ups (ugh!), climbing ropes, and running around the track enough to cause concern my lungs would burst. I swear I was panting and out of breath more often than normal—I didn't really know, and although there were always a handful of miserable heavy kids trailing way behind, I was usually in the last half. I was fine doing the routine exercises in the gym, and also tumbling on the padded gray mats; but for some reason I had less stamina for running, which made no sense because I was tall, weighed only 168 lbs., and was in good physical shape—largely, I assumed, because of the street football on 14th Ave. with what we referred to now as "the gang."

Speaking of which, September brought cooler "football weather," which caused all of us in the neighborhood to gather in the street every Saturday, at least. How come we didn't get to play dodgeball in high school? Some of the students had started to play after-school tennis, though, and pretty soon sophomores such as I were turning out for various after-school sports. I was more interested in trying out for school plays that were already being planned in the drama class, but that wasn't an immediate goal. In fact, I had no immediate goals at Roosevelt, which, along with a general lack of interest in any of the extracurricular activities, seemed to cause the school counselor to tentatively label me as antisocial. He wondered if I might show some interest in one of the activities such as sports or school politics or glee club or whatever I wished to join. It was clear his job was to make sure I wasn't going to just keep to myself. What the problem was with that I had no idea, and the whole issue had a whiff of conformity that had been a pet peeve of mine. Apparently, if I didn't sign up for some rah-rah school activity, and if I wasn't like other kids, something must be wrong with me that needed adjustment. This offended me, so I just shrugged, feeling a bit like James Dean in *Rebel Without a Cause*. What did they expect? I wondered. I'd barely started my sophomore year.

§ 43

As autumn took hold, I automatically looked forward to weekend relief from study obligations, saving Friday's homework until the last minute Sunday night. Those weekend days were often matters of wind, rain, reading. That fall I discovered something special at Craigen's Drugstore, this time on the revolving rack of paperback books: a collection of short stories by Ray Bradbury called *The October Country*. It was fitting, for October had begun, and as usual my literary mood was turning again toward Poe's stories and looking down the road toward Halloween, though of course trick-or-treat, per se, was long gone at age fifteen.

Luckily for me, Poe was an acceptable author (barely, it seemed) in English class, and I wrote an essay about "The Black Cat." But modern authors in the horror or science fiction genres were still snubbed by teachers, and there was little interest from the majority of students. I still found no friend at school who shared my attraction to these genres.

Before Ray Bradbury became known as a science fiction author (most would say science fantasy) with *The Martian Chronicles* and *Fahrenheit 451*, he'd written short stories in the genre of horror and the supernatural. *The October Country* contained the choicest of these earlier weird tales, and the cover illustration by artist Joseph Mugnaini of a small, dark figure walking against the wind in front of a fanciful Victorian house instantly attracted my eye. Also fascinating were Mugnaini's striking pen-and-ink interior illustrations. The evocative stories represented a phantasmagorical invocation of October and the apotheosis of an autumnal imagination.

Bradbury's preface described it perfectly:

> . . . that country where it is always turning late in the year. That
> country where the hills are fog and the rivers are mist; where
> noons go quickly, dusks and twilights linger, and midnights stay.
> That country composed in the main of cellars, sub-cellars, coal-
> bins, closets, attics, and pantries faced away from the sun. That
> country whose people are autumn people, thinking only autumn
> thoughts. Whose people passing at night on the empty walks
> sound like rain.

Here was a man who understood my own visions of autumn—a season of stark rural landscapes, haunting melancholy, and an atmosphere I'd found only in particular
passages by Poe: mysterious, transitory, and an indefinable
mood about a time of year I anticipated. The psychological
reasons were not to be solved, but the roots went deep. As
much as I admired *The Martian Chronicles*, these darker tales
seemed to be more at the center of Bradbury's oeuvre. They
represented his roots, too; they seemed somehow mine, as
well. The prose style and content of stories in *The October
Country* impressed themselves on my psyche and began what
was to be a memorable fall.

And so it was, but not a fall entirely in the way I anticipated, and for reasons I could never have predicted.

§ 44

Although my father had left an estate, I had received only one
dollar. Legally, this ensured I hadn't been left out of his will
and could not make a further claim. His full-time nurse, that
muscular woman of considerable size, had convinced him into marriage even while he was barely able to make himself
understood, and she took everything. It was a fait accompli in
that fall of '62. But I did not know my father had left something else to me as the result of his *second* marriage, the one

just after his with my mother. For vague reasons, some unexpected news had been kept from me, not only since my father's death, and I found out about it by a phone call from my mother before the end of September. She had a habit of dropping bombshells now and then by telephone.

After a brief chat, Mother said gently, "Philip, I have something to tell you." She paused to indicate importance. "We believe it's time to let you know that you have a brother."

The statement hung there, as I could only manage bewilderment.

"Vance's second wife Jean and I have decided it's time to let you and your brother know of each other. His name is Douglas and he is turning eleven this month. He is your half-brother because of your father's marriage to Jean. Do you recall that your father Vance had remarried sometime after he and I were divorced?"

"Yeah."

"Good."

"This is something . . ."

"You don't have to do anything. I just wanted you to know.

"I'm . . . well . . . ah, where does he live?"

"He lives with his mother and stepfather in Sunnyvale, California."

"Where's that?"

"Just south of San Francisco."

"Wow, I don't know what to think."

"Nothing to think, really. Just wanted you to know. You may wish to see him sometime in the future, but that will be up to you and him."

"Sure. OK."

"I'll say goodbye now. Don't forget to call me. Love you."

"Me, too."

"Bye."

"Bye."

And that was it. News most astonishing. I'd answered the phone in Peggy's bedroom, went back to my own room and flopped on the bed. How to consider this I had no idea. What did it mean to me, if anything? Yet something had changed. Since I wasn't advised of anything to do, I decided for the moment it wasn't too important. I wouldn't think of immediately writing to an eleven-year-old, for example. But the news that I suddenly had a little brother—did it matter that he was only a half-brother?—required some re-orientation. I'd been an only child my entire life. The thought that I wasn't quite that now seemed too abstract, which I guess it was and would likely remain so for some time, maybe for years. Yet it was *something*. I had this little kid brother in California. Might I assume the role of older brother at a distance? What might *he* be thinking? At his age, probably not much. I, on the other hand, was old enough to feel a change in status. I was no longer really an only child.

Yet by the time the sun went down that day, I'd set the news aside. Any consequence of this interesting change would likely be in the future.

§ 45

Then the unexpected: Would there *be* a future? Was it not often when life was rolling along in a comfortable routine, or when some pleasant new possibility came along to look forward to (such as an only child discovering he had a brother?) that the unpredictable intruded?

It had been there all along, of course, during my childhood, and it wasn't as if I, or anyone, had forgotten. There are differences between forgetfulness, acknowledgment, and denial.

Or was it a habit of numb concession that allowed the danger to take us by surprise that fall? The overall enjoyment of the times did not entirely obscure warnings or reminders. The lowest budget science fiction and horror movies reminded us throughout the '50s that we were living in the atomic age. More serious films like *On the Beach*—not to mention certain memorable episodes of *The Twilight Zone*—acted as dire warnings. Yet one could not live in constant fear of "the bomb"—so these themes, although part of one's mental landscape, were effortlessly pushed into the background. Not that I didn't pay heed, for I had gravitated to science fiction in which end-of-the-world scenarios were common. And although I hadn't actually read either of Herman Kahn's two significant non-fiction books, *On Thermonuclear War* and *Thinking About the Unthinkable*, I had kept pace through magazine articles and television with the madness of the nuclear arms race and the destructive increase demonstrated by the hydrogen bomb. I had also done a book report about the dropping of the atomic bomb on Hiroshima in the best-selling *Hiroshima* by John Hershey, and I knew that a single hydrogen bomb was 1,000 times more powerful than the atom bomb. Such a bomb could completely destroy Seattle (the Boeing aircraft plant would be a prime target) and both the Soviet Union and the United States had *thousands* of such bombs in their arsenals—bombs that could be delivered by Intercontinental Ballistic Missiles (ICBMs) to their targets in twenty minutes. Furthermore, tensions had risen during Khrushchev's construction of a wall dividing East from West Berlin, and it was possible the Soviet leader might also try to isolate *West* Berlin from the rest of Germany. That almost any conflict might result in nuclear war was hovering over the world like the dark wing of a colossal vulture.

But most of us weren't "thinking about the unthinkable." President Kennedy was scheduled to close the Seattle World's

Fair on its last day, October 21, 1962. Unfortunately, he begged off, saying he had a bad cold. I was disappointed, since a visit to Seattle by Kennedy was a pretty big deal. I was not thinking about the unthinkable. Neither was I when it was announced that President Kennedy would make an important address to the nation on national television. Not until after his speech on that evening of Monday, October 22—a speech that risked triggering a nuclear war—did the unthinkable sink in. As Grandfather, Grandmother, Aunt, and I watched the black-and-white TV in silence, he began:

> This Government, as promised, has maintained the closest surveillance of the Soviet Military buildup on the island of Cuba. Within the past week, unmistakable evidence has established the fact that a series of offensive missile sites is now in preparation on that imprisoned island. The purpose of these bases can be none other than to provide a nuclear strike capability against the Western Hemisphere.

Kennedy described the Soviet's installation of medium- and long-range nuclear missiles capable of striking nearly every major city in the Western Hemisphere, the deceit involved secretly placing such missiles, and the betrayal of promises made by the Soviet Union. Kennedy continued as we watched:

> To halt this offensive buildup, a strict quarantine on all offensive military equipment under shipment to Cuba is being initiated. All ships of any kind bound for Cuba from whatever nation or port will, if found to contain cargoes of offensive weapons, be turned back. This quarantine will be extended, if needed, to other types of cargo and carriers. . . .

My grandfather, sitting in his soft old chair, murmured to himself, ". . . an act of war."

> It shall be the policy of this Nation to regard any nuclear missile launched from Cuba against any nation in the Western Hemi-

sphere as an attack by the Soviet Union on the United States, requiring a full retaliatory response upon the Soviet Union.

The meaning of "a full retaliatory response" brought to mind a montage of total destruction. This was a decisive but dangerous move to stand up against Nikita Khrushchev, the Soviet leader who had belligerently built a wall to divide East and West Berlin and who had threatened us by saying, "We will bury you!"

We sat transfixed.

> I call upon Chairman Khrushchev to halt and eliminate this clandestine, reckless and provocative threat to world peace and to stable relations between our two nations. I call upon him further to abandon this course of world domination . . .

In the long hours to come, as the tension built in my family, at school, and throughout the country, my mind insisted on trying to encompass the horror of edging toward World War III. After his speech, Kennedy proposed a United Nations resolution that would force Khrushchev to dismantle and remove his nukes from Cuba. What were the chances? And what would happen if Khrushchev refused to honor the blockade of his ships *in the next few hours?*

Walking to school the next morning, I looked at the houses along the street and imagined them disintegrating in a massive shock wave as we'd seen in newsreels of a hydrogen bomb test. I saw Roosevelt High exploding in a paroxysm of flame and debris. What might be unleashed miles out of sight before the waves of destruction came from the sky? Death and destruction were in my imagination—still, in a way, unthinkable.

I knew too much. As frightening as immediate physical destruction was, if the worst predictions came true, the globe would be blanketed by a dark enveloping cloud, plant and animal life would die, the human species might not survive.

Everything I'd known or would know, everything human—all art, music, literature, science, would be eradicated and vanish into meaninglessness, and a barren Earth would continue around the sun in the endless night of deep space. The story would end barely after it had begun, the birth and death of every person who had ever lived would be rendered moot, including my own birth and death. All that anyone had ever known or shared or loved would be obliterated, if not instantly, in the afterglow of radiation and the suffering of starvation and barbarism.

My mind harkened back to that graphic portrayal of the birth and death of our planet in the big book I had treasured at age nine, and of the evolving graphic of the Earth being born, cooling, and ultimately dying as the sun became a red giant. Could it be that we ourselves—no!—two reckless, domineering men with unprecedented power—would irrationally cut off the natural progression of billions of years, ending everything in a nuclear holocaust?

The tension at school was relatively obvious in students and teachers alike. The hours went by. US Naval forces gathered to enforce the blockade of Russian ships on their way to Cuba. On the following night, the 23rd, the Joint Chiefs of Staff instructed the Strategic Air Command to activate DEF-CON 2, one level of preparedness short of DEFCON 1 meaning all-out nuclear war. Fear was worldwide. The world truly was on the brink of direct and horrific *indirect* annihilation by radiation after a launch of thousands of nuclear warheads. How did it come to this? One of my classroom discussions went back to Kennedy's attempted invasion of Cuba—the so-called Bay of Pigs—and whether Khrushchev found this a justification for expanding nuclear arms into the Western Hemisphere—to protect Cuba from a more comprehensive invasion in the planning stage. Or was Khrushchev's more likely motive to expand the reach of Soviet communism into this hemisphere with the help of Fidel Castro, the Cuban dictator?

Back to my immediate state of mind: Even if I somehow survived a nuclear war, everything I'd known back to my earliest days as a child would seem nothing more than a dream. Would the stubborn clash of two nations wielding weapons of mass death actually end the world? I was reminded of H. G. Wells's warnings. He had died a year before I was born, yet had lived to witness the atomic bombs dropped on Hiroshima and Nagasaki. He had predicted in 1913 the invention of the atomic bomb and had spent his life warning of the consequences of war, of environmental destruction, and of the *unexpected* nature of catastrophe. Such warnings had now come down to the very place and time in which I lived and breathed. It was not an abstraction now.

Yet contrarily, while the hours went by, I could not believe it would happen. In a sense, my imagination was frozen in the state I've described, but like most everyone else, I was just waiting while prayers were being said all over the world.

Of personal significance was that I was dismissive of prayer—of supernatural intervention—for me, a logical evolution from my rejection of Christian Science and "knowing the truth" about disease. My grandfather's lukewarm attitude came into play by an old adage he'd once mentioned: "The drowned sailors prayed just as hard as the survivors."

At school among a small circle of student acquaintances, my *eventual* reputation as the Holden Caulfield of Roosevelt High may have begun (one of the books we read as sophomores was *The Catcher in the Rye*) when I cynically noted the irony of those who thanked the Lord for their own or loved ones' survival after a fire, flood, or tornado. Their neighbors who died had "prayed just as hard as the survivors," I said. Moreover, an all-powerful, all-knowing, "loving" God, could have prevented these disasters in the first place, not to mention eliminated terrible diseases. Such was my sacrilege, and I waited silently along with most others as I went about my day and classes continued uninterrupted.

More hours went by, and then the news came: The Soviet ships were turning around. They were heading back.

The blockade had worked. Kennedy had faced down Khrushchev and was a sudden hero instead of a destroyer of civilization, a reckless adversary of communism. Of course we did not know everything of events at the highest levels, and the ordeal was not yet over. Remaining was Kennedy's demand that all of Khrushchev's missiles be removed from Cuba.

And then on the 25th, the Soviet ambassador to the UN, in an emergency meeting of the Security Council broadcast on nationwide television, *refused to admit that his country had any missiles in Cuba.*

What?! I watched as our UN Ambassador, Adlai Stevenson, showed enlarged photos taken by U-2 spy planes of the very missile installations the Soviets were denying existed. It was a stunning display of truth vs. lies.

§ 46

Should I describe this watershed crisis further? No. We know the outcome. Over the next few months, Khrushchev dismantled all his nuclear weapons in Cuba. But to report that fact, not to mention the days leading up to it, represents a problem with understanding history. To make clear the experience of the past, what it was *like*, would be to *not* know the outcome—in this case, an impossibility even a few hours after the news of Kennedy's gamble having paid off. Yet one who didn't live through it might bring to bear some imagination or contemplation.

The world did not end.

Time continued to weave a colorful pattern of life with only a momentary, albeit scary, interruption. The nuclear cloud was lifted from our minds once again, and the experience of the '50s continued right into the early '60s—accented, I decided, by Little Eva singing "Do the locomotion."

I did the locomotion by settling easily into the big high school whose complex society, intended or unintended, helped foster a sense of myself as a non-conformist, or at least with a feeling of separateness. This feeling would become true, even academically, and within a structure that wasn't designed for individual learning. My usual escape from the crowded halls and classroom routine was still, as always, to the movies. I went to see *How the West was Won* on a gigantic curved screen at the new Cinerama theater in downtown Seattle, followed at another downtown theater by a revival of my childhood crush on Hayley Mills, in Disney's *In Search of the Castaways*. Then the moodily adult *Two for the Seesaw* that prompted me to buy Andre Previn's wonderful melancholy soundtrack music—followed by two of the greatest films ever made, *Lawrence of Arabia* and *To Kill a Mockingbird*, the latter having premiered on Xmas day.

In music, the folk era was just beginning; I walked to Standard Records and bought Peter, Paul, and Mary's first album, and later on, *Joan Baez in Concert*. I stopped buying singles in favor of saving money for albums.

For Xmas, dear Peggy gave me my first 35mm camera, a new Argus Autronic I (Peggy remaining loyal to the brand). Unlike her C-4, it had its own built-in light meter with automatic exposure control. I went outdoors and began photographing all sorts of trivial things, including whichever poor soul happened to wander outside in the neighborhood. Would there be some professional photography in my future? Perhaps. At age fifteen, my mental viewfinder didn't see into the future, and no crystal ball was secreted in my upstairs room. But I was confident I could do whatever I set out to do.

And here the narrative must end but for two relevant observations: First, the story of my childhood thus far, if it is a story, does not naturally end here, for it is a truncated narrative brought to a random close until, perhaps, another time.

Second, and likely too late, I must ask the reader's indulgence, for I have come to learn in writing this memoir, that no matter how much one may remember, in detail or otherwise, the essence of one's life and particular slice of history—what it is *like* to be alive during a span of time in a certain place—is in the end impossible to convey. A backward peek at the past through a knothole is the best one can do.

As for the future, 1963 began with the President's promise of a New Frontier still in focus. I recalled Kennedy's speech about putting a man on the moon before the decade was out. It seemed incredible—yet the space program continued its breathtaking advance. Down on Earth, the Peace Corps was in full idealistic swing. Confidence in the future was the country's gift to the young. The seeds of change were planted in so many ways. My own life was also changing, an unopened book of possibilities; and succeed or fail, I knew I would always go my own way.

For so many of us growing up in those years, it was the best of times, and it felt like it would never end. That was the essence of being young.

Epilogue

One night that winter the very idea of time filled my thoughts. A light snow had begun to fall outside, and it reminded me of the walk my grandmother and I had taken from the big house on Ravenna Boulevard many years before. I became restless during this reverie and decided to take a walk around the block while the snow was still falling. I put on a warm coat, scarf, and my woolen watch cap, left the house, and walked slowly down the sidewalk toward Cowen Park.

At a silent, unlit intersection near the park was a two-story, early 1900s brick house of a higher stature than most of the surrounding houses. This involved not only the solid brick construction, but two lighted lamps on pedestals adorning each side of the steps up to the front door with its heavy iron knocker. The back yard of the house was surrounded by a high brick wall, and it was because of that wall, I think, that the house conveyed some hidden mystery. What was it that this house reminded me of? Yes, I knew. It reminded me of the Time Traveller's house in George Pal's movie *The Time Machine*. The final scene of the film was of the house at night, the glow from the windows, and the snow falling as the scene faded out. My imagination now took hold and I fantasized that this could *be* the Time Traveller's house, and if only I could see over the brick wall into the yard and the garden, I might find the greenhouse-glass entrance leading to the shop where the time machine stood.

For a minute, I stood gazing at that wall, bathing my imagination in the idea. It seemed as if I were standing at a crossroads between reality and fantasy. How much of our lives are of the former, how much of the latter? What of expectations? Was the future pre-determined, partly under our control, or a matter of chance?

The snow had stopped falling. I'd forgotten my gloves, and it seemed to be getting colder. I put my hands in my pockets and began to walk home.